Introduction

Ditties

I believe that a ditty is actually supposed to be a poem or a song, but I grew up with the Carolina colloquialism of a ditty being any short, pithy saying or writing. Having written only one noteworthy poem in my life, I'm definitely not a poet, but I do hope that these few thoughts I'm sharing in this little book will prove to be short and pithy enough to inspire a little something into your life each day.

I once read that it's plagiarism if you steal from one person, but it's research if you steal from several writers. Another thing that I firmly believe is that none of us really has an original thought. Every thought we have is a result of all the input we have received. For most of us, the old saying might apply very aptly: GIGO – "garbage in, garbage out." If there is any good thought that comes out of our minds, it is because some good influences have entered our hearts; the most important of those positive influences would be the Word of God and the inspiration of the Holy Spirit.

As you read my little ditties each day, I encourage you to enjoy each place where I have plagiarized (ah, done some research) and each place where something other than garbage has come out due to the inspiration of the Holy Spirit.

Since some holidays do not occur on fixed dates, the message for each movable holiday is given on the earliest possible date on which it can be observed: Martin Luther King Day, January 15; State of the Union Address, January 25; Presidents' Day, February 15; Palm Sunday, March 15; Good Friday, March 20; Easter, March 22; National Day of Prayer, May 1; Mother's Day, May 8; Pentecost, May 10; Father's Day, June 15; Labor Day, September 1; Election Day, November 2; and Thanksgiving, November 22.

New Year's Day
Happy New Year
I'm sure that I don't need to tell you that the number one New Year's resolution is to lose weight. And there is no wonder that it ranks at the top of the list since two out of three Americans are either overweight or obese. But did you know the annual cost for health care, sick days, loss of productivity, and extra gasoline (not counting food costs) for individuals considered overweight is $524 for a woman and $432 for a man? When we move to the obesity level, those numbers jump to $4,879 for a woman and $2,646 for aman. If we calculate in the loss due to shortened life expectancy, the new estimates come out to $8,365 for a woman and $6,518 for a man. It has actually been determined that seventeen percent ($2,800 per year) of all medical costs are due to obesity.

"Gruesome! What a way to start off my year! Why did you choose this topic to open your new book?" Well, I figured that this is the most likely day of the year for anyone to actually take these thoughts seriously and to actually act on them.

Now, let's take a look at this issue from a little different angle. You may be surprised to learn that the average American gives one penny per day to global missions. That calculates to $3.65, about three fourths of one percent of the average cost of being overweight and about one tenth of a percent of the average cost of being obese. Wow, just think how much impact we could have around the world if we simply stopped overfeeding ourselves and channeled our extra resources toward helping others.

> *Brethren, be followers together of me, and mark them which walk so as ye have us for an ensample. (For many walk, of whom I have told you often, and now tell you even weeping, that they are the enemies of the cross of Christ: Whose end is destruction, whose God is their belly, and whose glory is in their shame, who mind earthly things.)* (Philippians 3:17-19)

Daily Ditties from Delron's Desk Volume III

Delron Shirley

2013

Cover design by Jeremy Shirley

For permission to quote material from this book, contact:
Delron Shirley
3210 Cathedral Spires Dr.
Colorado Springs, CO 80904
teachallnations@msn.com

January 2
Metamorphosis

When Paul wrote in II Corinthians 5:17 that when a man is in Christ he is a new creature, he used words that spoke of going through a total transformation like that of a magnificent butterfly emerging from the cocoon that was once occupied by a lowly caterpillar. He also described this total transformation by saying that the old man that we once were has been killed and buried so that we can be resurrected to a radically new life. (Romans 6:6-7) However, all this is just theology and theory. But, there is a powerful statement in II Corinthians 7:2 that makes us realize that for Paul this was not just words and ideas; it was an actual life experience! *Receive us; we have wronged no man, we have corrupted no man, we have defrauded no man.*

We can only comprehend the power of this verse when we stop to look back at the life of Saul of Tarsus. We first encounter him in Acts 7:58 and 8:1 as he stood by consenting to the stoning of Stephen, the first martyr of the Christian church, by holding the coats of all those who actually threw the stones. Luke continues by telling us that he *made havock of the church, entering into every house, and haling men and women committed them to prison* (verse 8:3) and that he, *yet breathing out threatenings and slaughter against the disciples of the Lord, went unto the high priest, And desired of him letters to Damascus to the synagogues, that if he found any of this way, whether they were men or women, he might bring them bound unto Jerusalem* (verses 9:1-2). When God spoke to one of His servants to go minister to Saul, Ananias answered, *Lord, I have heard by many of this man, how much evil he hath done to thy saints at Jerusalem: And here he hath authority from the chief priests to bind all that call on thy name.* (verses 9:13-14) Even after his conversion, Saul found that it was impossible to join the church because the leaders were afraid of him. (verse 9:26)

Yet, this is the man who could confess that he had wronged no man. The evil person who did so many harmful things was no more. Saul was now Paul, a truly new creature as the result of divine metamorphosis.

January 3
Getting it Right
When I first started doing missionary work in Nepal, I decided to learn a little of the language. So I bought a Nepali-English dictionary, picked out a list of what I considered useful words, made flashcards with the English word on one side and the Nepali word on the reverse. After spending almost a full year learning a new word every day or so, I was ready to impress the people when I returned for my annual visit. Unfortunately, when I began to pray for people at the first church service, one of the elders came to me and politely asked that I not pray over the people in Nepali. Apparently, the phrase that I thought meant, "I bless you," actually meant, "I'm in love with you." When we went out to a restaurant after the service, I again put my foot in my mouth when ordering lunch. Instead of asking for beef, I had told the waiter that I wanted to eat a holy cow. Well, all this is an excusable stumbling over the language barrier; however, it does help point out how easy it is to say or do the wrong thing.

In the spiritual realm, we have a powerful helper who will direct us so that we can actually get it right rather than to continually wind up making serious mistakes and blunders. Paul said that if we simply walk in the spirit, we will not fulfill lust of flesh. (Galatian 5:16) That's a world of difference from trying to not walk in the flesh. In fact, trying to avoid fulfilling fleshly lusts through our own willpower is like trying to not think of an apple. Now that I've mentioned it, I'll guarantee you that you can't erase the idea of an apple out of your mind. I guess that you might say that this is an example of the power of God's grace versus the power of legalism. One actually frees you from the fault while the other brings you into continual bondage to the possibility of the fault. Grace must prevail, but we must not get our vocabulary mixed up and proclaim that grace eliminates our responsibility to follow the spirit of godliness.

Woe unto them that call evil good, and good evil! (Isaiah 5:20)

January 4
Muslim Healers

A growing number of Muslims are turning away from Western medical care in favor of the Medicine of the Prophet, a loosely defined discipline based on the Quran and other Islamic texts and traditional remedies. The trend in Islamic treatments is often associated with fundamentalists who charge that Western, chemically laced prescriptions aim to poison Muslims or defile them with insulin and other medicines made from pigs. The bulk of those seeking out Islamic clinics, hospitals and pharmacies appear to be moderate Muslims, reflecting a rise in Islamic consciousness worldwide. The industry's advertising is as gimmicky as any in the West. Capitalizing on the popularity of U.S. President Barack Obama, who spent four of his childhood years in Indonesia, one company produces a popular anti-stress concoction called Obahama – in a corruption of an Indonesian phrase for herbal medicine. Siwak-F, also exported to the Middle East, is hailed as "toothpaste just like the Prophet used to use."

Islamic medicine is grounded on the saying that "Allah did not create a disease for which he did not also create a cure." This is taken from Prophet Mohammed's teachings known as hadiths which, along with the Quran, make frequent references to diseases, remedies and healthy living. Practitioners say many ingredients in today's treatments were used in Mohammed's time, including honey, olive oil, bee pollen, dates and black caraway – which one ad claims is "a cure for every disease but death." Herbal medicine, bloodletting treatments, and twelve-dollar exorcisms in which a white-gloved therapist places a hand on a patient's head while chanting verses from the Quran are all part of this therapy.

> *And then shall that Wicked be revealed, whom the Lord shall consume with the spirit of his mouth, and shall destroy with the brightness of his coming: Even him, whose coming is after the working of Satan with all power and signs and lying wonders.* (II Thessalonians 2:9)

January 5
Eminent Domain

An American industrialist spent a huge sum of money building a manufacturing plant in a Latin American country, only to have the country nationalize his factory under their law of eminent domain.

Eminent domain, also known as "compulsory purchase," "resumption/compulsory acquisition" and "expropriation" in other countries, is an action of the state to seize a citizen's private property, expropriate property, or seize a citizen's rights in property with due monetary compensation, but without the owner's consent. The property is taken either for government use or by delegation to third parties who will devote it to public or civic use or, in some cases, economic development. The most common uses of property taken by eminent domain are for public utilities, highways, and railroads; however, it may also be taken for reasons of public safety. Some jurisdictions require the offer to purchase the property before resorting to the use of eminent domain.

A simple way of explaining this principle is that what you have is subject to be taken by the kingdom you live in. In the spiritual dimension, we live either in the Kingdom of God or in the kingdom of the devil. With that understanding, we can easily realize that everything we possess can be taken by either God or the devil. However, just as the country of Mexico has no right of eminent domain to property belonging to citizens in the United States, the devil has no right to seize anything belonging to those of us living in the Kingdom of God. On the flipside of that coin, God will not violate boundaries by seizing anything in the devil's kingdom. These two statements can really undo a lot of our theology because so many Christians are always blaming the devil for what happens in their lives and asking God to take away things from unbelievers so that they will come to themselves and repent as did the prodigal son. But we need to remember that Satan had to ask permission from God to take anything from Job and that Paul taught us to turn rebellious individuals over to Satan, not God, for the destruction of their flesh so that their spirits might be saved. (I Corinthians 5:5)

January 6
Lighten Up
When a student asked the professor about his opinion of the student's term paper, the professor responded, "It's absolute drivel." The student's retort was, "That's okay. I'd still like to hear it anyway."

No man can change his color or alter his stature (Jeremiah 13:23, Matthew 6:27), but a barber can lower your ears, and an eye doctor can lengthen your arms.

As far as I'm concerned, "whom" is a word that was invented to make everyone sound like a butler.

When an old maid schoolteacher asked her class to correct the sentence, "I don't have no fun at the beach," one student suggested, "Get a boyfriend."

Can a poisonous snake bite its own tongue?

Did you know that Stephen in the Bible was a hippie? He went to a rock concert and got stoned.

While in Korea, a friend of mine ordered seafood, thinking that he would get fish. When he was served eels, he not only learned something about the oriental diet, he also came to a new theological understanding – God is not a Korean, because the Bible says that if you ask Him for a fish He will not give you a snake instead.

Speaking of seafood, a man entered a restaurant and asked, "Do you serve crabs?" The waitress replied, "Yes, have a seat." He then tried to straighten out the situation by asking, "Do you have crab legs?" To this question, she replied, "No, this is from a childhood injury."

One of my students explained why he believes in planning ahead, "If you spend enough time planning, you never have to actually do any work."

Another student told me that he was a state champion – in the state of confusion.

One other student was stopped and given a ticket for DWM – Driving While Male.

As a college professor, my job description is, "Talk in other people's sleep."

January 7
Believe It or Not
Thinking that it was a casino, a man came into the Lincoln, Nebraska, police station to place a bet on a ball game. He was turned away by a staff member, but came back a few minutes later and asked for blackjack chips. At that point, he was arrested because his blood alcohol level was three times the legal limit for driving in the state.

A pastor gave a member of the congregation a videotape of what he thought was the sermon from the previous week's church service. When the parishioner returned the tape and explained that the pastor had apparently accidentally used the tape to record a football game, the pastor replied, "Well, I hope it blessed you."

One parishioner, in trying to explain how the Holy Spirit was dealing with her about some habits that she needed to break, said, "God is really getting on my nerves lately."

A billboard in front of a restaurant listed the fish of the day as "Beef."

In a British poll that asked if the survey audience thought that there were too may foreigners in the country, eight-two percent of the responses came back in Arabic.

A newspaper article announced that a psychic fair was being canceled due to unforeseen circumstances.

A sign displaying a public health announcement concerning the dangers of childhood obesity shared the same billboard with an advertisement for McDonald's.

A man who was concerned about a negative prognosis that the doctor gave concerning his mother's health shot the doctor, his mom, and himself. I guess that that is one way of making sure that the doctor's negative prediction doesn't come true.

A friend told me that he has a perfect memory but he seldom remembered to use it. He also was wondering if he might be bipolar because he had been to the Arctic and the Antarctic.

An exorcist got really excited when trying to cast out a demon and yelled, "Devil, come out or I'm coming in after you!"

January 8
Left-handed Compliments
A friend of mine once told me about being asked to write a job reference for one of his former employees. Although he didn't want to say anything negative that might keep the young man from getting the job, my friend certainly didn't want to be dishonest in writing the reference. He finally settled on saying, "You will be lucky if you can get him to work for you." If the new employer read the statement one way, he could assume that the candidate would be a great asset to the company. Read another way, the new employer would realize that the candidate was actually lazy, and would, therefore, make a poor employee.

This little story is an example of what is sometimes called a left-handed compliment – a statement that looks positive on the surface but is actually a derogatory statement when examined closely.

I heard a similar statement in a movie the other night. One of the lovers said to the other one, "Hurting you is the last thing I want to do." At first, we all think that this is a kind, endearing statement; however, when we really think the statement all the way through we can come to the conclusion that hurting her is still on the list. In fact, it is the guy's ultimate plan to finalize their relationship by hurting the girl. Maybe this is all just semantics, but in some individual's twisted minds, there could actually be a sinister plan to wind up seriously hurting the partner after gaining trust through a period of kind acts and loving words.

Well, be that as it may, I suppose that left-handed compliments actually originated in the Bible when Jacob crossed his hands so that he could lay his right hand on the younger grandson Ephraim and his left hand on the older grandson Manasseh, indicating that the younger boy would supersede his older brother. (Genesis 48:8-22) The ultimate left-handed compliment came from Ehud when he drew a concealed dagger from his garments with his left hand and slew the king of Moab while deceiving him by saying that he had a special message from God for him. (Judges 3:12-30)

January 9

"Amen"s and "Oh Me"s

Among the following random thoughts are some that we immediately agree with and others that make us take a second look at ourselves.

Is the definition of "platitude" the approach to life taken by a duck-billed, web-footed mammal?

I've probably already broken all seven commandments.

The early bird gets the Word.

It only takes one of me to change a light bulb since the world already revolves around me.

Stress is an ignorant state; I believe that everything is an emergency.

If you want to see a rainbow, you have to put up with the rain.

If you see ten troubles coming down the road, you can be sure that nine will run into the ditch before they reach you.

There will never be female referees because they will throw the flag but never tell you why. Later, they'll throw the flag and say, "I just remembered something you did in the first quarter."

Why is it that ninety-five percent of kids live outside the United States and ninety-five percent of youth workers work within the United States.

It's no accident that history's firebrands and ideologues are young, while its peacemakers, judges, and great theologians are more mature.

Everybody thinks of changing humanity, and nobody thinks of changing himself.

Resentment is like taking poison and waiting for the other person to die.

Misers are no fun to live with, but they make great ancestors.

Society works by putting opportunity and responsibility together.

Anecdotes to Ponder

A notice mistakenly read, "Your daughter Susan has received the top academic award in the university's biology department." The parents wrote back, "We don't know what kinds of experiments you are doing in your biology department, but we do know that our daughter Susan started school as our son Tim."

When the lady asked for a Coke but was told that they did not carry that particular brand, she replied with, "Just give me a dark, carbonated beverage." The young man behind the counter chuckled and asked if she wanted a cylindrical plastic sucking device to go with it.

When the teenage boy pulled a one-dollar bill out of his pocket to place in the offering, a gentleman in the row behind handed him a twenty-dollar bill. Thanking the man for his generosity, the boy also dropped in the larger bill. Just as the offering bucket moved past him, the man explained that the bill was the boy's and that it had fallen out of his pocket when he reached for the smaller one.

We have two regulatory systems: legal to keep us from killing one another and etiquette to keep us from driving one another crazy.

Michelangelo understood the power of touch when he painted the hand of God reaching out toward Adam on the ceiling of the Sistine Chapel. Waitresses who touch their customers get larger tips than those who don't. Politicians believe in "pressing the flesh."

An old man sat outside the wall of a great city. When asked what kind of people lived within the wall, he would ask the visitor what kind of people lived in their city. If someone answered, "Only bad people," he would reply, "Continue on; you'll find only bad people here." But if the traveler answered, that only good people lived in the place where he came from, then the old man would say, "Enter, for you will find only good people here."

January 11
Little Thoughts With Big Meanings

Teaching people about God is like teaching kids to ride a bicycle. You put the training wheels on. Then you hold the kids on the bike as they start to pedal. But, eventually, you have to let go and let them ride on their own.

When you believe in yourself, you can do it. When I hear, "It can't be done," I know that I'm close to success.

Ten to twenty percent of students are reluctant to make moral judgments. Asked about the Holocaust, one said, "Of course I dislike Nazis, but who is to say that they are morally wrong?"

All the bumped travelers waited patiently except for one man who treated the agent very rudely, demanding an aisle seat. Everyone was relieved when they learned that there would be room for all of them on the next flight, but the one man was still not happy until he was assured of his aisle seat. The gate agent announced that all the rest would be seated in first class.

After the midterm exam, the professor tossed the graded papers on her desk and announced, "Class, after I left here last week, the Lord spoke to me. He said, 'Thanks, professor. I haven't heard from some of those people in years.'"

The congregation advertised for a pastor who walks on water and moves mountains; the candidate showed up at his interview wearing a life jacket and carrying a shovel.

When I die, I want to go peacefully in my sleep like my grandfather – not screaming like the passengers in his car.

I feel a little sick each time I look in the mirror, but at least my eyesight is good.

I heard a family counselor say that we should place a cross in the room where the family argues the most to remind us that God is watching. My response is that most families would need a lot of crosses.

Plans are only good intentions unless they immediately generate into hard work.

January 12
Peladophobia

My favorite television show is <u>Monk</u>. I can really relate to the leading character, Adrian Monk, because he demonstrates all the classic symptoms of OCD, Obsessive Compulsive Disorder. Occasionally, my wife accuses me of suffering from OCD; however, I have two ready answers. First, I reassure her that I am not suffering; I enjoy it. Then I remind her that if I have any disorder, it certainly is not OCD. It would be CDO. That's OCD with the letters in alphabetic order – the way they should be.

The one thing that I can't relate to with Mr. Monk is his phobias. He suffers from fear of almost everything imaginable. However, I ran across a phobia the other day that even Adrian doesn't experience: peladophobia, the fear of bald people. Thank goodness, I don't have to worry with that; otherwise, I'd be afraid of myself!

When I read about this fear of bald people, I thought of all the wonderful bald people I know – including my father, several uncles, and even myself – and couldn't imagine why anyone would ever have any reason to be afraid of these great guys. Of course, that's the way with all fears. Fears are generally baseless. They haunt us and paralyze us for no reason.

The Bible is adamant that we should not be fearful. In fact, it commands us *fear not* three hundred and sixty-five times – one for every day of the year! So when you wake up each day, you have a fresh promise to claim against any fear that would try to overtake you during that day.

> *Though an host should encamp against me, my heart shall not fear: though war should rise against me, in this will I be confident.* (Psalm 27:3)
> *Therefore will not we fear, though the earth be removed, and though the mountains be carried into the midst of the sea.* (Psalm 46:2)

January 13
TSA
One of my mission students was going through the security check at the airport. Since she knew that she was going to have to bunk on the floor in Russia, she had taken an air mattress with her. The security officer was puzzled by the large folded-up object, but seemed at ease when she explained that it was an air mattress. However, when he pulled the pump out of her bag and heard her try to explain that it was the part that made it blow up, he did raise an eyebrow!

I've had a number of interesting encounters with these security agents over the years. Once, a couple were accompanying me on a mission when the lady was told that all her cosmetics were to be confiscated because they were in bottles bigger than three ounces. Even though none of the bottles contained three ounces of liquid, they all had to be discarded. The gentleman right behind her finished drinking a bottle of water just as he approached the checkpoint. The agent told him that he didn't have to discard the bottle since it was now empty. It's been several years since this happened, but I'm still scratching my head, trying to figure out how the lady's four-ounce bottles were dangerous but the gentleman's pint bottle was safe. If the fear was that she could have combined her liquids into one of her small bottles to create a threat, I'm not sure why they never thought that he could have been an even bigger threat by combining the liquids in his three-once bottles in the water bottle he took through the checkpoint. Of course, even if he had been required to relinquish his bottle, he could have bought a bottle of water in the airport and taken it onboard to do whatever dastardly deed he had in mind.

My point today isn't to bash the system, but to ask the question if we really think through all the rules we put on ourselves in life. Most of the regulations we impose upon ourselves and allow others to impose upon us do not really deal with the root issues. The same is true with all our religious rules. That's why Jesus came to bring us grace to release us from the bondage of the ineffective Law.

January 14
Chuckles
Incompetents invariably make trouble for people other than themselves.

The medical report stated that the female patient was experiencing mood swings because she suffered with PBS.

Another medical report confirmed that since the patient stopped smoking, his smell is beginning to return.

Still another medical document bore record that the patient, a 65-year-old woman who had experienced a fall, was suffering complications from the fall because a truck rolled over her while she was down.

The following prayer request was found in the church's prayer box: My daughter got her driver's license this week; pray for all of us.

An engaged couple stayed apart due to flu but decided, after they were married, they could spend the rest of their lives making each other sick.

When a juggler fell through a hole in the stage floor, someone in the audience yelled, "Don't worry, Jeff. It's just a stage you're going through."

A young boy wrote home from summer camp, "I am looking forward to the ultimate bummer experience at camp this year." Was he being truthful, or was his spelling off a bit?

We have all heard that the "Man upstairs" is watching us all the time, but the thing we didn't realize is that he is actually a helicopter cop.

To keep people seated while the aircraft was docking, the stewardess announced, "Those of you who would like to stay and assist with cleaning the plane, please stand up at this time."

While the men were fishing in the inlet, the girls were shopping in the outlet.

The would-be groom objected to the pastor he had asked to officiate the ceremony, "Why do I need premarital counseling? I've been married three times already!"

Life is not a laughing matter – but can you imagine having to live without laughing?

Martin Luther King Day
MLK Memorial
From the moment the Martin Luther King Memorial was unveiled in Washington, DC, it began to generate nothing but flak. Why did the King family have to be paid $800,000 for the rights to use his image and quotes? Why were some of his statements paraphrased to the point that they lost their original soul? Why was his most noted proclamation, "I have a dream" omitted? Why was the statue outsourced to China when so many of the American workers that Dr. King defended so adamantly are out of work? Why was a Chinese artist chosen rather than an Afro-American? Why does the sculpture depict Dr. King with his arms folded and face stern rather than as the determined but kind man he was? Why does his statue so closely resemble some communist leader of bygone years rather than a warm American set on liberating his people? But most of all, why is the statue carved of white stone?

Some critics have said that Dr. King is turning over in his grave, and others have said that, if possible, he would get up out of his grave and go straight for the offices of the memorial committee demanding, "How dare you!"

I guess that the whole scenario simply emphasized the point that no matter what we do in life, others may not know how to assimilate it. Thank goodness, that even though it is a $120 million statue weighing 1,600 tons, covering four acres of the National Mall, it is only a piece of rock. The life and legacy that Dr. King gave us stretches from coast to coast, through every village and city of our great nation, into every school, place of business, and factory. With such a great legacy and impact, I suppose that no memorial would ever be fitting – even if it were carved by a black man in ebony stone!

January 16
One-liners That Speak Volumes
The only disability in life is a bad attitude.

Ideas are like wandering sons. They show up when you least expect them.

Mistakes are a fact of life; it is the response to the error that counts.

It takes twenty years to build a reputation and five minutes to ruin it.

Confidence comes not from always being right but from not fearing to be wrong.

The reason men and women get together is that they can do different things; one is good at one thing and the other at something else; together, the job gets done.

Don't mind him; he's suffering from jet brag!

Try to do something that you'll enjoy remembering.

If you curse and swear, you'll be darned to heck.

It wasn't the apple on the tree that caused a problem in the Garden of Eden; it was the pair on the ground.

Eve in the garden thought the apple was "to die for."

People will accept your ideas more readily if you tell them that Benjamin Franklin said it first.

A synonym is a word that you use if you can't spell the word you wanted to use.

If "price" and "value" or "worth" are the same, why are "priceless," "valueless," and "worthless" the opposite.

I am willing to fail at what will ultimately succeed, but not willing to succeed at what will ultimately fail.

I wish the Lord didn't trust me so much. – Mother Teresa

When you ask for my "help" with something, do you really mean that you want me to do all the work?

The power of prayer is with One who hears it, not one who says it.

As long as Jesus is an option, He is not an option.

If we build a dam so that we have a reservoir of God's blessing, we turn the blessing into a curse because we have dammed (damned) it.

January 17
This and That

A mortgage company, trying to verify financial data for a psychic reader, received a letter from his employer, "He is a subcontractor for our psychic, not a regular salaried employee. We therefore cannot predict his income."

A notice in the church bulletin read, "Thanks to all for your prayers, love, support, faithful attendance, and financial giving. It is because of you that we have been able to pad all our bills."

A youngster learning the Lord's Prayer recited, "Lead us not into temptation, but deliver us some e-mail. Amen."

A supervisor, writing a review for one of his employees, noted, "You're our most valuable employee; your ineptitude consistently raises the self-esteem of all our other employees."

When the guy set off the airport security alarm, the security agent asked if he had any change; his reply, "Gee, you've got to tip everyone here!"

When Lady Nancy Astor – the first woman member of Britain's House of Commons – told Winston Churchill during a fierce debate, "If I were married to you, I'd put poison in your coffee," Churchill replied, "If you were my wife, I'd drink it."

The difference between a luncheon and lunch is that you use linen napkins.

A young boy called out to his mother, "In case you're wondering, I'm not doing anything wrong."

Prunes are dried up plums, raisins are dried up grapes, and grandparents are dried up parents.

Too many of us have ExD degrees – doctorates in excusiology.

If making wrong choices were an Olympic event, most of us would be on a Wheaties box by now.

A rather romantic reader bought the book <u>How</u> <u>to</u> <u>Hug</u> at the used book store, only to get it home and discover that it was one volume out of an unabridged dictionary.

Christ's return is near. Don't miss it for the world.

January 18
Steve Jobs

Steve Jobs, the creator of the Apple empire, left us with some significant words of wisdom:

Your time is limited, so don't waste it living someone else's life. Don't be trapped by dogma – which is living with the results of other people's thinking. Don't let the noise of others' opinions drown out your own inner voice. And most important, have the courage to follow your heart and intuition. They somehow already know what you truly want to become. Everything else is secondary.

When I was seventeen, I read a quote that went something like: "If you live each day as if it was your last, someday you'll most certainly be right." It made an impression on me, and since then, for the past thirty-three years, I have looked in the mirror every morning and asked myself: "If today were the last day of my life, would I want to do what I am about to do today?" And whenever the answer has been "No" for too many days in a row, I know I need to change something.

Your work is going to fill a large part of your life, and the only way to be truly satisfied is to do what you believe is great work. And the only way to do great work is to love what you do. If you haven't found it yet, keep looking. Don't settle. As with all matters of the heart, you'll know when you find it. And, like any great relationship, it just gets better and better as the years roll on. So keep looking until you find it. Don't settle.

January 19
Bill Cosby

I'm seventy-six. Except for a brief period in the 50s when I was doing my National Service, I've worked hard since I was seventeen. Except for some serious health challenges, I put in fifty-hour weeks, and didn't call in sick in nearly forty years. I made a reasonable salary, but I didn't inherit my job or my income, and I worked to get where I am. Given the economy, it looks as though retirement was a bad idea, and I'm tired. Very tired. I'm tired of being told that I have to "spread the wealth" to people who don't have my work ethic. I'm tired of being told the government will take the money I earned, by force if necessary, and give it to people too lazy to earn it. I'm tired of being told I must lower my living standard to fight global warming, which no one is allowed to debate. I'm tired of being told that drug addicts have a disease, and I must help support and treat them, and pay for the damage they do. Did a giant germ rush out of a dark alley, grab them, and stuff white powder up their noses or stick a needle in their arm while they tried to fight it off? I'm tired of hearing wealthy athletes, entertainers and politicians of all parties talking about innocent mistakes, stupid mistakes, or youthful mistakes, when we all know they think their only mistake was getting caught. I'm tired of people with a sense of entitlement, rich or poor. I'm really tired of people who don't take responsibility for their lives and actions; I'm tired of hearing them blame the government, or discrimination, or big-whatever for their problems. I'm also tired and fed up with seeing young men and women in their teens and early twenties bedeck themselves in tattoos and face studs, thereby making themselves un-employable and claiming money from the government. Yes, I'm darn tired. But I'm also glad to be seventy-six. Because, mostly, I'm not going to have to see the world these people are making. I'm just sorry for my granddaughter and her children.

January 20
Of War and Peace
In The Divine Intruder, James R. Edwards recounts this story:

Wilmer McLean was a small farmer in the Shenandoah Valley in 1861. In the spring of that year two powerful armies met on his property – the Union army under General McDowell and the Confederate army under General Beauregard. The bloodiest war in American history began at Bull Run, a creek that ran through McLean's property. McLean was not at all sure why the armies were fighting, but he was quite sure he did not want them fighting on his property. If he could not change the course of the war, he at least did not have to be part of it. McLean decided to sell out and go where the war would never find him.

He chose the most obscure place in the whole country – or so he thought: an old house in the village of Appomattox Court House, Virginia. Four years later, General Grant was pursuing General Lee through Virginia. In Appomattox County, Grant sent a message to Lee asking him to meet and sign a truce. The place where they met to sign the peace that ended the Civil War was Wilmer McLean's living room!

Coincidence? Divine orchestration? I don't know. But I do see an interesting lesson here. Wilmer McLean was obviously a man of conviction, and God honored that quality by letting him play a significant role in bringing about the peace that he so dearly believed in.

What do you have sincere convictions about? Stand up for what you believe in and just wait to see how God will make it come to pass.

January 21
College Majors May Shape Religiosity

Certain academic majors can influence students' religiosity – positively or negatively – over time, according to researchers at the University of Michigan Institute for Social Research. Education majors showed the most dramatic increase in religious attendance and religious importance. Biology, engineering, physical science, and math majors all increased their religious attendance but saw a decrease in religious importance. Humanities and social science majors are likely to dip slightly in religious attendance, but religious importance plunges. "College is one of the few times you have a neat little label about the sorts of ideas a person has come in contact with," economics professor Miles Kimball said. "Professions can have a profound effect on people's attitudes."

I must admit that these findings still have me baffled. Having spent my whole life in the academic world, I understand that the secular religion of humanism with its dogma of evolution has permeated all branches of study. This worldview leaves no place for religious attendance or importance in that it sees any form of religion as an enemy to its self-centered belief system. Even in the sciences where the wonders of our universe are explored, evolutionists have so captured the minds of the intellectuals that they see the most blatant proofs of God's existence and His creative imagination and power as the random results of almost endless un-orchestrated trial and error.

On the other hand, I have also seen that the college years can be the most fertile period for evangelism because the students are exploring and open to new ideas and experiences. It is in such an environment that a seed of the gospel planted with the fertilizer of divine logic and the irrigation of love can produce a most abundant harvest.

January 22

Arise and Depart

When we were considering making a move from Indiana where my wife and I had spent the last quarter century of our lives and where all our sons had spent their total lives, one of the places we had in mind for our new home was Colorado Springs because we felt that it would be a great place to connect and network with other mission-minded ministries. We decided to make an exploratory trip to feel out the town, but did not tell anyone about our plans or the reason behind our trip. As far as anyone knew, we were taking our sons on a skiing trip. However, God knew all about our plans – but, even more, He had some plans of His own. Just thirty minutes before we were to head to the airport, I received a phone call from a dear pastor friend from Nigeria. He was calling to say that the Lord had spoken to him that he should give me a word from Micah 2:10, *Arise ye, and depart; for this is not your rest.* That call impacted me more than anything I can remember. I can only sum up its effect as I felt like I was slain in the Spirit standing up. I was so into the spirit realm and out of touch with the physical realm that I couldn't figure how to open the door to leave my office or how to put the key into the ignition to start the car. I'm still not sure how I drove to the airport that day, but we did make the visit and eventually the move.

The Lord orchestrated everything precisely. Buyers came to look at our house the day we were packing the truck for the move. When they placed the offer, we were on our way to Chicago to meet with Andrew Wommack about the possibility of working with the Bible college in Colorado, so we made an arrangement for the realtor to meet us at an intersection where we could stop long enough to sign the papers. We arrived in Colorado the same week that a long-standing employee of the college left, creating a position for us on the faculty.

In addition, a prophet spoke to us that a house would be waiting for us – and it was. In spite of the fact that others had put in bids on the property, the owners rejected their offers in favor of our bid even though it was below their asking price.

January 23

The Man Who Feared the Lord

In I Kings 17:3-4, we read the story of how Obadiah, the governor over the house of the wicked King Ahab, hid and cared for a hundred prophets when Jezebel was executing all the spokesmen of Jehovah. The passage goes on to explain that he did this because he feared the Lord greatly.

In II Kings 4:1, we meet the widow of one of the sons of the prophets who came to Elijah's successor Elisha begging for help because her sons were going to be taken away in order to settle a debt left by her late husband. The passage goes on to explain that her husband was one who feared the Lord.

Because the same words are used in such close proximity, some biblical scholars have suggested that these two references to the man who feared the Lord were talking about the same individual. Although there is no indication that Obadiah was one of the sons of the prophets and it is unlikely that he could have served in his role as the governor over Ahab's house and been numbered among the sons of the prophets who traditionally were essentially mendicants, it is possible that he used all his funds supporting the prophets and may have eventually left his position at the palace to pursue the life of a prophet. If this is the case, he eventually wound up with nothing left, resulting in his own sons being in jeopardy.

If this explanation of the scriptures is true, it proves a powerful point – you can't out-give God. When the widow was faced with the total devastation of her poverty, God supernaturally provided for her with an abundance that was only limited by her diligence to collect vessels to hold it. (verse 6) She was essentially experiencing what Malachi described as blessing that we cannot contain. (verse 3:10)

Jesus Himself promised, *Verily I say unto you, There is no man that hath left house, or brethren, or sisters, or father, or mother, or wife, or children, or lands, for my sake, and the gospel's, But he shall receive an hundredfold now in this time, houses, and brethren, and sisters, and mothers, and children, and lands, with persecutions; and in the world to come eternal life.* (Mark 10:29-30)

January 24
The Leopard's Spots

It always amazes me when I read reports by the "geniuses" of this world that defy common logic and deny biblical truth. I recently read a report by an evolutionist who had been studying the spots on big cats such as leopards. His conclusion was that these body markings vary depending upon the environment in which the cats live. He said that his research suggested that the spot patterns would actually shift as the animals adapted to different environments. His conclusion was, "Perhaps in the future we will have striped leopards and spotted tigers."

As soon as I read his remark, my mind flashed to Jeremiah 13:23, *Can the Ethiopian change his skin, or the leopard his spots? then may ye also do good, that are accustomed to do evil.* I found it ironically amusing that, out of all the spotted animals he could have mentioned, he chose the one big cat mentioned in the scripture as not able to change its spots!

No, leopards can't change their spots, men cannot change their skin color, and sinners cannot volitionally change their sinful ways. The only way a leopard could wind up with stripes is that it would become a tiger. The only way an Ethiopian could wind up with white skin is that he would become a Caucasian. And the only way a sinner could become righteous is that he become a Christian. Obviously, leopards can't become tigers and Ethiopians can't become Caucasians; but, fortunately, sinners can become Christians by being born again.

> *Therefore if any man be in Christ, he is a new creature: old things are passed away; behold, all things are become new.* (II Corinthians 5:17)

I just hope that this evolutionist will wake up, recognize his misguided ways, and allow God to change his spots and stripes.

State of the Union Address
America Needs Revival

In what became known as the Panic of 1857, major New York financial institutions collapsed, leaving thirty thousand Americans unemployed. When businessman Jeremiah Lanphier asked people to pray in the financial district, he got five responses – then ten – and eventually thousands! Eventually, there were over ten thousand conversions being recorded weekly in New York City alone. This move of God, which became known as the Fulton Street Revival, spread throughout the nation with over one million salvations – three percent of the total population. This move of God led to major social reforms, including the abolition of slavery, and it set the stage for the Azusa Street Revival that birthed the modern Pentecostal movement. Since that great outpouring of the Spirit, there have been other periods of widespread spiritual refreshing in America such as the Latter Rain Movement, the Healing Revival, the Charismatic Renewal, the Jesus Movement. There have also been isolated pockets of revival such as the Toronto Revival and the Brownsville Revival. But every awakening has been followed by periods of moral decline and spiritual lethargy.

We must have continual revival because, as Dr. Lester Sumrall expressed it, we always live one generation away from paganism. All we have to do is look at the history of Israel to see that Hezekiah's revival (II Chronicles 29-30) was followed by Manasseh's fall into paganism (II Chronicles 33) and Amon's degeneration (II Chronicles 33:21-25) was followed by Josiah's awakening (II Chronicles 34-35).

All it takes is a simple look around to see that America is in serious need of a swing of the spiritual pendulum toward a fresh move of God and widespread revival.

If my people, which are called by my name, shall humble themselves, and pray, and seek my face, and turn from their wicked ways; then will I hear from heaven, and will forgive their sin, and will heal their land. (II Chronicles 7:14)

January 26

More

And I gave thee thy master's house, and thy master's wives into thy bosom, and gave thee the house of Israel and of Judah; and if that had been too little, I would moreover have given unto thee such and such things. (II Samuel 12:8)

The above passage comes from the message that Nathan the prophet delivered to King David after he had committed adultery with Bathsheba and had arranged the murder of Uriah her husband. The Lord through the prophet reminded David that He had prospered him with incredible gifts and then went on to declare that He was willing to give David even more. But in the middle of all this prosperity and increase, David desired to have -- and took – the one thing that God was not willing to give him, his neighbor's wife. I find it interesting that the story is so explicit in depicting Bathsheba's residence as being so close to David's home that he could see her clearly from his terrace. In other words, she was literally his neighbor. Thus, he defied the commandment against coveting one's neighbor's wife in a literal sense as well as in the figurative sense in which the passage is intended. (Exodus 20:17)

However, this malady was nothing new with David. In fact, it dated back to the very Garden of Eden where God was willing to give Adam and Eve every tree in the garden and all the fruit that they bore. They wanted the fruit of the one tree that God did not give them. God had promised to give the bounty of the Promised Land to the Israelites, but Achan wanted the goods from the one city that God had said was taboo. Ahab could have had any vineyard in the country, but he could not be satisfied without the one that belonged to Naboth.

Our lesson today is simple: if we will just curb the greed that makes us crave those things that do not belong to us, God is willing and able to give us even more than we can imagine.

Chasing Ten Thousand

When a lady came for marriage counseling, she described in detail her husband's refusal to admit the need for help and his unwillingness to work toward a solution. I explained that it takes both parties to make the marriage work, reminding her that one can chase a thousand, but it takes two to chase ten thousand.

I then explained that the only hope was for the husband to join in the struggle. "Until he decides that he wants the marriage to work and is willing to join in the battle, you won't be able to chase off the 'ten thousand imps' who are working to destroy your home. Until then, you must stand alone against the 'one thousand demons' who are attacking your sanity, your peace of mind, and your physical wellbeing."

I assured her that I was not saying to give up on the marriage. She must continue to pray that her husband will have a change of heart. However, in the meantime, she must remember that he has his own personal freewill. It is a gift from God, and God will not take it away from him – even if he is using it in a destructive manner, hurting both himself and her as well as other family members and friends.

If you are facing similar situations, let me be quick to add that I am not discouraging you from having faith for your marriage and standing firm for its restoration. Our God can and will do exceedingly great and mighty things beyond anything that we would ever dare to ask for or could ever think of! We must never limit Him in His ability. I'm just adding one aspect to consider in addition to His ability – His integrity. Because He gave each individual a freewill to make his own decisions, God's integrity will not permit Him to violate that freewill by making that person come back into a relationship that he does not desire.

My suggestion is that you attack the demonic spirit that is deceiving the unwilling individual into thinking that he does not want the marriage to work. If you can break off the spirit that is blinding and binding him, then he can think clearly and with a choice of his freewill decide to yield to the restorative plan of God.

January 28

Seeking the Lord

I was really struck by a couple verses when reading through the historical books of the Old Testament recently. The first one gave me a new perspective on pursuing a relationship with God, and the second one reemphasized the life-and-death necessity of having a relationship with Him.

> *And he did evil, because he prepared not his heart to seek the LORD...And they entered into a covenant to seek the LORD God of their fathers with all their heart and with all their soul; That whosoever would not seek the LORD God of Israel should be put to death, whether small or great, whether man or woman.* (II Chronicles 12:14, 15:12-13)

The story of Rehoboam presented me with a new angle to the principle of developing a relationship with God. Prior to reading this verse, I would have thought that people either sought the Lord or they didn't; however, this passage took the relationship back one further step. There is apparently a prerequisite step of preparing one's heart before we can even begin the process of seeking the Lord. Suddenly, a whole new world of worship and revelation came into focus. We may seek the Lord through scriptural study or prayer, but we must first lay a foundation upon which this seeking of God can be accomplished; we must prepare our hearts for the encounter we will have when we seek and find Him. It seems to me that such a preparation can be made only through praise and worship because it is through praise and worship that we get the focus of our attention off ourselves and onto Him. At that point, and only at that point, will our seeking of God be for relationship rather than for what blessing we might be able to obtain from Him.

The second verse emphasized the importance of commitment (actually a covenant) to having a relationship with God. For the people of Israel, it was a life and death matter. For us today, our lives also depend upon it!

January 29

Mrs. Einstein

When Mrs. Einstein was asked if she understood the theory of relativity, she replied, "No, but I understand Albert, and he can be trusted."

Even though there has been some recent news that Dr. Einstein's famed theory may have been disproved, the moral of the story about his wife is still valid. If you can trust an author, you can trust his words. I find this especially comforting when confronted with issues that I simply cannot fathom as I read the Bible. I don't claim to totally understand why God sent the Israelites into Canaan with instructions to kill everyone – women and children included. Yes, I understand the issue of the pollution they had brought into the land; however, I still have difficulty seeing the loving God depicted in the rest of the Bible giving such a directive. I can't understand why there is an eternal hell waiting to swallow up those individuals who have struggled all their lives to do the best they can but simply never had the opportunity to accept Christ because the gospel was never presented to them or it was presented in such a religious way that it was not effective. I cannot understand how some people will spend all their lives in misery, suffering from poverty, disease, abuse, addiction, or even the slavery of human trafficking and still face an eternity of agony if they have not accepted the gospel. I don't understand predestination and a whole list of other theological concepts so long that I'm embarrassed to admit it. HOWEVER, there is one thing that I do understand – God is a gracious loving Father who is always planning good things for His children. And since I understand Him, I can trust anything that He says or does.

> *Every good gift and every perfect gift is from above, and cometh down from the Father of lights, with whom is no variableness, neither shadow of turning.* (James 1:17)

January 30

Preserved

Two young Hispanic men were being considered for a position in a computer-based business. Throughout the application and interview process, the two seemed equally qualified for the job. The final elimination was to be made based on a timed computer skills test. As the two young men worked through the various levels of the skills test, Juan always seemed to be just a few steps ahead of Jesus; however, something tragic happened just as the clock was ticking down – the electricity went out. When the lights came back on, Juan stared in dismay at the blank screen, realizing that all his work had been lost. He frantically started over to try to get at least a little work done before the alarm sounded. Jesus, on the other hand, made a few final keystrokes and submitted his completed exam. The moral of the story: Jesus saves.

Well, when I first heard that story, I thought that it was tactless, sacrilegious, and disrespectful. However, I later came to realize that it actually did make a point that was worthy of discussion. Jesus does save, but that salvation also included preservation. What our young Hispanic friend had done with his computer work is commonly termed as "saving," but I would like to suggest that it really entails preserving, keeping it from being damaged, altered, lost, or destroyed. That is really what Jesus does in our lives as well. We too often think of being saved as simply our fire insurance policy to guarantee that we won't go to hell. However, when Jesus saves, He also preserves us from loss or damage.

> *I know whom I have believed, and am persuaded that he is able to keep that which I have committed unto him against that day.* (II Timothy 1:12)
> *The Lord shall deliver me from every evil work, and will preserve me unto his heavenly kingdom.* (II Timothy 4:18)
> *The Lord knoweth how to deliver the godly out of temptations.* (II Peter 2:9)

January 31
The Cabbie and the Preacher

The story is told of two men who appeared at the Pearly Gate at the same time. When St. Peter checked his roster, he realized that one of the men was a taxi driver and immediately promoted him to one of the choicest spots in heaven. Next, St. Peter checked the roster again to identify the second man and noted that he had been the pastor of a prominent church. The pastor, having seen the reward the cab driver had received, felt assured that he must have an especially magnificent reward awaiting him. Instead, St. Peter directed him to a rather modest mansion. Terribly perplexed as to how a man of the cloth could wind up relegated to one of the low-rent districts, he questioned St. Peter if he had been misidentified. Peter's answer was simple and straightforward, "Every Sunday, people fell asleep during your sermons, but no one ever fell asleep when the driver was behind the wheel. Instead, they were always actively praying, not like the people in your church."

Of course, heaven doesn't operate on anything that vaguely resembles the system depicted in this little story; however, maybe it is good for us to stop and think about how we influence others. The cab driver wasn't trying to get people to pray, but he did. The pastor was trying to help his congregants spiritually, but he wound up putting them to sleep. In your life and mine, the same things may also be true. Sometimes it is our unintentional actions – as opposed to our deliberate "ministry" – that have more impact on others.

> *Let your light so shine before men, that they may see your good works, and glorify your Father which is in heaven.* (Matthew 5:16)
>
> *Moreover he must have a good report of them which are without; lest he fall into reproach and the snare of the devil.* (I Timothy 3:7)
>
> *Likewise, ye wives, be in subjection to your own husbands; that, if any obey not the word, they also may without the word be won by the conversation of the wives.* (I Peter 3:1)

February 1

Follow the Leader

In <u>Life on the Edge</u>, Dr. James Dobson writes:

What are the characteristics of sheep that remind the Lord of you and me? What is he really saying when he refers to us in that way? Well, shepherds and ranchers tell us that these animals are virtually defenseless against predators, not very resourceful, inclined to follow one another into danger, and they are absolutely dependent on their human masters for safety. Thus, when David wrote, *We all, like sheep, have gone astray*, he was referring to our tendency to move as an unthinking herd and away from the watchful care of the Shepherd.

I observed this herd instinct a few years ago in a documentary on television. It was filmed in a packinghouse where sheep were being slaughtered for the meat market. Huddled in pens outside were hundreds of nervous animals. They seemed to sense danger in their unfamiliar surroundings. Then a gate was opened that led up a ramp and through a door to the right. In order to get the sheep to walk up that ramp, the handlers used what is known as a "Judas goat." This is a goat that has been trained to lead the sheep into the slaughterhouse. The goat did his job very efficiently. He confidently walked to the bottom of the ramp and looked back. Then he took a few more steps and stopped again. The sheep looked at each other skittishly and then began moving toward the ramp. Eventually, they followed the confident goat to the top, where he went through a little gate to the left, but they were forced to turn to the right and went to their deaths. It was a dramatic illustration of unthinking, herd behavior and the deadly consequences it often brings.

> *But when he saw the multitudes, he was moved with compassion on them, because they fainted, and were scattered abroad, as sheep having no shepherd.* (Matthew 9:36)

It Takes All Kinds

When we would meet people who were unusual – like for instance people who observe Groundhog Day – my mother would always comment, "It takes all kinds." Well, the world really is full of people of all kinds.

In El Paso County, Colorado, a man attacked his neighbor's home with a front-end loader, destroying much of the house and flipping over his six cars. The only reason he did not flatten the entire structure was because there were dogs inside one part of the house. The $150,000 in damages were the result of a disagreement over an $80 debt. The neighbor bought a flatbed trailer for $320 but didn't negotiate the $80 side rails. After being arrested and tried for the criminal mischief, the perpetrator committed suicide.

Alcohol Mary Road in Greenwood, Maine, is named after a famous Prohibition-era bootlegger in that area. Descendants sued to have the name changed because they felt that it defamed her name. Selectmen and residents refused, claiming that Alcohol Mary is an historical figure and a source of local pride.

India says that the poverty level for city dwellers is 578 rupees per person per month ($12.75) and 450 rupees for rural residents ($9.93). The ruling was set when the government was asked to explain why it had millions of tons of grain in storage while so many went hungry. The government claimed that it had limited resources to distribute grain to subsidized shops. Therefore, rather than doing their job, they simply changed the rules so that the people would no longer qualify for the benefits due them.

An escaped convict knocked on the door of a cabin in the state of Washington only to discover that it was rented out to a vacationing guard from the prison he had escaped from.

Amber Miller ran in the 2011 Chicago Marathon when thirty-nine weeks pregnant. She went into labor and delivered a healthy baby immediately after completing the twenty-six-mile run in six hours and twenty-five minutes.

February 3

Spin

The ice cream carton made the bold announcement that it contained two scoops more. Having piqued my curiosity, I couldn't help but wonder, "Two scoops more than what?" When I read the rest of the explanation, I discovered that this carton had fifteen percent more ice cream than the one-and-a-half-quart size. At that point, I simply couldn't resist wondering why the packaging company hadn't been honest enough to advertise that the container had two scoops <u>less</u> or fifteen percent <u>less</u> than the traditional half-a-gallon size.

What I had encountered was an obvious case of "spin," the practice of shifting the emphasis on a topic to cover up any negative aspect while trying to draw attention to any real – or imagined – positive aspects.

When I was having a physical exam in my teen years, the physician explained to me that I had one leg that was a fraction of an inch shorter than the other one. Being the sassy type of guy that I am, I couldn't resist asking how he decided that. When he looked back at me with a "Do I have to get the <u>Tape Measure for Dummies</u> for you?" expression on his face, I continued with, "How do you know that this leg is short? Maybe it's really that the other leg is long." Of course, it was just a stupid joke, but I didn't see any reason for emphasizing the negative aspect of a short leg when there was an equal possibility that we could look at the issue from a positive angle.

Politicians and salesmen don't have to have a monopoly on spin. In every area of life, we can decide to look for any possible positive aspect. And I'll guarantee you that you'll find it if you take the time to look for it. After all, the forecast that tells us that there is a thirty-percent chance of rain really means that there is a seventy-percent chance of sunshine!

> *Whatsoever things are true, whatsoever things are honest, whatsoever things are just, whatsoever things are pure, whatsoever things are lovely, whatsoever things are of good report; if there be any virtue, and if there be any praise, think on these things.*
> (Philippians 4:8)

February 4
Oh, Really?
Peggy and I had been invited as guest speakers at a new Bible college that had been in operation for only a few semesters. As the director of the school was driving us around the city, he began to share with us how God had provided miraculously for so many of the students who had come to school on faith. Just as we pulled onto the major thoroughfare that ran through the city, he was giving us the example of one student who had given up a lucrative career to come to Bible school. However, when he arrived in town, he came up with an idea for an independent business that was covering all his needs. The school director went on to explain that the gentleman had opened an escort service. Fortunately, the director was too busy watching the traffic on the busy road to see the shock on our faces. As he went on with the gentleman's testimony, the director explained that since the gentleman had to run his escort service at night only, he had all day free for school and assignments. I'm sure that both our jaws had dropped to the floorboard by this time, but the driver was still too occupied with watching all the other cars and trucks to notice. About that time, a small truck with a flashing yellow light approached us, and the school director exclaimed, "Why, that might just be our student right now!" Suddenly, it dawned on us that the student was running a business that escorts oversized vehicles through heavy traffic areas rather than the kind of escort service that we had been imagining.

We all, of course, had a great laugh when Peggy and I were able to catch our breath enough to share with the school director what had been going on in our minds. But in addition to the humorous string of events, we also had a great lesson: Don't jump to conclusions, no matter how obvious they seem.

> *Therefore judge nothing before the time, until the Lord come, who both will bring to light the hidden things of darkness, and will make manifest the counsels of the hearts: and then shall every man have praise of God.* (I Corinthians 4:5)

February 5

The Naked Prophet

The Jain religion in India has a number of interesting characteristics. Among them is ahimsa, the practice of being careful not to harm any living animal or bug. The Jain devotees usually cover their mouths with gauze so as to protect any wayward insect from flying into their mouths and being swallowed. They carry little brooms to sweep the path they are walking on so as to avoid accidentally stepping on a bug. They filter all their water to guarantee that nothing living that may be floating in the glass is accidentally ingested. Of course, they are vegetarians, but their dietary rules go even further than the average run-of-the-mill vegetarian. In addition to shunning meat, they are careful not to eat any food that might have involved the injury of an animal in the process of harvesting or preparing it. For instance, potatoes are off the menu because worms may have been cut in half in the process of digging up the tubers.

In addition to their practice of ahimsa, they also practice asceticism, a form of self-denial that leads them to reject any unnecessary material possessions. To indicate the level of self-denial they have achieved, Jains fall into two categories: white-clad and sky-clad. The white-clad Jains wear only white robes indicating that they have released all earthy ties. The sky-clad Jains have followed the path of self-denial so fully that they have even abandoned their white robes.

While traveling in India, a friend of mine had the opportunity to become acquainted with a sky-clad Jain priest and asked if he could take a photograph as a remembrance of the meeting. The prophet's response was, "Don't take a picture of me as a memory; become a vegetarian and you will remember me three times every day."

I believe that Jesus is also calling us to make such radical changes in our lifestyles so that we never forget that we have met Him!

February 6
Pulling Down Strongholds – Part I

For though we walk in the flesh, we do not war after the flesh: (For the weapons of our warfare are not carnal, but mighty through God to the pulling down of strong holds;) Casting down imaginations, and every high thing that exalteth itself against the knowledge of God, and bringing into captivity every thought to the obedience of Christ. (II Corinthians 10:3-5)

Paul tells us that pulling down the strongholds in our lives has to do with getting rid of the ideas that the devil has put in your head. He goes on to explain that pulling down these strongholds is done with a stronger force than the flesh and that the stronger force we need is the gospel. In other places in his epistles, Paul shows us that the authority of the gospel comes from believing it to the point that it actually manifests in life-changing demonstrations of power.

For I am not ashamed of the gospel of Christ: for it is the power of God unto salvation to every one that believeth...My speech and my preaching was not with enticing words of man's wisdom, but in demonstration of the Spirit and of power: That your faith should not stand in the wisdom of men, but in the power of God...But the natural man receiveth not the things of the Spirit of God: for they are foolishness unto him: neither can he know them, because they are spiritually discerned...For who hath known the mind of the Lord, that he may instruct him? But we have the mind of Christ. (Romans 1:16; I Corinthians 2:4-5, 14-16)

To pull down the strongholds that hold us in captivity, we must deliberately renew our minds with the truths of God's Word, believing them to the point that they actually become an effective force in our lives, not just a theological concept.

February 7

Pulling Down Strongholds – Part II

Yesterday, we learned that pulling down strongholds has to do with getting rid of the mental bondages and the mindset that the devil has imposed upon us. To fully comprehend how strong those bondages can be, it is important to understand exactly how such false ideas came into control in the first place. Paul gives us the full explanation in the book of Romans.

> *Because that, when they knew God, they glorified him not as God, neither were thankful; but became vain in their imaginations, and their foolish heart was darkened...And even as they did not like to retain God in their knowledge, God gave them over to a reprobate mind.* (verses 1:21, 28)

From this passage, we understand that it was through a deliberate disregard for the knowledge of God that these deceptive forces gained control over the human race and each individual human. Paul explained that this mind control is not a one-time event, but that it is an ongoing daily practice.

> *For they that are after the flesh do mind the things of the flesh; but they that are after the Spirit the things of the Spirit. For to be carnally minded is death; but to be spiritually minded is life and peace. Because the carnal mind is enmity against God: for it is not subject to the law of God, neither indeed can be.* (verses 8:5-7)

He gives the solution to this tragic state of human affairs by our being spiritually minded, and then he follows that statement up a little later in his epistle by explaining the process we can go through to become spiritually minded.

> *And be not conformed to this world: but be ye transformed by the renewing of your mind, that ye may prove what is that good, and acceptable, and perfect, will of God.* (verse 12:2)

February 8

Pulling Down Strongholds – Part III

In our last meditation, we were contemplating Paul's instruction in the book of Romans to renew our minds. It is in another of his epistles that we find his actual formula for doing this.

> *Finally, brethren, whatsoever things are true, whatsoever things are honest, whatsoever things are just, whatsoever things are pure, whatsoever things are lovely, whatsoever things are of good report; if there be any virtue, and if there be any praise, think on these things.* (Philippians 4:8)

Notice that he didn't simply say to think on things that are true. He qualified his statement by saying that the things we are to dwell on must also be lovely, of a good report, full of virtue, and praiseworthy. It may be true that you are sick or in poverty. But since these truths do not meet the other criteria, we cannot let our minds dwell on them. Instead, we must find other truths that do meet all the necessary conditions. Rather than thinking about our sickness, we must meditate on the truth that our God is a healer. Rather than focusing on our poverty, our solution is to concentrate on the truth that God wants us to prosper. Couple this instruction from Paul with the words of Solomon in Proverbs 23:7, *For as he thinketh in his heart, so is he*, and you will realize how you can be a person whose life is characterized by truth, honesty, purity, loveliness, a good report, virtue, and praise. When that happens, you can celebrate the fact that the strongholds have been broken off of your life.

In Ephesians 6:14, Paul wrote, *Stand therefore, having your loins girt about with truth, and having on the breastplate of righteousness,* showing us that truth coupled with righteousness – the product of allowing the truth of God's Word to actually manifest itself in our lives – that will give us authority to stand against the enemy and his strongholds. In this same passage, he tells us that the offensive weapon we take against the enemy is the sword of the Spirit, which is the Word of God. (verse 17)

February 9

Pulling Down Strongholds – Part IV

We concluded yesterday's thoughts with Paul's declaration that the Word of God is the sword of the Spirit.

Paul says that the sword belongs to the Holy Spirit, not necessarily to the believer himself. I believe that what Paul is trying to communicate here is the same principle that Jesus gave us in John 14:26, *But the Comforter, which is the Holy Ghost, whom the Father will send in my name, he shall teach you all things, and bring all things to your remembrance, whatsoever I have said unto you.* In other words, we are not to rely upon our own ability to figure things out. Rather, we are to rely upon the Holy Spirit to reach inside of us and pull out the portions of the Word of God that we have hidden in our hearts (Psalm 119:11) to use against the enemy at exactly the right time. In my own life, I have had many occurrences when, seemingly out of nowhere, a verse that I had learned many years before but had not really meditated on or thought about over those years would suddenly come bursting out of my spirit at just the moment when I would need the truth in that particular verse to deal with the specific situation I was facing at that precise moment. This was the work of the Holy Spirit as He wielded His sword – the Word of God – in battle on my behalf.

The second observation I want to make about this verse is that Paul used the term *rhema* rather than *logos* when he spoke of the word of God. The difference between the two Greek words available to him is that *logos* refers to a general truth, whereas *rhema* speaks of a specific individualized word or statement. What the apostle was trying to communicate is that we can't expect to be victorious in pulling down stronghold by simply relying on the general principle that God loves us and has a wonderful plan for our lives. Rather, we need to know the specific truths of the Word to face each specific challenge in life.

We must know the exact Bible answer to sickness, to lack, to sin, to fear, to depression… And when we do, the Holy Spirit will bring those truths like a two-edged sword (Hebrews 4:12) on our behalf when we need them!

February 10
Pulling Down Strongholds – Part V

Wherefore gird up the loins of your mind, be
sober, and hope to the end for the grace that
is to be brought unto you at the revelation of
Jesus Christ. (I Peter 1:13)

In addition to all that we have learned from the Apostle Paul concerning renewing our minds with the Word of God, the Apostle Peter adds to us the idea that we are to gird up our minds with the Word of God. The term he uses here means to wrap the Word of God around our minds. When we wrap our minds in the Word of God, it strengthens our minds in the same way that a back brace supports our physical backs so that we can lift heavy objects without injuring ourselves.

"Girding up" also conveys the image of gathering one's skirt tail in order to have more mobility. It's the image that we are all so familiar with from the Little House on the Prairie episodes when Mama would pull up her dress in order to run faster when there was an emergency. I've also seen the men in Sri Lanka and other Asian countries – where they wear sarongs rather than pants – wrap their skirts around their waists when working in the fields or on construction sites.

The message that Peter is conveying is that the Word of God gives us strength to do things that we would not otherwise be able to do just as the back brace enables workers to move objects they would not otherwise be able to lift safely. In addition, it gives us flexibility and mobility so that we can move more quickly and with more agility to accomplish the tasks before us. All these benefits come through the work that the Word of God does in our minds by giving us the ability to understand the truth of God as opposed to the deceptions and bondages of the enemy.

If we do not gird up our minds, we are easily and quickly entangled in negative and erroneous ideas that trap us and trip us up.

Stand fast therefore in the liberty wherewith
Christ hath made us free, and be not
entangled again with the yoke of bondage.
(Galatians 5:1)

February 11
Pulling Down Strongholds – Part VI

One classic example of the pulling down of a stronghold is found in the biblical story of David's conquest of Jerusalem. When the Jebusites possessed the city, they armed it with the lame and blind soldiers who were no longer able to serve in other positions in the military. (II Samuel 5:6) The reason that they didn't need strong able-bodied soldiers there was because the city was naturally fortified because of its position on a cliff with deep ravines surrounding it. This story becomes parabolic to us when we realize that the thoughts that the enemy had held us captive with are just like these Jebusite guards. (They are lame ideas because they don't have a leg to stand on.) They are blind ideas because the god of this world has blinded us from the truth. (II Corinthians 4:4)

My grandmother never believed that we actually had a man on the moon – even after seeing the pictures on the TV. I understand that twenty-seven percent of adult Americans still believe that the sun revolves around the earth. Obviously, these are radically incorrect thoughts – lame and blind – but they still control people's minds. In the spiritual arena, we can be controlled – and destroyed – by just as foundationless ideas.

> *For the creature was made subject to vanity, not willingly, but by reason of him who hath subjected the same in hope.* (Romans 8:20)
> *Because that, when they knew God, they glorified him not as God, neither were thankful; but became vain in their imaginations, and their foolish heart was darkened.* (Romans 1:21)
> *This I say therefore, and testify in the Lord, that ye henceforth walk not as other Gentiles walk, in the vanity of their mind.* (Ephesians 4:17)
> *Casting down imaginations, and every high thing that exalteth itself against the knowledge of God, and bringing into captivity every thought to the obedience of Christ.* (II Corinthians 10:5)

February 12
What Did You Mean to Say?

It is with serious trepidation that I take up today's topic. All of you who have carefully read any of my books will understand why when I tell you that I'm going to discuss spelling errors. Since I do my own typing and proofreading, my books are invariably seasoned with misspelled words that I simply read right over because my brain keeps inserting the words that I think should be there even when my eyes see something different on the page. But, let's take a stab at the topic anyway.

The other day, I noticed a sign on a plumber's truck that read, "No job to big or to small." Not a serious error, but a mistake nonetheless. Of course, it didn't engender any response like the handwritten sign next to the dog food display that read, "Free dog bowel with each purchase."

My favorite story comes from a college choral group that was making a trip to present a number of concerts, so they hired a sign maker to letter their bus before leaving for the trip. When he brought the bus back to the campus, both sides boasted the name of the college followed by the words, "Quire tour." When the conductor saw the wording, she was appalled and let the sign painter know in no uncertain terms that the tour had nothing to do with partial reams of paper and that the word she wanted was the one that started with a "ch." The next day, the bus was back with the error corrected. Now it read, "Chuire tour"!

While traveling in England in 2011, I had a chance to see The Adulterous Bible as part of an exhibit honoring the four hundredth anniversary of the King James Bible. Published in 1631 by the royal printers in London, the name is derived from the compositors' mistake of accidently omitting the word "not" in the sentence "Thou shalt not commit adultery." The publishers were fined and deprived of their printer's license.

Isn't it reassuring that other than such human errors as typos, we have a sure and dependable word from God?

We have also a more sure word of prophecy; whereunto ye do well that ye take heed. (II Peter 1:19)

February 13
Wearing the Badge

I ran across a really interesting study the other day: a survey done among atheists. The research presented in the study indicated that eight percent of atheists are certain that there is a God and that another twenty-six percent are pretty sure that He exists. Adding these figures together we can conclude that more than one out of every three so-called atheists actually is fairly well convinced that he is simply wearing the badge rather than really being an atheist. Actually, Paul addresses this specific issue in the book of Romans when he says that all men actually start out with the knowledge of God and have to deliberately disregard that original revelation in order to practice pagan religion or embrace atheism.

> *Because that which may be known of God is manifest in them; for God hath shewed it unto them. For the invisible things of him from the creation of the world are clearly seen, being understood by the things that are made, even his eternal power and Godhead; so that they are without excuse: Because that, when they knew God, they glorified him not as God, neither were thankful; but became vain in their imaginations, and their foolish heart was darkened. Professing themselves to be wise, they became fools, And changed the glory of the uncorruptible God into an image made like to corruptible man, and to birds, and fourfooted beasts, and creeping things. Wherefore God also gave them up to uncleanness through the lusts of their own hearts, to dishonour their own bodies between themselves: Who changed the truth of God into a lie, and worshipped and served the creature more than the Creator, who is blessed for ever. Amen.* (verses 1:19-25)

Valentine's Day

Accepted in the Beloved

To the praise of the glory of his grace,
wherein he hath made us accepted in the
beloved. (Ephesians 1:6)

Today's message is different from the usual Valentine love story. Rather than focusing on the normal audience of lovers, I want to say something to the ones who are alone, feeling unloved.

In India, girls are not considered to be valuable because their parents have to pay a very high dowry to get them married. In fact, many families wind up in financial bondage for the rest of their lives after borrowing the money to pay the dowry. Boys, on the other hand, are valuable because their parents collect a hefty sum from the dowry when they are married. As a result, many girls are simply abandoned and are given the names Nakusa or Nakushi, meaning unwanted. A recent program targets such girls and helps them get adopted, complete with a name certificate to prove that they are no longer unwanted.

This ministry of making the unwanted realize that someone really does want them dates back at least to the time of the Bible. When Paul said that we are accepted in the beloved, he used a term that appears only two times in the New Testament – here and in Luke 1:28, where the angel Gabriel used it to tell the Virgin Mary that she was *highly favored.* In other words, our acceptance is not just a toleration; it is a full-blown celebration of adoption. If we couple this understanding of the word with the context in which it is used here – to the praise of the glory of His grace – we will begin to get an insight into how exuberant God really is about having us as part of His family! Unlike Cinderella, who was unloved and rejected by her stepmother, our heavenly Father accepts and loves us.

Your life may be characterized by divorce, broken heartedness, abandonment, being forgotten, and being forsaken – not so with God. He not only accepts you in His beloved, He highly favors you!

Presidents' Day
Quotes from Our Presidents
We ought to be no less persuaded that the propitious smiles of heaven can never be expected on a nation that disregards the eternal rules of order and right which heaven itself ordained. – George Washington

Let me live according to those holy rules which Thou hast this day prescribed in Thy Holy Word…direct me to the true object, Jesus Christ, the way, the truth, and the life. Bless, O Lord, all the people of this land.–George Washington

The general principles on which the fathers achieved independence were the general principles of Christianity. I will avow that I then believed, and now believe, that those general principles of Christianity are as eternal and immutable as the existence and attributes of God.–John Adams

We have no government armed with power capable of contending with human passions unbridled by morality and religion…Our Constitution was made only for a moral and religious people. It is wholly inadequate for the government of any other.–John Adams

Can the liberties of a nation be thought secure when we have removed their only firm basis, a conviction in the minds of the people that these liberties are the gift of God? That they are not to be violated but with His wrath? I tremble for my country when I reflect that God is just; that his justice cannot sleep forever.–Thomas Jefferson

I have always said and always will say that the studious perusal of the Sacred Volume will make better citizens, better fathers, better husbands…the Bible makes the best people in the world.–Thomas Jefferson

Before any man can be considered as a member of civil society, he must be considered as a subject of the Governor of the Universe. And to the same Divine Author of every good and perfect gift we are indebted for all those privileges and advantages, religious as well as civil, which are so richly enjoyed in this favored land.–James Monroe

February 16

Order

I have always been a neat freak. In fact, my roommates in college used to make fun of me by saying that they always thought it strange that after I had been in the bathroom all the shampoo bottles, shaving cream cans, and aftershave containers would magically be in order of size. I also discovered that one of their pastimes was to sneak into my dresser when I was out to look at the display of all the socks folded and arranged by color while their socks were simply tossed into their dresser drawer without even being matched into pairs. However, I believe that order is part of God's nature and that He expects it to be part of the lives of those who follow Him.

Researchers in the Netherlands demonstrated that an orderly environment versus a disorderly environment actually changes people's moods. During a strike by workers at a railway station, the researchers did a survey in which they asked people to sit down and answer questions about Muslims, homosexuals, and Dutch people. They repeated the same survey after the strike had ended and the station was back to normal. When the station was messy, those responding to the survey were ten percent more likely to stereotype people and sat twenty-five percent further away from people of other ethnic backgrounds than when the station was tidy.

Order my steps in thy word: and let not any iniquity have dominion over me. (Psalm 119:133)

In those days was Hezekiah sick unto death. And the prophet Isaiah the son of Amoz came to him, and said unto him, Thus saith the LORD, Set thine house in order. (II Kings 20:1)

And if any man hunger, let him eat at home; that ye come not together unto condemnation. And the rest will I set in order when I come. (I Corinthians 11:34)

Let all things be done decently and in order. (I Corinthians 14:40)

February 17

How to Get Ahead Part I

The story is told of a cannibal who jumped out of the bush to attack a passerby. When the startled stranger yelled at the headhunter, "What are you trying to do?" he replied, "Oh, I'm just trying to get a head."

Well, we all want to know how to get ahead in life, and, fortunately, we have a manual that tells us exactly how to do it – the Bible.

One of the first principles to remember is that we are first and foremost responsible to God for all our actions, attitudes, and decisions. In the story of David's adultery with Bathsheba and his murder plot against her husband Uriah, we find a very interesting conclusion in the king's prayer of repentance recorded for us in Psalm fifty-one. In verse four, David acknowledges that his sin was against God and God alone. Uriah was dead and Bathsheba was defiled, but David recognized that the real crime was in his broken relationship with God. A similar observation can be found in Genesis 39:9 where Joseph refused to allow himself to be seduced by Potiphar's wife, acknowledging that he could not sin against the Lord.

What we can learn from these examples is that the primary key to successful living is to always guard the heart relationship we have with God. When David realized that he was not going to get away with trying to cover up his sin, his repentance prayer was for a new spirit and a clean heart. The result was that the New Testament record of his life is that he was a man after God's own heart. (Acts 13:22)

From the very beginning of David's life, the thing that set him apart from others was that heart relationship he had with God. (I Samuel 16:7) After this failure with his neighbor's wife, David learned to continually keep his heart under surveillance (Psalm 139:23-24) and to keep it full of the Word of God as a safeguard (Psalm 119:11).

David's key to getting ahead in life and winning a place in history was to first of all guard his relationship with God.

February 18
How to Get Ahead Part II
Another key to getting ahead in life is to keep yourself motivated. At one point in David's life, it seemed as if the bottom had fallen out. Upon returning from battle, he and his men discovered that their camp had been raided in their absence. All their possessions had been stolen, and their wives and children had been kidnapped. The men in David's army – all of whom had been his most loyal and trusted companions since he took them from being misfits in society to being heroes and champions – turned against him. Accusing him of not taking proper security measures by leaving some of them behind to protect the families and goods, they were plotting a mutiny against David and were actually scheming to kill him. On top of all this, David was exhausted from his military campaign, and could barely "put one foot in front of the other." At his very rope's end, he turned to the one source of strength that he knew would not fail him – his God. First Samuel 30:6-8 records that he encouraged himself in the Lord and inquired if he should pursue after the marauders and overtake them. The Lord answered him that, yes, he should do the two things he had in his heart – to pursue and to overtake. Then the Lord added one more bit of encouragement – that, without fail, he would recover everything that had been taken.

In Hebrews 10:34, we learn that the New Testament Christians took joyfully the spoiling (confiscation, plunder, and destruction) of their goods because they knew that they had a better and an enduring substance in heaven. Paul was able to count all the trouble he endured – including imprisonment, floggings, being stoned and left for dead, shipwreck, perils of robbers, hunger and thirst, exposure, and hypothermia (II Corinthians 11:23-27) – as just light afflictions (II Corinthians 4:17) because he was so focused on the heaven he was going to that he barely noticed the hell he was going through.

To get ahead in life, we have to encourage ourselves that there is always light at the end of the tunnel – and it is not a freight train headed toward us. It is the light of men that shines in our darkness – Jesus. (John 1:4)

February 19
How to Get Ahead Part III
Another important aspect of getting ahead in life is to repent for any self-motivated agendas. Notice that David did not head out after the marauders without first seeking God's direction. When we do make plans without His counsel, they will fail. In fact, Solomon felt that this principle was so important that he repeated it twice for us in the book of Proverbs, *There is a way that seemeth right unto a man, but the end thereof are the ways of death.* (verses 14:12, 16:25) On the other hand, Solomon explicitly spelled out his formula for success in the third chapter of the same book:

> *Trust in the LORD with all thine heart; and lean not unto thine own understanding. In all thy ways acknowledge him, and he shall direct thy paths. Be not wise in thine own eyes: fear the LORD, and depart from evil. It shall be health to thy navel, and marrow to thy bones.* (verses 5-8)

When we do make a mistake by trusting in our own ideas, we simply need to understand what it was that went wrong and where it was that we made the mistake. At that point, we must go back and pick up the remaining pieces and start over. Like making a wrong turn when on a trip, the easiest way to get back on course is to go to the place where we made the erroneous turn and make the correct turn this time. Of course, there is the possibility that we might just find someone who knows another route to get to where we are going. In that case, it would be wise to ask him for directions. That is, of course, assuming that you are not a man! It is so well known that men refuse to stop and ask for directions that some women have calculated that the reason it took Israel forty years to get through the Sinai is that Moses, rather than Miriam, was in charge. Seriously, we should always look for godly counsel from other spiritually mature people and from the Word of God. This principle is so significant that Solomon repeated it three times in the book of Proverbs. (verses 11:14, 15:22, 24:6)

How to Get Ahead Part IV

The next principle to getting ahead in life is so obvious that I am afraid I'll insult your intelligence by even mentioning it – take action.

Proverbs 24:16 tells us that even a just man may fall seven times, but he will rise up again. Solomon goes on to add that, when the wicked falls, he winds up in mischief. The difference between falling and failing is the determination to get up and move forward. Paul encouraged Timothy along these lines, *Wherefore I put thee in remembrance that thou stir up the gift of God, which is in thee by the putting on of my hands.* (II Timothy 1:6) James tells us three times that no matter how much faith we have, it is dead or useless unless we take action on it. (verses 2:17, 20, 26)

The story of the four lepers in II Kings chapter seven exemplifies this principle in that they were starving to death as they camped outside the besieged city of Samaria. Knowing that they would not be allowed to enter the city and that there was no food inside even if they could get in and that they would starve to death where they were, they decided to try to seek mercy from the enemy. Their conclusion was, *Why sit we here until we die?* (verse 3) The action that they took resulted in their finding abundant prosperity for themselves, food to save the entire city of Samaria, and their claim to fame that made them heroes in not only their own day but legends for centuries to come.

In Acts 1:11, the angels had to stir the apostles into action as they stood gazing up into heaven after Jesus' ascension rather than following through on the Lord's directive that they go forth as witnesses unto Jerusalem, Judaea, Samaria, and the uttermost part of the earth.

Let's put feet to our prayers and remember that we'll get ahead as we go ahead!

February 21

Miracle Provision

Did you ever notice that God created grass on the third day of the creation week (Genesis 1:11-13) but didn't create cattle until the sixth day (Genesis 1:24-25, 31)? Because He was thinking ahead, God supplied the grass long before there would be a need to feed the cattle. Otherwise, can you imagine the chaos on the sixth day when all the animals suddenly appeared and there was nothing to feed them? Just imagine God running around in heaven trying to think of a quick fix to the problem He had just created! No way!!

Because God knows the end from before the beginning (Isaiah 46:10), He is never caught off guard with an unexpected emergency. He always prepares the answer to every problem before there is even a need. He was Jehovah Rapha before there was even any sickness to be healed. He was Jehovah Jireh before there was ever any lack to be filled. He was Jehovah Nissi before there was ever a battle to be fought. He was Jehovah Shalom before there was ever any conflict to be resolved. He was Jehovah Shamma before there was ever any loneliness to be dispelled. He was Jehovah Tsidkenu before there was ever any sin to be dealt with. And, best of all, Jesus was the Lamb that was slain for our sins before the earth was even created (Revelation 13:8), meaning that there was absolutely no way for there to have been a need for His sin offering because there was no Eve, no Garden of Eden, no Tree of the Knowledge of Good and Evil, no serpent…

My encouragement today is to always remember that nothing ever takes God by surprise. There is no accident or incident in your life that will ever catch God from the "blind side." He knows what's coming, and – more importantly – He has already made provision in advance for the situation. A promise to hold on to in those unexpected (from our point of view) situations is found in Exodus 23:20, *Behold, I send an Angel before thee, to keep thee in the way, and to bring thee into the place which I have prepared.*

February 22
God Façade
Back in August of 2006, the South African Catholic Bishops' Conference warned their priests to stop moonlighting as witchdoctors. Amazing! Supposed men of God were making a little on the side working for the enemy.

As strange as it may sound, this is not really an unusual situation. In fact, much of the church is filled with people who are simply wearing the façade of Christianity without actually having the true nature of Christ inside of them.

I'm sure that we've all heard the famous quote of Mahatma Gandhi that he liked Jesus and would have become a Christian if he hadn't met any Christians. And most of us have also heard the expression that a lot of Christians should just claim to be non-believers and help the cause in reverse. What all these expressions say to us is that we need to take off the masks and take a serious look inside to see who we really are.

> *You can't keep your true self hidden forever; before long you'll be exposed. You can't hide behind a religious mask forever; sooner or later the mask will slip and your true face will be known.* (Luke 12:2 MSG)

Paul made the determination to eliminate all facades and let the whole world see who he truly was so that he would not be exposed by God. Let's do the same.

> *We refuse to wear masks and play games. We don't maneuver and manipulate behind the scenes. And we don't twist God's Word to suit ourselves. Rather, we keep everything we do and say out in the open, the whole truth on display, so that those who want to can see and judge for themselves in the presence of God.* (II Corinthians 4:2 MSG)

February 23

Apple Seeds

We have all heard the expression that you can count the seeds in an apple, but not the apples in a seed. But the fruitfulness of a seed is most dramatically demonstrated in the multiplication power of the gospel in its printed form.

In an isolated village in the Himalayas where only the Hindu priest is able to read, the one entertainment the people enjoy is to gather around the priest as he reads to them each evening after a hard day in the fields. Someone in the village somehow obtained a Bible that he asked the priest to read to them. Eventually, the entire village became Christians simply by hearing the scriptures read to them by, of all people, their Hindu priest! Another story comes from the tarai, the flatlands in the plains below the mountains. A pioneer missionary with Every Home for Christ trekked to this distant village that is a day and a half's walk from the nearest civilization center. Here, he gave a gospel tract to each family and left literature at the huts if no one was at home. Weeks later, a letter arrived at the EHC offices explaining that someone had found the pamphlet at his door when he returned that evening. He was so intrigued by its message that he walked the long journey into town to send a letter to the address on the back of the brochure. After several follow-up correspondences, an EHC worker decided to visit the village only to find that there was by then a group of four hundred believers – none of whom had been witnessed to by any outside witness! It was all the result of that one little tract!

My wife Peggy came to the Lord through a tract that someone shared with her while she was in a hospital many years ago. That simple seed planted in her life has produced more apples than we could ever dream of counting through the women she has mentored in the Bible college classes, in her home cell group, in women's conferences all around the world, and in her prison ministry.

He that goeth forth and weepeth, bearing precious seed, shall doubtless come again with rejoicing, bringing his sheaves with him.
(Psalm 126:6)

February 24
Farmers in the Pulpit

I recently attended a cowboy church. It was an interesting experience with the preacher and worship leaders dressed in jeans and cowboy hats. We all sat on wooden benches, and they literally "passed the hat" when it came time for the offering as the ushers pulled off their ten-gallon hats and handed them down the rows. The one thing that I really appreciated about the service was that the preacher had grown up on a ranch and really understood what it meant to be close to the land. He told a story about a farmer who won a million dollars in the lottery. When someone asked him what he was going to do now that he was rich, he replied, "Oh, I guess I'll just keep farming until it's all gone." When he told that story, all the farmers in the audience immediately understood that he had a real connection with the economic challenges that today's farmers face.

And that is exactly what made the ministry so effective – he knew what he was talking about. In fact, I was so impressed by his ministry that I sent him an email the next day to tell him about a note that I had scribbled during a sermon a few weeks prior at a different church. As I listened to a city preacher try to explain the Parable of the Sower, I noted, "We need more farmers to be preachers. They will understand parables and harvesting."

Jesus and all the prophets, as well as most of the apostles, were men who were close to the land. Because of their sensitivity to how God works in nature, they could use illustrations that the people around them could easily relate to. Today, in our urban society, we are often too far removed from the natural life to know the power of many of the biblical messages and parables. Perhaps we should require that all ministers-in-training have not only Bible classes and homiletics courses, but also a semester as a farm hand. If they learn how seeds and crops really work, maybe they'll also understand how to deal with the hard soil, the rocky soil, and the thorny soil so that they can reap a harvest in every situation, not just in the good soil.

February 25
The Spirit of Travel and Adventure

A missionary told me recently that she had been accused of just having a spirit of travel and adventure. She said that she responded to her accuser that God made her that way because you have to have a spirit for travel and adventure to be a missionary. I could totally relate to what she was saying because I believe that I inherited something from my great-uncle Bramlet who was an official hobo, back in the days when such people weren't called "homeless drifters." He was the kind of guy who would "ride the rails" just to see where they would take him. And those rails took him to all sorts of places that left all the rest of us wide-eyed as he would spin his tales of all the places he had been and all the things he had seen. Yes, I believe that that wanderlust got into my bloodstream for a purpose – to equip me to travel all around the world to teach and minister the gospel.

I've had so many ministers approach me with comments like, "I don't know how you do it," "I can't even imagine going back and forth across all those time zones," or "I just couldn't adjust to living and working in a different culture." My response is always, "Well, this is what I was born for." They weren't born for it, but they were certainly born for something else. The Bible scholar is born with a temperament to sit quietly and study, analyzing all details of the passage. The healer is born with a temperament to get excited about seeing people's problems and challenges solved through the power of God. The apostle is born with a personality to step into leadership. And the list can go on and on.

The point is that we are all made differently because the Lord has a different position for each of us. We must learn to celebrate those differences so that we can all work together to accomplish God's overall plan and purpose.

> *If the whole body were an eye, where were the hearing? If the whole were hearing, where were the smelling? But now hath God set the members every one of them in the body, as it hath pleased him.* (I Corinthians 12:17-18)

February 26
Lost in Translation

Many years ago, there was a popular movie based on the then-emerging technology of email. The title of the film was, <u>You've Got Mail</u>; however, when it was showing on an Air France flight that I was taking on a mission trip, the head stewardess announced it as <u>You've Got a Message</u>. Apparently, rather than having an original English script in front of her, the stewardess was translating into English while reading from a French announcement sheet.

I've seen way more than I'd care to believe examples of this sort of thing happening on the mission field when inexperienced preachers try to minister in a foreign culture. They introduce ideas and images that the local people cannot relate to or they use words that simply do not translate or translate with totally different meanings. One classic example was a sermon entitled "Get Right or Be Left." The play on words was based on the similarity of the words for the directions right and left with the words that communicate the ideas of getting in proper relationship with God or facing the consequences of missing the Rapture. Obviously, the words were not the same in the foreign language, and the poor interpreter never knew when to translate with the word for the direction or the word for the spiritual message. Of course, since the words were not identical in the interpreted language, there was nothing clever in the presentation – just confusion.

I've seen American preachers talk about soap operas – a concept that was totally foreign to the culture in primitive Africa where the people usually didn't even have televisions and the words soap and opera had no connection to television programming. I've seen missionaries try to tell American jokes and use English acrostics that left only blank stares on the faces of their audiences.

In similar fashion, I all too often witness Christians fail in trying to explain their faith to the people they live around everyday because they use only churchy terminology that does not relate to the everyday guy.

February 27
Faith, Hope, Love

We all know the reference in I Corinthians 13:13 to the three hallmark Christian qualities of faith, hope, and love; most of us never stop to consider how intricately these three qualities are intertwined.

Paul commended the Thessalonians for their work of faith, labor of love, and patience of hope (I Thessalonians 1:3) and challenged them to put on the breastplate of faith and love and the helmet of the hope of salvation (I Thessalonians 5:8). To the Romans, he wrote that we have access to the grace of God by faith and the glory of God by hope. (Romans 5:2) In II Corinthians 10:15, he explained that increased faith manifests itself in hope, and, in Galatians 5:5, he clarified for us that it is by faith that we can have the hope of righteousness. In the following verse, he then tied in the connection between faith and love by saying that faith works by love, literally meaning that it is through love that faith becomes effective. In fact, Paul repeatedly focused on the fact that he was continually looking for the combination of faith and love in believers. (Ephesians 1:15, 3:17, 6:23; Colossians 1:4; I Timothy 1:14, 6:11; II Timothy 1:13; Philemon 1:5) It would seem that he was looking for faith that had been activated through love, not just faith that was so many words. In I Timothy 6:10, he spoke of those who had erred from the faith by misplacing their love on money rather than the things and people of God.

Although Galatians 5:22 described both faith and love as the fruit of the Spirit, we are not to believe that they will simply manifest themselves without any involvement on our part. The Apostle Peter showed us how to diligently focus on making these qualities foremost in our lives.

> *And beside this, giving all diligence, add to your faith virtue; and to virtue knowledge; And to knowledge temperance; and to temperance patience; and to patience godliness; And to godliness brotherly kindness; and to brotherly kindness charity.*
> (II Peter 1:5-7)

February 28

God Forbid

Because he had so strongly stressed the doctrine of God's grace in Romans, Paul had to also address the question of whether we could continue to live in sin. If we do not raise the question about the possibility of continuing in sin, we have not preached grace the same way Paul did. Paul made it clear that our motive for living a holy life is not to earn credit but because it is the outgrowth of our new nature and it is a defense against the devil having an in-road into our lives. Holiness is a by-product of our life in Christ, not a means for establishing it. It is the fruit, not the root, of our relationship with God. Forty-seven out of forty-nine times that "sin" is used in Romans, it is referring to the nature of sin rather than to specific acts of sin. Once the nature of sin is properly dealt with, the specific acts of sin no longer become an issue. We can sin without deliberately attempting to, or we can come to the place where we live righteously as part of our second nature.

Ten different times in the one book, Paul uses the term *God forbid* to describe his (and His) adamant disapproval of the idea that Christians have a license to continue in sinful acts because God has extended His grace to them. (verses 3:4, 3:6, 3:31, 6:2, 6:15, 7:7, 7:13, 9:14, 11:1, 11:11)

> *What shall we say then? Shall we continue in sin, that grace may abound? God forbid. How shall we, that are dead to sin, live any longer therein?...For sin shall not have dominion over you: for ye are not under the law, but under grace. What then? shall we sin, because we are not under the law, but under grace? God forbid.* (verses 6:1-2, 14-15)
> *For, brethren, ye have been called unto liberty; only use not liberty for an occasion to the flesh, but by love serve one another.* (Galatians 5:13)

Leap Year's Day
Our Complicated Calendar

Have you ever wondered why October is the tenth month, November is the eleventh month, and December is the twelfth month? Since the word "October" comes from the word meaning "eight," "November" comes from the word meaning "nine," and December comes from the word meaning "ten," it appears that we have the whole calendar off by a couple months. In fact, there was a time when the new year began in the spring instead of in the middle of the winter. At that time, these months really were in the correct numerical sequence. The Jewish calendar, by the way, still holds to the spring beginning for the year in that the observed new year Rosh Hashanah, which usually occurs in September, occurs in the seventh month of the year. Thus, the beginning of the calendar roughly coincides with early March – fairly close to spring. Of course, since the Jewish calendar is based on the lunar cycle, it winds up with extra days at the end of the year, requiring the Jews to add in a full extra month every so often to keep in sync with the sun.

The calendar as we know it, called the Julian Calendar, was instituted in 45 BC and revised in 1582 as the Gregorian Calendar. Because the actual length of a year is 365.242216 days, the system of leap years to accommodate the extra part of a day by adding an extra day every four years is still off by eleven minutes and fourteen seconds, a problem that is solved by dropping the leap year in each centennial year except in years that are divisible by four hundred.

Leap years that don't leap, thirteen-month-long years, New Year's celebrations in the seventh month of the year, months that lie about their age – what could possibly be more confusing? Isn't it comforting that God has all of this in His control?

> *And he said unto them, It is not for you to know the times or the seasons, which the Father hath put in his own power.* (Acts 1:7)

March 1

Never on a Sunday

God told us to honor the Sabbath day, but we often simply go overboard about it. When Dr. Lester Sumrall was living in Israel, he took his family to lunch in the King David Hotel one Saturday. After the meal when he asked the waiter for the check, the shocked response was, "You didn't pay in advance? This is the Sabbath!" He quickly learned that money transactions could not be made on the Sabbath. The only way he could cover his bill was to leave the cash on a shelf for the waiter to pick up the following day. Dr. Sumrall also told the story of his neighbor who would ask him to light his cigarettes on the Sabbath because he was prohibited from lighting fires on the holy day. Bro. Sumrall even told a story about a Jewish man who blocked the drive to his house to keep the fire trucks from coming up to put out the fire that was destroying his house because he did not want the firemen to work on the Sabbath, even though it would save his home! Elevators in the hotels in Jerusalem are preprogrammed to stop at every floor on the Sabbath so that the passengers don't have to push the buttons to select their floor. Some homes have preprogrammed timers to turn on and switch off the lights so that the residents don't have to exert the effort on the holy day. One winter Sabbath, all the Orthodox Jews were stranded in their homes because a freak snow broke down the wire that is erected around the city to make it a "walled city." Since they were not permitted to travel outside the walled city, they were confined to their own residences.

In the US, many "blue laws" which prohibit or restrict Sunday activities are still on the books. On Sundays, it is still technically illegal to auction a turtle in Kansas City, go tadpole hunting in Pennsylvania, buy a television in Spokane, buy an ice cream cone in Winona Lake, IN, play dominoes in Alabama, make cabbage soup (unless you cut the cabbage the previous day) in Ocean City, NJ, sell hamburgers in Evansville, IN, fish for bay scallops in New York, sell cherry pie in Kansas, buy corn flakes in Columbus, OH, and give a haircut in New Jersey.

March 2

Knowing God

Psalm 103:7 makes an interesting suggestion that there is a difference between knowing acts of God and knowing His ways when it says that God made known His ways unto Moses and his acts unto the children of Israel. Apparently, the people of Israel could recognize when God <u>did</u> something while Moses was able to tell when God <u>was going to do</u> something. The people knew God well enough to be able to pigeonhole the events that happened to, for, through, and around them as activities of God. On the other hand, Moses knew Him so intimately that he could see into the very motivations and motives of the Almighty, allowing him to not simply analyze the actions, but to actually understand and move with the operations of God. If there is anything to be learned from this verse, it is that we should pursue such an intimate relationship with God that we can sense His moving even before He totally manifests Himself.

Two different Old Testament prophets predicted a time when the whole world would be inundated with a flood of the knowledge of the Lord. Both Isaiah (verse 11:9) and Habakkuk (verse 2:14) predict a time when this knowledge will flood the earth just like the waters cover the sea. When I think of those prophecies, I am reminded of the time when God literally filled the earth with floodwaters during the time of Noah. Genesis 7:11 describes how this happened. It was not just from rain out of heaven, but also the opening of the fountains of the deep. This is exactly how the Bible predicts that the flood of knowledge of God will sweep over the earth. In Acts 2:17, Peter reaffirmed the prophecy of Joel 2:28 that God would pour out His Spirit on all flesh in the last days – the latter rain of the Holy Spirit. On the other hand, Jesus explained in John 7:37-39 that the Spirit of God would flow out of the innermost bellies of His Spirit-filled followers – the opening up of the fountains of the deep to flow out of the rivers of the hearts of believers. When the Holy Spirit comes, He will give us all the intimate knowledge of God that we need. (John 16:13-15)

March 3

Circumcision

Circumcision has recently been declared illegal in San Francisco. Until the recent move against the practice, circumcision was an automatic procedure for newborn baby boys in most hospitals in the US unless the parents specifically requested that it not be done. Of course, it is no surprise that it was in San Francisco, where male sex is a major focus, that the movement was spearheaded. Of course, there have been challenges to the ruling based on the religious practice of Jews and Christians. The counter is that the procedure is forced upon the child without his consent and that it should be postponed until he has the ability to decide for himself. Obviously, there is a flaw in such an argument in that we are all subject to having many long-lasting decisions being made for us before we reach the age to decide for ourselves.

As I read about this new law, I couldn't help but think that maybe there may be some validity to letting young men make their own decision about the operation. After all, for most people, it is only a ritual without a lot of meaning – especially when it is done in the Christian setting where a doctor does it unceremoniously in the hospital as opposed to the Jewish setting where a rabbi performs a full liturgical in the process.

On the other hand, there is more than just a sign of people's attitudes at play here. There is a totally malevolent spiritual element at work. It is a blatant attack against the covenant of God with His people. Don't get me wrong here. I certainly am not reverting to the Old Testament covenant. I fully understand the New Testament principle that circumcision is an unnecessary and ineffective vestige of legalism. There is certainly no spiritual benefit from the cutting of the flesh. However, my point is that when we criminalize the procedure, we stand headstrong against the symbol of God's intervention in the lives of men. Certainly, it is the circumcision of the heart, not the flesh, that God desires; however, this adamant stance against the physical symbol must certainly be motivated by an even more adamant hatred for the spiritual circumcision as well.

March 4

March Forth

Today is one of my most favorite days of the year simply because of how the name of the date sounds: March fourth (march forth). It sounds like a command from General Jesus for His army to get the Great Commission done.

Unfortunately, as I look around me, I see way too many of us in retreat rather than in advancement. Statistically, only one out of ten pastors stay in the ministry until retirement – if there is such a thing as retiring from the ministry. Since being a minister is who you are rather than what you do, I'm not sure that it is possible to retire. However, I'm sure that you understand what I mean here: they quit rather than continuing until their physical limitations force them out of an active roll. In fact, I understand that four hundred ministers quit each week and that four thousand churches close each year. Certainly, there is a whole plethora of reasons for this attrition in the ministry. Probably one of the foremost reasons is discouragement and disillusionment. Ministers begin their work with a vision that simply doesn't work out or they face challenges, such as squabbling within the body of believers or lack of finances, that they simply are not prepared to handle. But I suspect that these issues are only symptoms of much deeper underlying problems. Additionally, I have observed that the basic underlying condition that is a setup for an upset in ministry is a basic lack of clarity as to what ministry really is. Because most of us have all grown up in a church environment where all we saw were pastors and an occasional evangelist doing the work of God, we have assumed some very limited stereotypes for ministry. I believe that there are thousands of individuals who enter ministry each year, knowing that they have a call of God upon their lives but don't really know what that call is all about. Therefore, responding the only way they know how, they try to gather a few people around them and open a church. When things don't work out exactly as they dreamed, there is no other option but to close the doors. Today, my prayer is that we all see more clearly what our calls are and march forth in them – in the pulpit of life that God has granted to us.

March 5

It Is Illegal

To sell doughnut holes in Lehigh, NB

For women to play Santa Clause in Minnesota

To snore loudly enough to wake your neighbor in Dunn, NC

For pet goldfish to make a disturbance on public buses in Seattle

To play pinball in Athens, GA

For dentists to advertise that they sell false teeth in Maine

To ride on the roof of a car in Los Angeles

For vendors to sell candy or peanuts in California parks

To eat garlic before attending the theater in Gary, IN

To take a bite of someone else's hamburger in Oklahoma

To be a male librarian in Mississippi

To throw a banana peel in front of a horse in Detroit

To disturb bullfrogs in Hayden, AZ

For jury members to knit in New York

To flip a coin to see who pays in restaurants in Richmond, VA

To disturb honeybees in Nebraska

To sell hollow logs in Tennessee

To sleep under the stars in Chicago

To drive a horse-drawn sled without three bells in Massachusetts

For chickens to lay eggs in Seattle

To climb trees in New York City

To appear in court barefooted in Hawaii

To drive a car barefooted in New Jersey

To throw a ball at someone's head in New York

To have a disco dance contest lasting more than eight hours in Tennessee

To plow a cotton field with an elephant in North Carolina

To carry an ice cream cone in your pocket in Lexington, KY

March 6
More No-Nos
To slurp soup in a restaurant in New Jersey

To conduct an automobile safety inspection without smiling in Tallahassee, FL

To juggle in Chicago

To make goo-goo eyes at girls in Houston

To shoot a rabbit from the back of a trolley in Brooklyn

To keep snowballs in your refrigerator in Scottsbluff, NB

To remove the lid from another person's garbage can in Marysville, OH

For a woman to pick her husband's pockets while he's asleep in Maryland

To eat chocolate chip cookies on the beach in Fire Island, NY

To set fire to a mule in Maine

For kids to hitch their bikes to airplanes in Utah

To kill your neighbor's chickens unless all the other people in the neighborhood agree in Cleveland

To wear a bathing suit on a street unless you are accompanied by a policeman in Kentucky

To enter a restaurant on horseback in California

To carry a banner for your favorite cereal in Virginia

To serve wine in teacups in Topeka, KS

To whistle for your escaped canary before 7 AM in Berkeley, CA

To block the street by playing hopscotch in Griffin, GA

To race horses on the turnpike in New Jersey

To have a messy house in Norfolk, VA

To throw snowballs at men in top hats in Watertown, NY

For barbers not to visit their doctor at least every six months in Kansas City

To fall asleep while getting a shave in Erie, PA

For barbers to eat onions between 7 AM and 7 PM in Waterloo, NB

For buffalo herds to roam the streets in Denver

To put tomatoes in clam chowder in Massachusetts

March 7
It's The Law

In addition to all the rules and regulations we have seen in the last couple days, it is also illegal for dogs to growl in Arlington, VA; to grow poison ivy in a window box in New York City; for donkeys to sleep in bathtubs in Brooklyn, NY; and to walk backwards while eating peanuts in Green, NY.

As humorous as all these laws may seem, I'm sure that there was a logical reason for each one of them when they were instituted. However, as the times have changed, all of them have served their useful purpose and become archaic. The same is true with all the requirements of the Old Testament Law. They had a very legitimate purpose until Jesus Christ came and fulfilled them. Paul said that they were a schoolmaster to bring us to Christ (Galatians 3:24-25) and that once we have been freed from them, we should be careful not to get re-entangled in their bondage (Galatians 5:1). Jesus Himself explained that He didn't come to destroy the Law but to fulfill it. (Matthew 5:17) This does not mean that the law is evil and that we should not live by the moral standards it sets forth. On the contrary, the grace of God that we live in today should compel us to live even more righteously than we would if we lived under the bondage of trying to fulfill the obligations of the law. (Matthew 5:20)

> *But now we are delivered from the law, that being dead wherein we were held; that we should serve in newness of spirit, and not in the oldness of the letter.* (Romans 7:6)
> *For the law of the Spirit of life in Christ Jesus hath made me free from the law of sin and death.* (Romans 8:2)
> *That the righteousness of the law might be fulfilled in us, who walk not after the flesh, but after the Spirit.* (Romans 8:4)
> *But if ye be led of the Spirit, ye are not under the law.* (Galatians 5:18)

Hope

Therefore being justified by faith, we have peace with God through our Lord Jesus Christ: By whom also we have access by faith into this grace wherein we stand, and rejoice in hope of the glory of God. And not only so, but we glory in tribulations also: knowing that tribulation worketh patience; And patience, experience; and experience, hope: And hope maketh not ashamed; because the love of God is shed abroad in our hearts by the Holy Ghost which is given unto us. (Romans 5:1-5)

Paul introduces almost all the cardinal elements of the Christian faith: faith, grace, hope, patience, love, God, Jesus, the Holy Spirit. A few verses later, he continues with the same theme and adds prayer to his list, *Rejoicing in hope; patient in tribulation; continuing instant in prayer.* (verse 12:12)

The element that I want to focus on today is hope – an all too neglected quality in the church today that emphasizes the right-now quality of faith versus the slow-growth process of hope. From the two verses quoted in today's lesson, we might easily associate hope with trials since both passages put hope in juxtaposition with the endurance of tribulations. The truth is that hope doesn't come from trials any more than children come from schools. The schools only develop the children that are already there. Likewise, our difficulties only enhance the confidence in God that we already have.

Hebrews 6:19 describes hope as *an anchor of the soul, both sure and stedfast.* With this thought in mind, let me encourage you that when you come under a difficult circumstance, you focus on the rainbow rather than the thunderheads. Genesis 28:15 in the New Living Translation gives us a powerful thought to keep in mind in such times, "I will be with you constantly until I have finished giving you everything I have promised." Philippians 1:6 in the Message Bible declares that the end result of such confidence will be a *flourishing finish.*

March 9
Come Hell or High Water

There's a story about an unusual sighting of a hat going back and forth in the front yard of a home that was inundated with about five feet of water after the levy broke during a flash flood. When the search and rescue team came through the area, they were puzzled by why the hat seemed to be moving in deliberately straight lines rather than to be floating on the water or being swept away by the current. When they paddled their rescue boat close to the hat to check out the intriguing phenomenon, they discovered that the hat wasn't floating on the water but was rather actually on a man's head. Querying for an explanation as to why the man was pacing back and forth in the yard rather than trying to rescue himself, the search team got his answer, "Well, I was cutting my grass when the levy broke, and I'm just trying to finish the job before I run."

Now, that's what I call determination, single-sightedness, and purpose – not to mention stupid.

Certainly, we don't want to get so focused on our tasks that we lose our grip on reality and fail to deal with the urgent issues of life while zeroing in on the mundane. On the other hand, success is waiting for those who know how to maintain their focus and determination in the face of all deterrents.

Sometimes, those things that hinder us from fulfilling our tasks are people. (Genesis 24:56) Sometimes, they are our own sins and emotional or physical encumbrances. (Hebrews 12:1) Often, they are circumstances that arise. (Romans 15:22) In Paul's case, his circumstances included everything from jail to shipwreck. Our challenges my not be quite so severe, but lack of funds, broken-down vehicles, or just last-minute phone calls often stand in our way of accomplishing what we know we need to be doing. Frequently (and possibly always to some degree), it is Satan himself who is deterring us from accomplishing our goals. (I Thessalonians 2:18)

As one old gentleman once expressed it, "Ya gotta wanna." If you really want to do something strongly enough, you can and will overcome every obstacle that presents itself! Put on your athletic shoes and just do it!

March 10

Climbing Up to Heaven

There is a legend about a little place in the eastern Himalayas called Daramden. The story says that the Lepcha people who inhabit that region once tried to climb up to heaven by making a tower of clay pots. They never accomplished their goal due to miscommunication among the workers. As a result, the tower was broken down, and they could not reach heaven. There are still the pieces of clay pots that can be found on the spot, and it is reported that a piece of one of those clay pots is preserved in a museum in London.

There are a couple thoughts that come to me when I think about this story. The first is the fact that certain stories are common to the human race. The story of a deception and fall of the original father and mother of the human race, the story of a great flood, and this story of an attempt to reach heaven are essentially universal. Why? Because they really happened! Of course, the stories have been grossly distorted as they have been passed through generation after generation of oral communication, but that doesn't disprove the premise that these stories are real. On the other hand, it actually validates them and helps us find the true story that has been preserved without distortion. For example, the story of the flood is a significant element in Sumerian literature; however, the ark in this legend was a cube, which would have been totally unstable in the floodwaters. Imagine the topsy turvy ride Noah and his animal would have had with the cube tumbling willy nilly for all those months. The dimensions of the biblical ark, on the other hand, have been aerodynamically proven to be perfect for a free-floating vessel. It would not have capsized, no matter how big the waves that it encountered were.

My second thought is concerning the heart condition of the human race that makes all men have the desire to be able to go to heaven but the inability to get there. No tower, no religion, no good works will ever get us there. There is only one way to God – through His Son Jesus. (John 14:6)

March 11
Could Jesus Have Sinned?

We've all heard the question about the omnipotence of God. If He is really all-powerful, can He make a stone so big that He can't move it? Obviously, He is not limited in His ability to create. Just look at the universe! So, making the stone is not an issue. Obviously, moving things is not a problem for God. Just look at the universe that He orchestrates, moving all of the planets, stars, comets, and asteroids precisely through their positions. The problem in this question is not with God but with the phrasing of the question. The issue is between possibility and potential. Yes, God has the potential of making a stone so massive that it would fill all the universe, but that stone would not have the possibility of outweighing God's ability to move it.

Now, let's take that same reasoning to the question that often arises concerning Jesus' earthly life: "Could He have sinned?" If not, then could He really relate to our fallen condition? If so, then was the redemption plan faulty through the fact that His sin would have negated Plan A while there was no Plan B? Again, the answer lies in the difference between potential and possibility. Jesus would not have been human without the potential to sin; however, He would not have been God if He had the possibility of sinning. It was the unique character of Jesus – totally God while totally man – that gave Him the potential but not the possibility of sinning.

Notice in the description of His incarnation in John 1:14, *And the Word was made flesh, and dwelt among us, (and we beheld his glory, the glory as of the only begotten of the Father,) full of grace and truth*, that He still retained the total qualities of divinity (glory, grace, truth) while becoming totally human (flesh). Hebrews 4:15 explains that He had the total human experience of being touched with the feelings of our infirmities and being tempted in every way as we are while maintaining His divine personality as our sinless high priest.

This understanding of potential and possibility helps us answer the other question of what would have happened if Adam had not eaten the forbidden fruit after Eve had taken her bite. But that's another ditty for another day.

March 12
Quick Thoughts
It's about time for Old Man Winter to take a spring break.

"They" haven't found a way to tax you for laughing yet.

If a man can be found faithful in hard places, he can usually be trusted in high places.

At the graduation ceremony from the school of hard knocks, the valedictorian fell off the stage.

Your quality of life is determined by two things: what you eat and what eats you.

We are called to be port-a-temples because our bodies are the temples of the Holy Spirit and we take Him everywhere we go.

If you can get your opponent angry, he'll start making mistakes, and you'll be able to take him out of the game. – Reggie White (NFL champion)

Hypochondriacs can get addicted to placeboes.

The best men are still men at their very best.

You cannot make a difference until you are made different.

What our fathers called work we call stress.

When God shows up, He doesn't take sides; He takes over.

Pressure shows what you are on the inside. You only get juice from an orange when you squeeze it.

Character is how God sees you; reputation is how men see you.

Old men dream dreams because they have insight; young men see visions because they have foresight.

Some people speak because they have something to say; others talk because they have to say something.

Blocks must be interconnected or they will be just a pile of stones. The church is built from lively stones (I Peter 2:5) that must be built together (Ephesians 4:16).

Pray before you become prey.

Relocate before you suffocate.

There is dignity in labor, whether by head or hand. The world owes no man a living, only the opportunity to earn one. – John D. Rockefeller Jr.

March 13
Grace, The Power of God to Resist

Someone once said that the way we could tell when grace is working in our lives is that we don't panic when a need arises. He followed up the explanation that falling from grace (Galatians 5:4) is when we start trusting in ourselves. These ideas can actually help us to get a new perspective on what grace is. Generally, we perceive grace as a great cover to deal with our faults and errors. However, the perspective presented in these two observations helps us to see grace as an actual trust in God's work in our lives. It is not so much that God's grace causes Him to ignore our shortcomings as it is a power that works in us to give us the ability to live beyond such shortcomings.

Let's take a look at what the Apostle James said about the operation of grace in our lives. In chapter four, he referred to those who were involved with moral failures (adulterers and adulteresses), asking if they didn't understand that friendship with the world is enmity with God and whosoever is a friend with the world is an enemy of God. (verse 4) He follows up in verse six with the assertion that, in such cases, God gives more grace with the result in verse seven that they can then resist the devil.

In two places in his short letter, James refers to the law of liberty (verses 1:25, 2:12), which seems to be an alternative description for grace in that it is the New Testament antithesis of the Old Testament law of obligation. In making reference to this law of liberty, the apostle says that some people just ignore it even when it points out their need and the opportunity to correct their shortcomings. He then follows up with the statement that such people will be judged by this law of liberty. In other words, they will be held accountable for the fact that there was grace given them to deal with the flaws in their lives and they didn't take advantage of that privilege and potential.

Perhaps this is what Paul was referring to when he mentioned frustrating the grace of God. (Galatians 2:21) He explained that he no longer was in control of his life, but had come to the place where that he lived by the power of God within him.

March 14
McDonald's Culture

The other day, I was still poring over the menu in a restaurant when the waiter asked if I needed a few more minutes to make a decision. I responded that I thought I should just go to McDonald's where it was easy to make a decision since there is basically only one item on the menu.

Perhaps we don't really realize how much McDonald's has dominated our society today. So much of our thinking and way of doing things have been redefined by the standardized method introduced by this one fast food chain. Occasionally, we see this influence showing up in the most unusual aspects of life. For example, I read an article about million-dollar-plus homes that were labeled as McMansions because they were built from a standard "cookie cutter" pattern even though they were still high-end homes. In previous generations, no one would even dream of not having a totally personally designed, individually drawn by an architect, and custom-built house if he was going to invest in a top-dollar home.

Unfortunately, the same cultural shift has also occurred in the church where we have seen the remake of Jesus into a McJesus and the revision of the Bible into the McBible. By these terms, I mean that we have turned our faith into a drive-through experience where we get a little presentation of the gospel but little or no in-depth quality encounter. Issues and questions that really need serious soul-searching are too often answered by quick, pat McAnswers rather than genuine loving counsel and intercessory prayer. I even heard of a drive-through funeral home where friends can show their respect for the departed without even getting out of their cars!

Is what McDonald's has done to and for society wrong? Absolutely not! Their efficiency and streamlining has greatly improved our everyday life. On the other hand, the church is not McDonald's with a packaged product. There is a whole other side of living that we must not readily lump into our fast-paced schedules. The things that have to do with our faith are eternal and must not be relegated to drive-through answers.

Palm Sunday
So, Why Are We Partying?
The catalytic event that precipitated the Triumphal Entry on the first Palm Sunday was a dinner that Mary and Martha (well, most likely Martha) gave in honor of their brother who had been raised from the dead. According to the story in John chapter twelve, there were lots of people there who came because they wanted to see Lazarus. John goes on to specifically point out that they weren't really there because of Jesus, but because of Lazarus. In the emotion of the event, they headed toward Jerusalem, celebrating the miracle worker who had brought Lazarus back to life. We can only suspect that many of these same emotion-driven people were also among the crowd that just a week later were calling out for Jesus to be executed.

When seen in this light, the story bears some striking similarities to an earlier story in the same gospel. In chapter six, John tells us about the time that Jesus fed a multitude of more than five thousand with just a few loaves and fish. In verse fourteen, the beloved disciple records, *Then those men, when they had seen the miracle that Jesus did, said, This is of a truth that prophet that should come into the world.* But in the immediately following verse, he reveals that Jesus was able to discern what was really in their hearts regardless of what came out of their lips, *When Jesus therefore perceived that they would come and take him by force, to make him a king, he departed again into a mountain himself alone.* Of course, we are perplexed as to why He hid Himself at this point. After all, the people were so intent on following Him that they rushed across the Sea of Galilee to "head Him off at the pass" when He tried to go to Capernaum. (verse 24) When they did catch up with Him, Jesus explained what it was that He had seen about their hearts – that they didn't want to follow Him because of who He was but because of the free meal He had given them.

Today is a good opportunity to examine our reasons for following Christ. Is it really because of who He is?

March 16

Whoa

I received a phone call from a lady asking for prayer. I was really drawn into her story as she began to describe her problem. She described in detail how her husband had gone into the garage at the normal time that he left for work each morning, and she had naturally assumed that the day was off to its usual course. Several hours later, she headed out to do some errands; however, when she opened the garage door, she was greeted by her husband's lifeless body hanging from the rafters. At that point in the story, she had an emotional breakdown. Of course, I was also in somewhat of a state of shock by the unusual turn of events in the story and the obviously overwhelming grief the dear woman was experiencing. From the way she was so vividly describing the details of the event and the uncontrollable emotion she was displaying, I could imagine that the husband's corpse must still be dangling from the end of the noose. Almost certain that the 911 response team had not yet reached her home, I asked how long ago it had been that she found her husband's body. Her answer was even more shocking than I was prepared for – thirty years! To say that it took my breath away may be a little misleading. What actually happened is that I wanted to burst out laughing and had to hold my breath so that I wouldn't. I couldn't believe that the freshness of the wounds and the vividness of the imagery had not been softened in spite of the three decades that had transpired. I tried every possible polite way of counseling her, even though what I really wanted to do was to simply demand, "Get over it!"

Unfortunately, most of us harbor wounds, insults, and injuries far longer than is healthy. If you realize that something is taking longer than normal to heal, there is just one reasonable way to deal with it: say *whoa* to the *woe*. We need to simply tell the devil that we've had enough – actually more than enough – and refuse to allow him to continue to torment us. What has happened has happened, and no amount of remorse on our part can change anything in the past. However, dwelling on the past can totally cripple your future!

St. Patrick's Day

With a little help from Wikipedia, I finally figured it out. I've always wondered why St. Patrick's Day is such a big deal around the world, especially among people who have no Irish blood in them. Or course, it's always a big party, and everyone loves a party. But why did this particular saint get picked to be the universal party animal. The Wikipedia article on the holiday explains, "The day is generally characterized by the attendance of church services, wearing of green attire (especially shamrocks), and the lifting of Lenten restrictions on eating and drinking alcohol, which is often proscribed during the rest of the season. Saint Patrick's Day is a public holiday in the Republic of Ireland, Northern Ireland, Newfoundland and Labrador and in Montserrat. It is also widely celebrated by the Irish diaspora, especially in places such as Great Britain, Canada, the United States, Argentina, Australia, and New Zealand, among others. Today, St. Patrick's Day is probably the most widely celebrated saint's day in the world." The lifting of the restrictions against alcohol consumption on this one day during the forty days of fasting during Lent is the key to the holiday's worldwide popularity. Catholics from non-Irish backgrounds, who otherwise would have no reason to relate to the saint, have adopted him as their patron simply because it justifies their carnal desires. They can party without any blame. In fact, I remember a few years back when the Pope had to actually announce a special dispensation because of a conflict that arose because the holiday fell right in the middle of Holy Week.

Isn't this the general condition of humans? We are all looking for an opportunity to sin and get by with it. When Paul taught us about the wonderful freedom we have in Christ, he had to make a special point to emphasize to us that this did not give us a license to sin without consequences. God's grace is not a St. Patrick's Day amnesty from God's standards.

> *For, brethren, ye have been called unto liberty; only use not liberty for an occasion to the flesh, but by love serve one another.*
> (Galatians 5:13)

March 18

Guarding Your Tongue

Calvin Coolidge was well known for being a man of very few words who carefully guarded his speech. When someone bet him that he would be forced to say more than two words, the President replied, "You lose."

Think of any bottle that you might purchase in the supermarket. When you open the cap and start to pour out the contents, the only thing that comes out is what is inside. I'm sure that you are thinking that this is such an obvious truth that it is strange for me to take the space in this lesson to even mention it. However, have you ever stopped to consider that the opening in the top of the bottle is called its "mouth"? If the bottle has pure water in it, only pure water will come out of its mouth. If the bottle contains poison, only poison will come out through its mouth. The same is true with our mouths; what is in our hearts will eventually spill out through our lips. It is true that we can sometimes guard our speech so that what is inside our hearts is not revealed through our lying lips which are cautious to conceal the true heart. We've all had those moments when we had to "bite our tongues." (Isaiah 29:13) However, what is in the heart will eventually come out. (Luke 6:45)

In Psalm 141:3, David expressed his desire to guard his mouth and even acknowledged that his lips were a gateway. *Set a watch, O LORD, before my mouth; keep the door of my lips.* However, it is in the following verse that we see that the true heart of the matter is the matter of the heart. *Incline not my heart to any evil thing, to practice wicked works with men that work iniquity…* His son Solomon confirmed that the heart is the source in Proverbs 4:23, *Keep thy heart with all diligence; for out of it are the issues of life.* Even though he also wrote that life and death are in the power of the tongue (Proverbs 18:21), the very wellspring for those issues of life is in the heart of the man. In Proverbs 10:19, Solomon explicitly described the danger of an uncontrolled tongue and the benefit of one that is under restraint, *In the multitude of words there wanteth not sin: but he that refraineth his lips is wise.*

March 19

Funny Money

When my wife and I were on our honeymoon on a beach in North Carolina, we strolled through the sand singing a song that accurately described our situation, "Ain't got a barrel of money..." Today we are billionaires. Yes, billionaires! I have a fifty billion dollar note that I brought home from Zimbabwe. Unfortunately, it is worthless outside Zimbabwe, and of little value inside the country. I also have a copy of a "one million US dollar" note that a friend from Aiken, S C, got for me after a man was arrested there for trying to pass off the bills as real US dollars. As we've traveled through many different countries, we have collected all sorts of currencies printed in the various nations we have visited. In most cases, the currency from one country is totally useless once you cross the border. Peggy learned that lesson the hard way when she got confused by having money from several different Asian countries in her wallet at the same time. She couldn't pay for her purchase because the store clerk could not accept her Thai, Nepali, or Indian money in Korea. I was once left penniless in a remote area of India because there was no bank in the region that could cash a traveler's check. My friends thought it funny that when a beggar asked me for loose change, I had to tell him that he actually had more money than I did. I actually had hundreds of dollars, but it was in a medium that could not be used in that particular place. In the spiritual dimension, we must also learn that there is a designated medium of exchange in the kingdom of God that is different from the currency of the natural world. In the book of Revelation, Jesus spoke to the church at Laodicea, encouraging them to get this spiritual currency because – even though they were rich in physical wealth – they were wretched, and miserable, and poor, and blind, and naked in His sight. (verses 3:17-18) Simon the magician's money was to be destroyed with him (Acts 8:20) and the wicked will cast their silver into the streets in the day of judgment (Ezekiel 7:19), but the righteous can preserve their treasures in heaven for eternity (Matthew 6:19-21). The currency of the kingdom is faith and trust in God manifest through our righteous lives and generosity.

Good Friday
The Divine Sacrifice
As many were astonied at thee; his visage was so marred more than any man, and his form more than the sons of men: So shall he sprinkle many nations; the kings shall shut their mouths at him...he hath no form nor comeliness; and when we shall see him, there is no beauty that we should desire him. He is despised and rejected of men; a man of sorrows, and acquainted with grief: and we hid as it were our faces from him; he was despised, and we esteemed him not. Surely he hath borne our griefs, and carried our sorrows: yet we did esteem him stricken, smitten of God, and afflicted. But he was wounded for our transgressions, he was bruised for our iniquities: the chastisement of our peace was upon him; and with his stripes we are healed. All we like sheep have gone astray; we have turned every one to his own way; and the LORD hath laid on him the iniquity of us all. He was oppressed, and he was afflicted, yet he opened not his mouth: he is brought as a lamb to the slaughter, and as a sheep before her shearers is dumb, so he openeth not his mouth. He was taken from prison and from judgment: and who shall declare his generation? for he was cut off out of the land of the living: for the transgression of my people was he stricken. And he made his grave with the wicked, and with the rich in his death; because he had done no violence, neither was any deceit in his mouth. Yet it pleased the LORD to bruise him; he hath put him to grief: when thou shalt make his soul an offering for sin, he shall see his seed, he shall prolong his days, and the pleasure of the LORD shall prosper in his hand. He shall see of the travail of his soul, and shall be satisfied: by his knowledge shall my righteous servant justify many; for he shall bear their iniquities. Therefore will I divide him a portion with the great, and he shall divide the spoil with the strong; because he hath poured out his soul unto death: and he was numbered with the transgressors; and he bare the sin of many, and made intercession for the transgressors. (Isaiah 52:13-53:12)

March 21

Corruption

The book of I Peter makes some very insightful observations concerning corruption and incorruption. Peter begins in verse 1:4 with a reference to our inheritance in heaven that is *incorruptible and undefiled and that will not fade away.* In verse eighteen of the same chapter he speaks of the fact that we are not redeemed with such corruptible things as silver and gold, and, in verse twenty-three, he says that we were *born again, not of corruptible seed, but of incorruptible, which is the word of God.* He reconfirms the enduring nature of the Word of God again in verse twenty-five when he proclaims that it will last forever. The theme seems to carry into chapter two when the apostle says that we must *desire the sincere milk of the Word of God* so that we can grow in our faith. In chapter three, he again comes back to his terminology of corruptible versus incorruption when he describes the *hidden man of the heart* of a sincere woman of God as not being corruptible and adds that in the sight of God such a heart is of great value.

Let's contrast this with the teaching in Isaiah 64:6 that our own righteousness is as filthy rags in God's sight. This verse actually makes our own righteousness even more repugnant than most of us would imagine in that the actual Hebrew context refers to menstrual cloths – a concept which is certainly detestable in any context, but even more so in light of the Jewish laws concerning the uncleanliness of a woman during her period. Even the furniture in her room was considered unclean.

The summation of the discussion is that anything we try to do to save ourselves is putrid corruption; whereas, the work that God has done is totally pure, flawless, and eternal.

I make a joke out of all the medication commercials on television because they give the disclosures of possible side effects. Some even list death as a possible result of using the "health" product. One anti-depressant says that its use could result in suicidal tendencies. Human cures are always corruptible.

Easter

Resurrection Power

Yea doubtless, and I count all things but loss for the excellency of the knowledge of Christ Jesus my Lord: for whom I have suffered the loss of all things, and do count them but dung, that I may win Christ, And be found in him, not having mine own righteousness, which is of the law, but that which is through the faith of Christ, the righteousness which is of God by faith: That I may know him, and the power of his resurrection, and the fellowship of his sufferings, being made conformable unto his death; If by any means I might attain unto the resurrection of the dead. (Philippians 3:8-11)

The Apostle Paul told us that his objective in life was to know Christ in the fellowship of His sufferings and in the power of His resurrection. In fact, he said that he counted everything he had ever accomplished as rubbish in comparison to this quest to know Christ in His fullness. The *fellowship of His sufferings* refers to the humanness of Jesus, while the *power of His resurrection* refers to His divinity. Paul recognized that he needed to comprehend both aspects of his Savior, but – as he expressed in a following verse – he realized that the real power of his relationship with Christ was that he was the one who was comprehended by that revelation.

Many of us relate to the resurrected Christ in His victorious majesty and glory. Others of us relate to the suffering servant nature of the earthly Jesus. But Paul stressed that, to be genuine Christians, we need to be able to know Him and relate to Him in both aspects. This all-encompassing revelation of Jesus is like the treasure hidden in the field and the pearl of great price; it is worth giving up everything else. The true goal of the transformed life, however, is to come to the place in our lives where everything that we do, think, or feel – our very existence – is determined by the revelation.

March 23

Difficulties

All around us we observe a pregnant creation. The difficult times of pain throughout the world are simply birth pangs. But it's not only around us; it's within us. The Spirit of God is arousing us within. We're also feeling the birth pangs. These sterile and barren bodies of ours are yearning for full deliverance. That is why waiting does not diminish us, any more than waiting diminishes a pregnant mother. We are enlarged in the waiting. We, of course, don't see what is enlarging us. But the longer we wait, the larger we become, and the more joyful our expectancy. (Romans 8:22 MSG)

What a wonderful way to view life, especially the difficulties we encounter in life – a period of gestation. I remember all the changes that occurred round our house as my wife went through her pregnancies with our three boys. Everything was in a constant state of flux. Nothing remained the same, and when things did change, they didn't stay that new way very long. I remember that Peggy got really upset with me because my breath smelled after I had eaten a peanut butter sandwich. No problem – I just went and brushed my teeth. Yes problem – the toothpaste smell on my breath was even more offensive than the peanut butter aroma!

Well, all those inconveniences during the pregnancies were certainly worth it since the end result was an enlarged family. The same thing happens in our spiritual dimension as we go through the pregnancy of difficulties – we are enlarged in many dimensions. Our faith is enlarged. Our ability to recognize and follow the voice of God is fine-tuned. Our capacity to discern the work of the enemy from the hand of the Lord moves to a new level. Our patience is enhanced. And our love for God and the Body of Christ who endured with us is magnified.

That is if we don't abort during the process!

March 24

Flying the Unfriendly Skies

When you fly as much as I do with mission travel, you're certain to experience some interesting things in the air. I was once seated in one of the very back seats of the plane on a trans-Atlantic flight when one of the passengers had a heart attack. In order to give him the necessary medical care, the flight attendants brought him to the back of the plane and created a little bed for him on the floor in the galley. For the next several hours, the area around me was a beehive of activity as the attendants and all the nurses and doctors on the flight hovered around the ailing man. On another flight before the imposition of the three-ounce limit on carry-on liquids, an already inebriated passenger started to open up a bottle of duty-free liquor that he had brought onboard. There was a heated altercation with the flight attendant who had to make numerous threats of arrest before the passenger relinquished his bottle. Of course, that was just one passenger. Multiply that by about a hundred to get an idea of the commotion that occurred on a delayed flight into Haiti. Haitians in general are already known for having rather volatile emotions; but, since these passengers were from a more privileged class, they felt that they could boss the airline employees around like they were accustomed to doing when dealing with other Haitians from lower classes of society. Needless to say, the departure gate became the scene of a very boisterous protest – essentially, a mini-riot. When we finally did get on the plane, there was a further delay, and the disturbed passengers refused to take their seats while passing around a notebook to collect names on a petition to have airline personnel fired and the ticket money refunded. When it was decided that the plane could not fly that day due to need for maintenance, the protest escalated into somewhat of a sit-in as these angry passengers refused to exit the plane. I know that it is totally out of context, but on such days, I claim the promise of Psalm 55:4-6, *My heart is sore pained within me...Fearfulness and trembling are come upon me, and horror hath overwhelmed me...Oh that I had wings like a dove! for then would I fly away, and be at rest.*

Advice for Young Men

In I John chapter two, the beloved apostle shares some powerful insights and counsel with the young men in the Body of Christ.

The first thing that he says is that they are strong. The Greek term used here to refer to these young men defines them as forcible, mighty, powerful, strong, and valiant. Young men in the kingdom of God must be forcible; however, it is important to note that the term used here is not the same Greek word as in Matthew 11:12 where Jesus spoke of the violent men who try to take the kingdom of God by force. This Greek word is used a number of times in the New Testament, but two occurrences are of special interest: Luke 11:22, where Jesus speaks of the stronger one who is able to subdue the opponent who has held the goods of a house captive, and Hebrews 11:34 that speaks of warriors who waxed valiant in their fight and were, therefore, able to turn to flight the enemy armies. Young men in the kingdom of God need to learn to be aggressive and vigilant against the enemies of God. They are the forcible ones who can advance the kingdom. Immediately upon acknowledging the power and potential for the young men to overpower the enemy, John sends up a red flag – that it is possible for them to be entrapped by loving the things of the world – the very enemy they are fighting. Achan was lured into sin by the treasures of Jericho (Joshua 7:20-21), Saul couldn't resist the best of the goods of the Amalekites (I Samuel 15:15), and Demas loved the things of the present world more than the things of the kingdom to come (II Timothy 4:10).

Even though they are twice listed as overcomers, they are still warned about passing away versus being able to abide by doing the will of God. (verse 17) Men of authority must allow the Word of God to abide in them. (verse 24) Men of power must allow the anointing of God to abide in them and they must be careful to always abide in Christ. (verse 27)

March 26
God and Economics
I recently heard a rather prominent minister make a statement with a very definitive attitude. He declared that God speaks to nations through their economies. Since our own country was going through a recession at the time, all the people in the congregation gave him a big "Amen," confirming that God was making a loud announcement to America through the difficult times. When I heard him make the statement, I immediately questioned inside myself, "Is God saying something different to the Caymans and Switzerland than He is to Haiti and Zimbabwe?" I really doubt that He is.

The statement did, however, prompt me to do a little Bible study on the subject of poverty and prosperity in which I discovered a couple interesting points. Proverbs 13:18 declares, *Poverty and shame shall be to him that refuseth instruction: but he that regardeth reproof shall be honoured.* That verse seemed to confirm that those who refused the instruction of the Lord would result in poverty, a way that God could speak to nations through their economies. On the other hand, Psalm 73:3 reads, *For I was envious at the foolish, when I saw the prosperity of the wicked*, suggesting that, even though some nations are in rebellion and wickedness, they can continue to experience prosperity. That verse certainly doesn't seem to validate the idea that God is speaking to them through a downfall in their economies. In Ecclesiastes 7:14, we read, *In the day of prosperity be joyful, but in the day of adversity consider: God also hath set the one over against the other, to the end that man should find nothing after him.* Here, the scriptures seem to indicate that there is one lesson to be learned from both abundance and lack – that God is trying to tell man that he is not able to create or even predict the future. The stock market and all other economic indicators fluctuate beyond our control and often in contradiction to our forecasts. The only thing in life that is predictable is the love and security of our God. If He is speaking to us through our economy, He is saying that we must learn to trust Him in good times and in bad.

March 27
Good God! Bad God!
*Though he slay me, yet will I trust in him: but
I will maintain mine own ways before him.*
(Job 13:15)

The idea of cursing God is a major point in the book of Job. Twice, Satan claims that he can get Job to the point that he will curse God. (verse 1:11, 2:5) Job was continually in intercession for his children, fearing that they might have sinned through cursing God in their hearts. (verse 1:5) The solution that Job's wife offered to all his troubles was that he should curse God and die. (verse 2:9) Actually, the entire book centers around the same theme even though the exact terminology doesn't surface again. All of Job's friends tried to convince him that he was at fault in some way; otherwise, these calamities could not have come upon him. Job refused to admit fault because he knew that he simply was not guilty. In addition, he refused to relinquish the assessment that the Lord had twice made of him, *perfect and upright, and one that feared God, and eschewed evil.* (verses 1:1, 1:8) Had he decided to side with the opinions of his friends or his wife, he would have essentially been calling God a liar and, therefore, cursing Him. The lesson we can learn from this book is that we desperately need to learn what the scriptures say about our God and never believe anything different. We need to learn everything our God says about us and tenaciously refuse to believe or accept anything that even vaguely disagrees.

In this verse, Job seems to be blaming God for the tragedies that have struck his life. The first thing that we need to understand is that the book of Job was actually the first book of the Bible to be written down. It is only in the narrative that sets the heavenly context for the story that we see mention of the involvement of Satan. From Job's earthly perspective, there is never mention of the devil. To him, since God allowed these things to happen, it was the same as if God had actually done them. The wonderful thing about this verse is that it shows us that even when we don't understand exactly what is happening or why it is happening, we can still trust Him.

March 28
Where Does Your Money Go?

The average family spends $35,083 per year, with those expenditures falling into the following major categories:

$8,026 for health and family
$5,477 for getting around
$6,514 for food and drink
$8,668 for shopping
$6,398 for home-related expenses

However, the average amount donated to charity by residents of Oklahoma – the most generous state – is $1,587.

> *There is that scattereth, and yet increaseth; and there is that withholdeth more than is meet, but it tendeth to poverty. (Proverbs 11:24)*
>
> *I have shewed you all things, how that so labouring ye ought to support the weak, and to remember the words of the Lord Jesus, how he said, It is more blessed to give than to receive.* (Acts 20:35)
>
> *Now he that ministereth seed to the sower both minister bread for your food, and multiply your seed sown, and increase the fruits of your righteousness;) Being enriched in every thing to all bountifulness, which causeth through us thanksgiving to God. For the administration of this service not only supplieth the want of the saints, but is abundant also by many thanksgivings unto God...by the experiment of this ministration they glorify God for your professed subjection unto the gospel of Christ, and for your liberal distribution unto them, and unto all men.* (II Corinthians 9:10-13)
>
> *Cast thy bread upon the waters: for thou shalt find it after many days. Give a portion to seven, and also to eight; for thou knowest not what evil shall be upon the earth.* (Ecclesiastes 11:1-2)

Lazarus, Come Forth

J. Lee Grady, former editor of *Charisma Magazine*, once interviewed two people who were raised from the dead during an evangelistic meeting in the Indian state of Andhra Pradesh. He said of the experience, "During my twenty-six years as a journalist I've interviewed some interesting people and heard some amazing stories. But this week set a new standard when I met two people in southern India who experienced biblical-style resurrection."

The first person Grady interviewed was six-year-old Jyothi Pothabathula. Her father explained that, while en route to the crusade, Jyothi stopped breathing. The father carried her lifeless body to the stage where the evangelist was praying for the sick. "I know Jesus is a great God because he raised my daughter to life," the father explained. The miracle prompted his brother and two other family members to give their lives to Jesus.

The other resurrection occurred at another crusade led by the same evangelist, when forty-five-year-old Mesheck Manepally collapsed at the meeting and began foaming at the mouth. His son flagged down an ambulance to take his father to the hospital, but, when the evangelist heard of the emergency, he stopped preaching and walked through the crowd of over one hundred thousand attendees to pray for the man. By then, he had no pulse, and his body was stiffening. The evangelist laid his hands on the man and prayed for his life to return. Within a few minutes, Mesheck sat up in the back of the vehicle with a dazed look on his face. Mesheck's wife says that Hindu villagers came to see her husband for ten days after the incident. "They came to view him as a Lazarus. The people were saying, 'Your God is the true God.'"

The evangelist, who has witnessed five dead people raised during his fourteen years of doing crusades, explained, "Every time it happens it boosts the people's faith. In the Bible we are told that the crowds came not just to see Jesus, but to see Lazarus. As the word about these miracles spreads, everyone's faith is elevated."

March 30
Deception
When I was a college student back in the 1970s, the Charismatic Movement was in full swing, sweeping through all the Protestant denominations as well as the Catholic Church. In reaction, many of the denominations made official statements concerning their acceptance of or rejection of this fresh wind of God. Two particular campus organizations officially forbade our charismatic groups to use their facilities. However, these same organizations opened their doors for transcendental meditation and yoga classes.

I believe that it was Dr. Lester Sumrall who once said that if you neglect the power of God, you will follow after demon power. Of course, we can see this principle at work in the life of King Saul who slipped from godliness to witchcraft. Judges 16:20 tells us about a similar experience in the life of Samson who didn't even realize that it had happened when the Spirit of God had left him.

Why is it that such things happen? I believe that the reason behind such spiritual shifts is that people in church are there looking for something beyond themselves. If the church doesn't provide it or even recognize the true spiritual reality, they won't stop looking until they find something to fill that spiritual void in their lives.

How can we turn the current? As far as I know, there is only one way to do so, and it is not through forcing our way into the traditional framework of the church. I once knew a Presbyterian woman who received the baptism in the Holy Spirit and decided to force her church to convert to a Spirit-filled church by having a message in tongues during every service. She would blatantly interrupt at any point in the service – whether the choir was singing or the pastor was preaching – with her message from God. Such disorder would not even be accepted in a Holy Roller Pentecostal church, much less in a staid traditional congregation. Needless to say, she was soon kicked out. The Bible teaches that the way to change things is through prayer for the leadership.

March 31

Seven Wonders of the Ancient World

Dating back as far as the fifth century BC, scholars have made early lists of Seven Wonders of the World, but unfortunately the most ancient ones have been lost and the oldest surviving list dates to the Middle Ages. The most reliable listing we have today includes the Great Pyramid of Giza, the Hanging Gardens of Babylon, the Statue of Zeus at Olympia, the Temple of Artemis at Ephesus, the Mausoleum of Mausolus at Halicarnassus, the Colossus of Rhodes, and the Lighthouse of Alexandria. Some ancient lists substitute the Ishtar Gate instead of the Lighthouse of Alexandria. Since I was a child, I've always been fascinated by these ancient achievements of human endeavor and dreamed of being able to see them. Of course, only one of them – the Pyramid of Giza – still stands today. And I have had the privilege of climbing to the top of it! Pieces of the Ishtar Gate have been dispersed into museums around the world, and I have had numerous occasions to gaze in awe at the massive display in the Oriental Institute in Chicago. But, on my travels in Europe, I had the occasion to visit Olympia, Rhodes, and Ephesus to see where their famous monuments once stood. I was impressed to learn that it took a caravan of nine hundred camels to carry away the scrap metal after the demise of the Colossus at Rhodes. I was awestruck to see the diagrams depicting the Statue of Zeus in Olympia. But it was the visit to Ephesus that really struck me. As we walked for hours through the ruins of the city, our tour guide never even mentioned the Temple of Diana (or Artemis as she is also known). Finally, when I asked about the structure that was once one of the Seven Wonders of the World, she pointed out one simple piece of rock and said that that stone was all that remained. The thought that impressed me so much that day was how the Bible depicted the demise of worship in that temple when Paul preached the true gospel in the city. (Acts 19:26-27)

April Fool's Day
Idiosyncrasy
We all have our own little quirks, but some people are just plain quirks. We all have our personal idiosyncrasies, but for some they are idiot-syncrasies.

One man shot his television because he couldn't stand any more of Bristol Palin's Dancing with the Stars performances.

When a lady shot her identical twin sister and then herself, the authorities who investigated could not immediately identify which one was which.

In Rio de Janeiro, Brazil, a man was charged a $6,500 fine for calling off the wedding at the last minute because it caused the bride-to-be emotional pain and suffering.

In Africa, many believers show their faith by giving their businesses spiritual sounding names. One dry cleaner establishment sports the sign out front, "Holy Ghost Cleaners." But the one that really "takes the cake" is the "God is Able Beauty Salon." I'm afraid to see what the women must look like who chose to go there.

A Colorado Springs police arrested a man for jumping on a moving car, forcing his way into the car, and biting the driver on the head. When he tried to force his way into the car of an off-duty police officer, the patrolman rolled up the window on the suspect's arm and bit his hand. I guess that one good bite deserves another.

A group of students at a Bible college paid their way through school by robbing convenience stores. They had held up at least fourteen stores before they were apprehended.

Two Lakeland, Florida, Domino's Pizza managers burned down the local Papa John's restaurant in hopes of gaining more of the local market share of pizza customers.

Maybe we all have at least a little stake in today.

Happy April Fool's Day!

April 2
If You Have an Ear, Hear

A missionary friend of mine in the Dominican Republic had a problem with the portable generator he needed for a crusade he was doing. When one of the local mechanics could not figure what was wrong with the machine, my friend resorted to calling a friend of his on the cell phone. By simply listening over the phone to the sound that the generator was making, Juan Carlos was able to diagnose the problem with the generator and explain to the missionary what needed to be done to get it working properly. That's what I call an attentive ear.

God is looking for people with that same kind of spiritual hearing. That's why He insisted to each of the seven churches in Revelation that if anyone has an ear he should hear what the Spirit is saying. In addition, He gave us that same admonition at least nine times during His earthly ministry. (Matthew 11:15, 13:9, 43; Mark 4:9, 23, 7:16, 8:18; Luke 8:8, 14:35)

James warns us that we must not be forgetful hearers (verse 1:25) who hear but not with an attentive ear that causes us to remember and act upon His instructions. In verse twenty-two, James explains that the root cause of such hearing problems lies not in our ears themselves but in the fact that we deceive ourselves – a malady which Jeremiah describes as being a condition of the heart. (verse 17:9) James makes a parallel statement when he equates heart deception with an unbridled tongue. (verse 1:26) He makes another intriguing comment concerning wicked men, saying that they nourish their hearts as in the day of slaughter. (verse 5:5) Many translations render this phrase *to fatten the heart,*" but a couple make it even more graphic: "indulged your fancies (Twentieth Century New Testament) and *stupefied yourselves with gross feeding* (Weymouth's New Testament). So what is the bottom line? Our human inclination is to be so self-absorbed that we can't control our lips or our ears. We are always so self-focused that we simply can't force ourselves to talk about the things of God or listen purposefully when He tries to talk to us.

April 3
Leadership
Today, I'd like for us to consider a few almost random thoughts that can serve as attitude checks for people in leadership and for those of us who are in "followership." Both leaders and followers need to stop occasionally to double check that we are not leading or being led blindly. *Can the blind lead the blind? shall they not both fall into the ditch?* (Luke 6:39)

"Service" in certain parts of the country sounds more like "serve us." That's a good reminder of what real leadership is all about.

Remember, it is the owner of the sheep, not the shepherd, who is responsible for feeding them. The shepherd only has to lead the sheep to the place where the owner has stored up the provision.

We need to understand that there are things that leaders can do for the congregation while there are other things that the leaders must encourage the congregation in as they take on these responsibilities. First Corinthians 16:15 speaks of the ministry of saints, but Ephesians 4:12 speaks of the ministry to saints.

It takes apostolic covering and care to ensure that we can finish strong. (Philippians 1:1-6)

Will your name open doors or slam them? When leaders have honor and a good name, the Lord opens doors for them.

The test of real leadership is whether you are willing to do all the work and let your followers get all the credit. David drew up all the blueprints for the temple and worked hard to raise all the money to build it, knowing that it would be named for Solomon.

Speaking of working hard in leadership, remember that people will never work harder than their leaders do, so put in more effort than you might think necessary.

True leadership requires discernment of what is really pertinent. If you are a zoo director, there may be times when you must realize that your focus must be on the fence rather than the animals.

April 4

Extravagance

In the book of Ephesians, Paul makes several references to the extravagance of God in providing for us. In verse 1:19, he speaks of the exceeding greatness of His power that is working in us according to the working of his mighty power. In verse 1:8, he says that God has made wisdom and prudence to abound toward us. One translation says that He has given these things to us lavishly. Verse 3:20 says that He gives us everything exceedingly abundantly above all that we ask or think.

When I read these passages, I think of the time when I stopped at a fast-food restaurant for a sandwich. The girl who was serving me took a handful of roast beef and put it on the scale. When she saw that there was just over four ounces of meat in the portion she had picked up, she began to pick off little pinches until she had balanced the scale precisely. I was actually offended as I watched her meticulously protect the company's profit margin. The next time I wanted to buy lunch, I went across the street to an all-you-can-eat buffet where, for just about a dollar more than I paid for my carefully portioned four-ounce roast beef sandwich, I could get unlimited servings of salads, hot dishes, and desserts. Now, that's what I call lavish and abundant extravagance.

Spiritually, this is exactly how God wants to treat us. He has set before us a banqueting table laden with more than we can ever imagine. He continually causes our cups to run over. The only limits that we have are our own ignorance that such blessings are available to us, our feelings of unworthiness that cause us to feel that we don't deserve to "belly up" to the table, and our rebellious attitudes that make us want to sit in our own corner rather than join the fellowship around the table of the family of God.

Today, God is calling us, *Come and dine...Ho, every one that thirsteth, come ye to the waters, and he that hath no money; come ye, buy, and eat; yea, come, buy wine and milk without money and without price.* (John 21:12, Isaiah 55:1)

April 5
Y Generation
Y Generation, those young Americans who were born between 1980 and 2000, are the new force that is shaping our world today. The leading edge of this generation is just now reaching the age where they are stepping into careers and taking leadership positions in business, military, education, media, and every other segment of society. Since they are the emerging generation, it would be good for the rest of us to get to understand them a bit. After all, who they are and what they think will mold our future. Here's a spiritual profile of the Y Generation:

> 65% rarely attend church
> 70% feel that church is irrelevant
> 26% believe that they will go to heaven
> 15% are true Christians
> 13% consider spirituality important

Notice that only about one in three have any relationship with organized Christian faith and practice, and only that number are considered to be true believers. Unless this trend can be reversed, our nation is headed for serious difficulties.

Twice, the Psalmist told us that the key to happiness and success is acknowledging the Lord as our God.

> *Blessed is the nation whose God is the LORD; and the people whom he hath chosen for his own inheritance.* (Psalm 33:12)
> *Happy is that people, whose God is the LORD.* (Psalm 144:15)

Interestingly enough, there are other titles for this generation, including "The Worst Generation." Truly, the lack of God in their lives will certainly lead them to live up (or should I say "down"?) to that description.

The root cause of the Y Generation? The previous generations have given them a religion that lacked a vital relationship with God. After all, if you have an empty wrapper, you trash it. The cure? Let's stop pretending and start living a true and vital life of faith before them.

April 6
Living to be 100
I've run across several articles lately about living to be a hundred years old. Most of them present statistics claiming that the present generation is very likely to produce an overwhelming number of centenarians due to our advancement in medical care and our ever-growing consciousness of a healthful lifestyle, including a good diet, plenty of exercise, proper sleep, and avoidance of harmful habits such as smoking. One other physical factor that some of these articles mention is periodic fasting, a process that allows us to literally cleanse our physical insides while also spiritually cleansing our spiritual inner man. In addition to these obvious factors, the articles often add being socially connected. Many times, the social connections are specifically related to being part of a community of faith. Another non-physical factor that is often included is having a purpose bigger than yourself. If we have a reason to live that focuses on others rather than ourselves, an inner force is activated that rejuvenates and regenerates us.

The Bible also has keys for long and meaningful lives.

He shall call upon me, and I will answer him: I will be with him in trouble; I will deliver him, and honour him. With long life will I satisfy him, and shew him my salvation. (Psalm 91:15-16)

My son, forget not my law; but let thine heart keep my commandments: For length of days, and long life, and peace, shall they add to thee. (Proverbs 3:1-2)

Honour thy father and thy mother: that thy days may be long upon the land which the LORD thy God giveth thee. (Exodus 20:12)

Of course, the real target that the Bible wants us to focus on is not simply living a hundred years, but having eternal life.

For God so loved the world, that he gave his only begotten Son, that whosoever believeth in him should not perish, but have everlasting life. (John 3:16)

April 7
Taki-Taki

I have just discovered a new language – the Taki-Taki language, which is spoken in Suriname. I'm excited to learn about it because it has only a few hundred words as opposed to English that has the most words at a quarter million. The question in my mind is, "Why didn't God call me to be a missionary to the people who speak that tongue?" Considering my difficulty with learning languages, it would have been a very considerate thing on His part. When I do master a few phrases in the local languages, I seem to have a tendency to use the right words – but in the wrong countries.

I have had to learn five languages to get through school: Latin and French were the only two languages offered in my public high school, and they were required for students in college prep studies. Since my undergraduate degree was in chemistry, I was not required to study any languages in college; however, my seminary studies required Hebrew and Greek, and my doctoral degree required German. I generally did pretty well in class, but once I earned the necessary credits, I basically forgot everything except the blood, sweat, and tears I went through to get the grade.

When I started doing mission work in Nepal, I made an attempt at learning the language by making a stack of flash cards based on words I took from a Nepali-English dictionary. Returning to the country for my annual visit after having mastered the words and phrases on a fairly sizable stack of my homemade cards, I proudly began to use my new vocabulary. Praying for people after the church services, I boldly proclaimed what I thought was "I bless you." That is until my Nepali friend suggested that I not say that anymore since I was really saying, "I'm in love with you." Next, I decided to show off my language skills in a restaurant by ordering in Nepali. When the waiter looked at me with a totally stunned expression on his face, I assumed that it was an expression of shock that I was speaking such fluent Nepali. My friend explained that the server's expression was actually one of horror at my blatant request to eat a holy cow!

April 8

New Creation

As new creatures in Christ, the old sinful nature has actually been done away with out of our lives. (II Corinthians 5:17) They have been expiated, not propitiated. In the King James Bible, we find the word "propitiation" a number of times. In more modern translations, that word has been exchanged for the word "expiation." Propitiation means "to cover up." Expiation means "to eliminate." In our lives, the new creature has had expiation. An old creature may have had his problems covered up, but a new creature has them totally removed, washed away. Dr. Sumrall always described the difference as washing a wall white and whitewashing it.

And he is the propitiation for our sins: and not for ours only, but also for the sins of the whole world. (I John 2:2)

Whom God hath set forth to be a propitiation through faith in his blood, to declare his righteousness for the remission of sins that are past, through the forbearance of God. (Romans 3:25)

Herein is love, not that we loved God, but that he loved us, and sent his Son to be the propitiation for our sins. (I John 4:10)

As new creatures, we are also empowered by the Holy Ghost to live a new life that we could never live in our own strength.

That ye put off concerning the former conversation the old man, which is corrupt according to the deceitful lusts; And be renewed in the spirit of your mind; And that ye put on the new man, which after God is created in righteousness and true holiness. (Ephesians 4:22-24)

Even the Spirit of truth; whom the world cannot receive, because it seeth him not, neither knoweth him: but ye know him; for he dwelleth with you, and shall be in you. (John 14:17)

April 9

The Portrait

I once heard a story of a very wealthy man who had only one child. Unfortunately, this son was killed while serving on the frontlines in the military. After the tragic loss, the father had an artist to paint a portrait of the young man. This portrait became one of the gentleman's most valued possessions; so, he left careful instructions that, upon his death, the art piece be the first item to be auctioned when his estate was liquidated.

On the day of the estate sale, a large crowd gathered, hoping to obtain the deceased's houses, lands, furnishings, and other treasures at Black Friday prices. Everybody had their eyes on the massive estate holdings and were rather irritated with the auctioneer's first item on the table since they saw no value in the simple painting compared to all the property holdings also ready to go up on the block. Disinterested, they sat impatiently waiting to get the formality over with so they could move on to the houses, lands, and other holdings. Finally, one buyer bid ten dollars simply to get the auctioneer to move on. To everyone's amazement, the auctioneer began to close up shop as soon as the transaction on the painting was completed. What no one knew, as the painting was being displayed, is that the old gentleman had written into his will that he was leaving his entire estate to whomever would purchase the painting of his son!

This story – whether fact or fantasy, I know not – gives us some great insights into the gospel. Jesus is the Son of God who is despised and rejected by men; yet, in Him are hidden all the treasures of the kingdom of God. Once we accept Jesus, we obtain all that the Father has! In addition, we see the value of the Bible as a portrait of Jesus because it is through the Word of God that we can understand who He is and what great treasures we obtain through Him.

April 10

One-liners Worth a Second Glance

A son differs not from a servant while he is training.

A sovereign is a son by birth but a servant by rebirth.

There are no shortcuts to the foot of the cross.

Go for the gusto; don't accept Gospel lite.

There is no life worth living until there is a cause worth dying for.

Retreat is not defeat; failure is not forever.

A good waiter anticipates his customer's need in advance; he should never have to ask.

We leak out our heavenly deposit to the point that we live on spiritual fumes instead of godly fire.

The church has symptoms of heart disease.

Lay down the "bless me" milkshake.

Repent or relent.

Don't strike back; you cannot absorb the bitterness of revenge.

The Word of God is a sword; use it properly, not on yourself.

We can come out of the trials of life smelling like a rose (Rose of Sharon).

True spiritual warfare can be fought by remote control – like Desert Storm. Jesus didn't have to go to the centurion's house; He spoke the word and healed the servant from a distance.

A church on its knees keeps its pastor on his feet.

The widow's mite is when we decide to put Monday's lunch in Sunday's offering.

While praying for and giving to ministries in the 10/40 Window, we must not forget to be a witness on our own 9/5 Window – our workplaces.

Most of us walk past our ministry on the way to go minister; remember the priest and the Levite in the story of the Good Samaritan.

Evangelism is supposed to be fishing, not hunting; fishermen use bait.

The presence of God is not for escape, but for empowerment.

Signs and wonders are the dinner bell that calls people to the supper table.

April 11
Gifts and Calling

Romans 11:29 tells us that the gifts and calling of God are without repentance. Notice that we may have multiple gifts but there seems to be only one calling since the word is expressed in the singular. As ministers and laypeople alike, we need to find out exactly what our individual calling is and separate it from the list of gifts that we might have. If we can do that, we will be able to restrict ourselves to the areas where we have a vision, a calling, and an anointing. Otherwise, we will waste our lives doing good things simply because we have the ability to do them rather than to fulfill the higher calling upon our lives by finding the exact spot where God wants us to be.

Someone once said that the church will tolerate what would not be allowed in the secular world. If a plumber showed up at your house trying to be an electrician, you would not allow him to start tampering with your wiring – that is, unless you were willing to risk having your home burn down from faulty wiring. But in the church, we allow – and often even encourage – people to function outside their divine calling. Honestly, we put our spiritual house at risk of being destroyed because of this sort of undiscerning negligence.

I was once interviewed for a faculty position at a Bible college that was run by a denomination. The president of the school really wanted to hire me. In fact, he drove several hundred miles to come to interview and recruit me. Unfortunately, there was one little roadblock that kept him from hiring me; the denomination had a policy of hiring from within. Since I was not part of that denomination, he could not offer me the job. However, he had a way around the obstacle; he wanted me to accept an interim pastoral appointment at one of their churches that was in transition between permanent pastors. His idea was that I could serve in the church for a couple years and, thus, qualify for the job at his school. I told him that I could not accept his offer since I would be working outside my calling even though I'm certain that I have the gifts necessary to fill the position. I didn't want to put their church in jeopardy of a fire.

Love

In II Timothy 3:5, Paul spoke of people who would have a form of godliness but deny the power thereof. I'm sure that most, if not all, of us have heard this passage preached as an accusation against denominational churches that don't operate in the gifts of the Holy Spirit. However, I believe that there is an entirely different meaning to this verse. If we couple it with another of the Apostle's statements, we can begin to see it in a whole new light. In Galatians 5:6, we learn that the power behind faith is love. Is it possible that Paul is telling us that we can try to operate while denying the power of love that motivates it? That is exactly what he had to deal with in the Corinthian church, *Though I have all faith, so that I could remove mountains, and have not charity, I am nothing.* (I Corinthians 13:2)

Jesus taught us that the only way to have fruit that will remain is through love.

> *Ye have not chosen me, but I have chosen you, and ordained you, that ye should go and bring forth fruit, and that your fruit should remain: that whatsoever ye shall ask of the Father in my name, he may give it you. These things I command you, that ye love one another.* (John 15:16-17)

In Ephesians 3:20, Paul speaks of the mighty power of God at work in our lives; however, in the preceding verses, he lays the groundwork for that revelation by telling us that that power really is God's unfathomable love.

> *May be able to comprehend with all saints what is the breadth, and length, and depth, and height; And to know the love of Christ, which passeth knowledge, that ye might be filled with all the fulness of God. Now unto him that is able to do exceeding abundantly above all that we ask or think, according to the power that worketh in us.* (verses 3:18-20)

April 13
Foreign Language 101
To qualify for the doctoral program in seminary, I had to pass a competency test in German. The requirement was put in place because so much of the theological scholarship in the first part of the twentieth century was written in German. The easiest way for me to learn the language was to take a class at my alma mater, North Carolina State University, which was less than an hour's drive from the seminary. Since I lived in the same city as the university, I found taking the classes at the campus convenient – well, somewhat. I started my day by teaching at a high school in the outskirts of town, followed by driving to the seminary and taking a couple classes. After class, I would drive back to Raleigh and park at a hotel where I had worked while in college. Since I didn't want to pay for a parking permit at the university for just one class, I had requested permission from the hotel manager to use a spot in their lot each day. Then I would speed walk about a mile to my German class. By the time I sat down in class, the class was just ready to begin. Of course, I was exhausted from the hectic pace I had kept all day – and I usually dozed off for a couple minutes as soon as I was relaxed in my seat. On one particular day, the professor began the class by telling a joke in German. I woke up just before he got to the punch line and immediately caught the gist of the story. Since the rest of the students in the class were busy trying to translate through the whole story, none of them were able to catch the point. I was the only one who laughed at the story. Of course, the instructor recognized that I had slept through most of his story and told me later that he was amazed that I was able to understand the joke. At that point, I really did understand German.

In many things in life, including our faith, the important thing is not that we are able to work through all the details but that we are able to use the truths when the "rubber meets the road."

Presbyterians

Several years ago, I attended a free concert that was presented by a local Presbyterian church as an evangelistic outreach to the community. It was a great concert by a well-known Christian recording group. They sang powerful worship songs interspersed with their personal testimonies and some spiritual teaching. At the close of the concert, the pastor of the church came to the stage to present an evangelistic message and an invitation. As he presented the altar call, he told those who wanted prayer that there were a number of Presbyterians available to pray with them. I'm sure that he didn't intend to come across with the attitude that Presbyterians are different from other Christians. I have no doubt that this was nothing more than a slip of the tongue; but instead of saying that there were trained counselors or good Christian men and ladies to help, he communicated that the best (or possibly, only) way to get help was through Presbyterians. Obviously, this was not his intent, and I hope that it was not the lasting impression that the people took away from the concert.

A couple years later, I had another interesting experience with Presbyterians when one of the local Presbyterian churches presented a diversity festival with the intent of communicating to the community that people of all backgrounds should be welcomed into the community. With the intent of fostering a better understanding of people from diverse beliefs, the church invited witches, New Agers, and people from all sorts of occult practices to have booths where they were able to interact with the community and explain what they believe and how they practice their faith. I'm not exactly sure how much the church intended to endorse these various groups, but the festival certainly left a message in the minds of the community: Jesus is not the only way to God.

From these two radically different messages presented by these two Presbyterian churches, we must learn that neither message is right. The truth is that we may have many ways for finding Jesus, but there is no other way to God except through Him.

Tax Day
Wealth of the Wicked

As we pay our taxes today, all of us must be wondering if the government is looking to us to clear up the national debt. As I'm writing this article, the debt level according to www.usdebtclock.org, which gives a real time view of the US debt, is over fifteen trillion dollars; however, as the numbers swirl across the screen right before your very eyes, there is no guess how big they will be by the time you read this ditty. Can you believe that our national debt level was at only one trillion dollars during the Reagan administration?

I somehow doubt that there is ever going to be a tax payment or financial transfer that is going to clear up all the economic difficulties of the US and the world; however, the Bible does predict a significant wealth transfer in the end times. Proverbs 13:22 tells us that the wealth of the sinner is laid up for the just. James 5:3 furthers the discussion by adding that these wicked men have heaped their treasure together for the last days. In the parable of the wheat and tares in Matthew chapter thirteen, one line is of real significance to this discussion, *So shall it be at the end of the world: the angels shall come forth, and sever the wicked from among the just.* (verse 49) This verse is likely prophesying the exact time when the resources that the wicked control will be transferred to the just. Verse forty-three says that the just will *shine as the sun* – likely a reference to the transfer of resources into their hands. Now the punch line – since this parable is speaking of the final harvest and the ultimate destruction of the wicked, the transfer of wealth to the righteous cannot be for the purpose of evangelizing the world as is often thought when people make reference to the prophecy. Biblically, this transfer of wealth is simply a part of establishing the millennial kingdom. Thus, we Christians must stop relying on the "pie in the sky" inheritance from the wicked in order to fund the last great thrust of world evangelism. It is no more likely than seeing our taxes – no matter how high they are – settle the national debt.

April 16
Say What You Mean and Mean What You Say

When I was studying Greek in seminary, I had an awful time figuring out all the pronunciation rules. I could never decide whether the accent was supposed to be on the penult, antepenult, or ultima. In fact, I'm not sure I ever even figured out what all these various syllables were in the first place. And then there were the vowels that sounded differently if they followed certain consonants or appeared in a diphthong – not to mention the iota diphthong that camouflaged itself as a simple vowel by the disappearance of the iota. Well, one day I totally embarrassed myself when the professor called on me to read a passage aloud to the class. I stumbled through the reading, mispronouncing every word except the very simplest ones. The professor then called on one of my classmates to read the passage. After he read the verse as if Greek were his native tongue, the student bumbled through the translation, butchering it as badly as I had massacred the pronunciation. I was so pleased with myself when the professor gave me an opportunity to redeem myself from the botched reading by giving a flawless translation of the text. The lesson to be learned from Greek class that day was not about the Greek language itself, but about our lives in general: it is not what you say, but what you mean that really counts.

Back in 1987, Alan Greenspan, who later became head of the Federal Reserve Board, said, "Since becoming a central banker I have learned to mumble with great incoherence. If I seem unduly clear to you, you must have misunderstood what I said." I can't remember what political figure it was who said, "You can't even misquote me correctly," and a Google search didn't help me find the originator. I did find a similar quote, but then I would have to misquote that individual to put these exact words into his mouth. But the truth is that the world revolves around misquotes, misinterpretations, and misunderstandings. As Christians who want to carefully guard our speech so that we always communicate the truth and never misrepresent the gospel, we must rely upon the Spirit of Truth.

April 17

The Race

A friend of mine went to visit one of his relatives and discovered that his visit happened to coincide with a 10K race that his relative was scheduled to run in. Since my friend didn't want to just sit at his relative's house the whole day or to simply stand on the sidelines waiting for the race to be over, he decided to enter the race himself. Although my friend is actually fairly athletic for a guy his age, he had not trained for a foot race and was not in shape for running a 10K. Although he soon fell to the back of the pack, he continued running with the intent of finishing the course – even if he would come in last. He told me that he had a police escort the whole way through the course because the patrol that followed the runners to warn drivers that there were pedestrians in the road ahead was continually tailing him. When he did eventually cross the finish line, he enjoyed the rest of his visit with his relative and returned home, thinking nothing more of the race.

A few days later, my friend was surprised to receive a package in the mail containing a medal and a letter congratulating him for placing first in his particular age bracket in the race. Even though he came in last in the whole race, he actually won first place in his special category since there were no other runners in that group!

We can learn some valuable lessons from this little story that we can apply to our everyday lives. First, we must remember that because every one of God's creatures is unique, we must never compare ourselves to others. Perhaps we may look like losers if we compare ourselves to someone else, but the truth is not in competing with others but in making sure that we don't fail in our individual calling. The next lesson is in endurance. Had my friend not crossed the finish line, he would not only have been in last place – he wouldn't have placed at all. The tasks we are given to complete in life are usually not timed tests. The thing that matters is that we complete the task, not the time it takes us to do so. One other significant point is that we must not live our lives always expecting a reward for our efforts. Just do what's right. If you get recognition for it, great; if not, great!

April 18

Quick Thoughts with Long-Lasting Truths

Knowledge is sight; wisdom insight.

Rank-to-rank combat requires a brave man, but it is suicide; be smart and brave.

Set your mind like you do your TV or VCR to pick up only one specific channel – the wisdom of God. (Isaiah 55:3, Romans 8:5)

Live life in the crosshairs of the horizontal relationship of your love for your brother and the vertical relationship of your love for God.

We can learn some important lessons from the pigs in the story of Legion, the demoniac. Pigs have more authority than people because the demons couldn't enter without permission. Pigs also have more sense than people because they drowned themselves when they got possessed; we have parades.

When the Israelites left on their journey from Egypt to the Promised Land, they were facing an eleven-day trip. They probably left with enough provision and had no need of manna. Their rebellion was the reason for the miracle supply. God will go to miraculous lengths to take care of His children, even when they are in disobedience.

You can't be big in a small office.

Christians ought to stand out like a healed thumb.

Always sandwich your requests between praise. Look at the pattern in the Lord's Prayer; the request for daily bread comes after the proclamation of the hallowedness of God's name and before the declaration of His kingdom, power, and glory.

God would be unjust to give a command we couldn't keep.

When Jesus told the disciples not to let their hearts be troubled, He was declaring that we are to be in control of our emotions. (John 14:1, 27)

Satan chose a snake – a subtle animal rather than a forceful one – to tempt Eve because he really doesn't have force, only persuasion.

April 19
Quick Insights for Ministers

The Israelites had to learn to stay with the cloud rather than their own agenda. How long would your ministry keep moving if God stopped?

The unjust steward was unwilling to beg and dig. If we are to be just stewards in our ministries, we must be willing to do both.

Make sure that you are raising up a body of believers, not just a group of receivers.

Don't talk about your authority as a pastor; that makes the people feel that you want to drive them like goats. Tell them that certain things are your responsibility; that way, they recognize that you are leading them like sheep.

If you don't have faith to refuse when men offer you gifts with strings attached, you won't have faith to receive when God hands you blessings.

Don't turn giving into grieving by coercing the people. (II Corinthians 9:7)

Learn to rest in your labors rather than to have to rest from them.

Learn to trust God to the point that you don't have a breakdown when things break down.

Not every growth is good; sometimes growth can be cancerous.

Don't count your harvest at the altar call. The harvest isn't over until the grain is threshed and the grapes are pressed.

The workers who came at the end of the day had been waiting for a job all day and were probably willing to work as hard as the ones who had worked for eleven hours. Those of us in the end-time harvest must be diligent and determined.

The laborers are few because we have been too selective.

Make sure that you are a mouthpiece for God, not a mimic of others.

The scriptures teach that the husbandman is to be a partaker of fruit, not the seed.

Shepherds with dull hearts will scatter the sheep. (Jeremiah 10:21)

April 20

Interesting People I Know

A Nigerian man went to the US to have eye surgery because he didn't trust local doctors. When he checked into the hospital here, he discovered that his doctor was Nigerian.

When another Nigerian came to the US, his traveling companion noticed how careful he was to drop his candy wrapper in a trash bin. However, his friend was quick to note that he reverted to tossing the papers on the street as soon as they returned to Africa.

One of my friends wrote about her mom, "She'll be eighty-nine next month; so, she has had a long life – but says she's not ready to die because she has two little girls (both of us in our early seventies) that she has to take care of!

A man had petitioned authorities for permission to walk across a tightrope to be stretched above Niagara Falls. The city of Niagara Falls, NY, favored the stunt, thinking that it would promote tourism, but authorities in Canada where the other end of the rope would have to be anchored refused permission. The last time this stunt was done was in 1910 by the famous French aerialist Blondin.

I have a cousin who suffers from a crippling foot disease. She is very limited in her mobility and has to undergo rather frequent surgeries and hospital stays. In spite of her hindrances, she is probably the happiest person I know. She raises bunnies and takes them for walks on a leash. If you want to see something funny, just imagine a lady with a walker and a rabbit on a leash. When a friend brought her to visit us recently, we decided to meet at a restaurant for lunch. I arrived a bit early and stood in the parking place just in front of the door to reserve it so that she wouldn't have to walk very far. Communicating with cell phones, I tried to direct her friend to the parking place. She went the wrong way on the street, turned into an alley instead of pulling into the parking place, went down the wrong block, and finally almost ran me over when she did find the parking spot. I'm thinking that she should stick to walking bunnies.

April 21

Auntie Ruth

Auntie Ruth was a little old lady from our church in Indiana who used to do a lot of mission work in Asia. She traveled with me to Burma and Nepal on a couple of occasions and made a real impression on the local people as well as on us as missionaries. I don't know how many times she corrected me that people are not "slain in the Spirit" because they are not dead; rather, they are "out under the power." Even more frequently, she corrected me that we must designate that we are talking about Jesus Christ of Nazareth, not just Jesus or Jesus Christ. She had met many "Jesus"es in her mission work, but knew of only one biblical Jesus Christ of Nazareth who could save, heal, and deliver! One of my fondest memories was the day we were traveling into the remote mountains of Nepal on a road that had just enough pavement to hold the potholes together as we bumped over the trail, I could hear her praying, "Lord, don't let me get bunions on my buttocks."

One of my most interesting stories about Auntie Ruth is based on her insistence that all pastors' wives must have the gift of giving messages in tongues and all pastors must have the gift of interpreting messages given in tongues. Although she had no biblical basis for her belief, she was insistent and refused to relent. Once, when she was teaching in a Bible college in Nepal, she was determined to get all the married couples to begin to exercise these gifts. Otherwise, she was not willing to qualify them for the pastorate. All the students eventually qualified except for one young couple from a remote region in the Himalayas. After Auntie Ruth's repeated insistence that the wife must be able to give a message in unknown tongues so that the husband could interpret it into Nepali, the young lady came upon a plan. She spoke several paragraphs in her regional language which none of the other Nepali students could understand. Of course, her husband was able to fluently translate it into the national Nepali language. Everyone was happy, but Auntie was none the wiser as to what had happened.

Auntie Ruth lived to be just short of one hundred years old, and she made every year of her life count for Jesus.

April 22

Sea of Forgetfulness

We've all heard the expression that our sins are cast into the sea of God's forgetfulness, and often the comment that He has put up a "No Fishing" sign is tagged on. In fact, we've probably heard this saying so often that most of us assume that it is a quote from the Bible. Actually, this quote does not come from the Bible, and I have not been able to find the exact origin in any of my research. I suspect that the phrase must take its roots from a couple biblical references: *He will again have compassion on us; he will tread our iniquities underfoot. You will cast all our sins into the depths of the sea,* (Micah 7:19) and *I, even I, am the one who wipes out your transgressions for My own sake; and I will not remember your sin.* (Isaiah 43:25). It is possible that there may even be an allusion to Psalm 88:12, *Shall thy wonders be known in the dark? And thy righteousness in the land of forgetfulness?* in the phrase.

Regardless of the background of the term and the message it is intended to convey, we must remember that just because things are dumped into the ocean does not mean that they cease to exist. They are very likely to resurface – and often in the most unlikely places. I remember being shown bean pods in South America that were referred to as "Africa beans." When I asked why they were given that name, the gentleman explained that they are carried all the way across the ocean by the currents. I've also read articles about debris from the tsunami in Japan showing up in Alaska and Hawaii, but the most amazing discovery of sea trash that I've heard of was the discovery in Ireland of a tag from a lobster pot that was swept off the New England sea floor two decades ago during what came to be known as "The Perfect Storm." After a journey of three thousand miles and twenty years, the flotsam proved that just because it was lost at sea did not mean that it was non-existent. Not the case with our sin! When God forgives our sins, He eradicates them so that they can never be remembered again – no matter how many miles and years may pass.

April 23

Becoming an Antique

When we arrived in Livingstone, Zambia, the young man driving our taxi from the airport to our hotel wanted to give us a little history lesson en route. He was pointing out the fact that the city had made a special effort to preserve its historic buildings in their original state. As he pointed out one specific structure, he proudly explained, "Now this building dates <u>all</u> <u>the</u> <u>way</u> <u>back</u> to 1949!" After I commented that three out of his four passengers were born in 1949, he seemed to lose his interest in the city's "antiquities."

At a recent missions conference, the emcee made an interesting comment as he was introducing me, "After sixty, you can say anything you want – you are a father in missions." I'm certain that there is a compliment hidden in the statement somewhere, but I'm still trying to sort it out. I guess that it just takes a little longer to work through things when you get to be my age.

Of course, there is one good thing about being over the hill – you pick up speed.

Another good aspect of aging is that the older you get, the more friendly He becomes.

When a younger guy noticed one elderly gentleman who seemed to be spending a lot of extra time reading his Bible, he asked his elderly friend why. His answer, "I'm studying for my final exam."

Of course, getting older can mean a bit of memory loss, but it doesn't have to mean that you lose your wit. Try this story as an example: When the becoming-an-antique gentleman forgot his wife's birthday, he was able to cover his mistake by explaining, "But you never look any older, my dear!"

Speaking of looking older and becoming an antique, you can tell when you hit the mark that qualifies you because you get the furniture disease: your chest falls into your drawers.

By the way, a piece of furniture is classified as an antique when it is fifty years old. At that point, it is no longer considered old, worthless, used, or second-hand. It suddenly becomes valuable and on its way to becoming an heirloom.

April 24

Inside Prison Walls in India

An Indian pioneer missionary was severely beaten by an angry mob of radical Hindus. When the police came to break up the riot, the young man was imprisoned because the officers thought that he was the one who had incited the riot. When one of his cellmates in prison asked why he had been attacked, the young Christian shared his testimony and eventually led his cellmate to the Lord. One of the wardens in the jail overheard the whole conversation between the two inmates and asked the missionary if he would like to share his story with the whole prison body. He accepted the invitation and boldly preached the gospel to the entire prison population. As a result of that message, seventeen more inmates received salvation!

One important detail of the story is that during the beating the young man had suffered on the street, someone had kicked him in the genitals with the result that he will never be able to have children. However, the young man gladly testifies that even though he will never father any physical children, he is happy to have eighteen spiritual sons in that dank Indian jail. He is happy that God has allowed him to be spiritually fruitful and to multiply the kingdom of God.

In the Apostle Paul, we see a testimony of the effectiveness of the message that is not bound even when the messenger is.

> *For which I am an ambassador in bonds: that therein I may speak boldly, as I ought to speak. (Ephesians 6:20)*
> *So that my bonds in Christ are manifest in all the palace, and in all other places.* (Philippians 1:13)
> *Be not thou therefore ashamed of the testimony of our Lord, nor of me his prisoner: but be thou partaker of the afflictions of the gospel according to the power of God.* (II Timothy 1:8)
> *I beseech thee for my son Onesimus, whom I have begotten in my bonds.* (Philemon 1:10)

April 25

Plan B

When Dr. Lester Sumrall was alive, he did not receive a salary from the church, TV station, or any other aspect of his ministry. The only income he received was from two offerings each year – one at his birthday and one at Christmas. It was during his birthday offering one year that I felt the Lord directing me to give a hundred-dollar gift. Unfortunately, money was very tight at that particular time, and all I could afford without having to go into debt was a ten-dollar bill. I dropped the bill in the plate and figured that this was the end of the matter. However, in the service the next week, Dr. Sumrall took time to thank the congregation for his offering of $5,910 – a generous offering back in those days. He then made a comment about the fact that it was ninety dollars short of six thousand and mused that someone with the extra money must have been absent that day. Well, that person wasn't absent; he was right there in the service, but he was just lacking in the faith it took to obey the direction of God.

I learned a valuable lesson that day about trusting God when He speaks to you. Too often, we simply assume that our disobedience doesn't make a big difference in the long run. We somehow think that God has a back-up plan with someone else to take over the responsibility He gave us. The birthday offering that day disproved that assumption. The amount I held back was the exact amount that the offering lacked. If this principle is true in offerings, I'm sure that it applies to every area of obedience.

When God spoke to Dr. Sumrall about going to the prison in the Philippines to pray for a demon-possessed girl, the Lord warned him that the girl would die if he didn't go because there was no one else to do the job.

What is God asking you to do today? Please be faithful to obey because God simply doesn't have a Plan B up His sleeve.

April 26

Promotion

*For promotion cometh neither from the east,
nor from the west, nor from the south. But
God is the judge: he putteth down one, and
setteth up another.* (Psalm 75:6-7)

The Bible teaches us that God is the one who is in charge of promoting us in His kingdom; however, it also illustrates to us that there are certain principles that come into play in this promotion process. The parable of the talents in Matthew 25:14-30 portrays the difference between the unprofitable servant and the one who was promoted as knowing but not acting on the nature of the master. He knew that the master was one who reaped where he didn't sow; however, he did nothing with the master's money to ensure him a harvest. The promoted servant recognized this prosperity characteristic in his master and acted in faith, expecting that he would have something to reap. In Luke 17:7, we get a revelation that the servant is actually unprofitable unless he is looking for the second mile that he can go in service for the master.

Those of us who would desire to be promoted in the kingdom of God need to have only one thing in our hearts – doing the will of God. (Ephesians 6:6, Colossians 3:22) We must remember that a double-minded man is unstable in all his ways and will not receive anything, including promotion, from God. (James 1:5-8) Romans 8:6 speaks even more to us about the mental focus we must have, calling it being spiritually minded rather than being carnally minded.

To understand how to fulfill the will of God, we must first understand the nature of God and live in accordance with the attributes of the nature of Christ:

Servanthood – Matthew 23:11
Childlikeness – Matthew 18:4
Willingness to be the Least – Luke 9:46
Willingness to Take the Last Place – Matthew 19:30
Humbling Oneself – Matthew 23:12

April 27

Knowing God

Genesis 4:16 bears a disturbing statement about Cain, saying that he went out from the presence of the Lord. Imagine, being with God and deliberately walking away! Of course, this is not a testimony unique to Cain. The vast majority of people throughout history have done exactly the same thing, even though they didn't get their deeds so graphically recorded in scripture.

While Moses was on the mountain getting the Ten Commandments, the people of Israel were making a golden calf. But one interesting thing that is often overlooked is the fact that they weren't attempting to create a different god; rather, their desire was to remake the image of God to one that was more familiar to them. The fact that they didn't see the golden calf as different from the God Moses had introduced to them is evident in the fact that they declared that this statue represented the God who brought them out of Egypt (Exodus 32:4, 8) – a name that distinctly refers to Jehovah (Deuteronomy 8:14, 20:1; I Kings 12:28; Micah 6:4).

Cain deliberately decided to ignore God while the Israelites wanted to continue to acknowledge Him – yet on their own terms. Contrary to both these scenarios, the only way to true fulfillment in life is to pursue a vital knowledge of Him. Colossians 3:10 directs us to be renewed to a true knowledge according to the image of God. Psalm 103:7 emphasizes the necessity of knowing the difference between knowing Him objectively through recognizing His acts and knowing Him subjectively through understanding His ways. When Paul directed the Ephesian church not to be drunk with wine but to be filled with the Holy Ghost (verse 5:18), he was acknowledging the need we all have to fill our inner God-shaped vacuum with the knowledge of God. Anything else that we use to try to fill that void will be unsatisfying and will lead to bigger and bigger cravings because we are craving something we are not getting. Marijuana will lead to cocaine, promiscuous sex to homosexuality, and wine to hard drink. What we really want is Jesus.

April 28

Parenting

Someone once said that God gives us children so we can understand what He goes through with us. If that is true, then we can learn a lot about dealing with our children by looking at the way He deals with His.

1) Set boundaries. He has made a practice of setting protective boundaries since He warned Adam about the Tree of the Knowledge of Good and Evil in the Garden of Eden.

2) Don't be overly protective. God always allows us to live by our free will, even when He knows that we are going to use that liberty to get ourselves in trouble. He could have stopped Eve from talking to the serpent, but He allowed her the freedom to make her own choice.

3) Remember that nagging is negative reinforcement. God never badgers us about our errors. He deals with them – either through correction if we refuse to repent or through forgiveness if we do repent – and then moves on.

4) Don't praise too much or too badly. God is always quick to honor His people, but never gives them false security through flattery or undeserved praise. (Deuteronomy 7:7)

5) Don't punish too harshly. In the midst of each correction, God continues to hold out a promise of restoration. *Behold, at that time I will undo all that afflict thee: and I will save her that halteth, and gather her that was driven out; and I will get them praise and fame in every land where they have been put to shame.* (Zephaniah 3:19)

6) Don't tell your child how to feel. When Jesus said that the Holy Spirit will reprove us (John 16:8), He used a term that meant to cross-examine. In other words, He was saying that the Holy Spirit will give us an opportunity to rethink how we feel about our decisions and actions. He doesn't tell us; rather, He gives us the right to deal with our own thoughts and feelings.

7) Don't forget to have fun. *The LORD thy God in the midst of thee is mighty; he will save, he will rejoice over thee with joy; he will rest in his love, he will joy over thee with singing.* (Zephaniah 3:17)

April 29

People Perish Because of Lack of Knowledge

My people are destroyed for lack of knowledge: because thou hast rejected knowledge, I will also reject thee, that thou shalt be no priest to me: seeing thou hast forgotten the law of thy God, I will also forget thy children. (Hosea 4:6)

This is a very well worn passage. Well, at least the first clause out of the verse is. However, I would be willing to bet that probably less than one percent of the preachers who preach about the concept of God's people perishing from lack of knowledge could even quote the rest of the verse. They use the verse to expound on the necessity of Bible study or church attendance in order to learn the truths of God so that we will not perish. Their sermons may sound something like this: "It has been said that what you don't know can't hurt you; however, this is a totally erroneous statement. Any one of us who has touched poison ivy without knowing what the plant was can testify that our ignorance certainly did hurt us." Now, this is a true principle and one that needs to be reiterated constantly among the people of God. However, this is not the message that the verse is intended to communicate.

The context of the passage dictates that Hosea is speaking of one specific kind of knowledge – rejected knowledge. He is talking of a deliberate walking away from the revelation we already have, not our ignorance about things that we haven't had the opportunity to learn. In other words, he's making reference to the person who knows exactly what poison ivy looks like and what effects it will have on a person yet decides to rub it on his skin anyway.

The value of a piece of real estate is determined by three factors: location, location, location. The same is true about determining the meaning of a biblical passage. The context of the passage is the story of Hosea and his unfaithful wife. Gomer left the loving home he had provided for her and turned to a life of prostitution. She rejected the knowledge that Hosea loved and cared for her. We must never allow ourselves to reject the knowledge of how much God loves us.

April 30

Twenty Questions

One game I always enjoyed playing with my boys was "Twenty Questions" where the contestants had to search for clues by asking no more than twenty questions. During His ministry, Jesus actually asked one hundred questions. I've selected twenty of them to help us find the clues to eternal life.

1) Why do you notice the splinter in your brother's eye? (Matthew 7:2)
2) Why are you anxious? (Matthew 6:28)
3) Why do you harbor evil thoughts? (Matthew 9:4)
4) Can the wedding guests mourn as long as the Bridegroom is with them? (Matthew 9:15)
5) Do you believe I can do this? (Matthew 9:28)
6) How can you say good things when you are evil? (Matthew 12:34)
7) Why do you break the commandments of God for the sake of your tradition? (Matthew 15:3)
8) Who do people say the Son of Man is? (Matthew 16:13)
9) What profit would there be for one to gain the whole world and forfeit his life? (Matthew 16:26)
10) What do you want me to do for you? (Matthew 20:32)
11) Did you never read the scriptures? (Matthew 21:42)
12) Are you asleep? (Mark 14:37)
13) Where is your faith (Luke 8:25)
14) When the Son of Man comes, will he find any faith on earth? (Luke 18:8)
15) Was it not necessary that the Messiah should suffer these things and then enter his glory? (Luke 24:26)
16) If I tell you about earthly things and you will not believe, how will you believe when I tell you of heavenly things? (John 3: 12)
17) Has no one condemned you? (John 8:10)
18) Why do you not believe me? (John 8:46)
19) Do you love me? (John 21:16)
20) What concern is it of yours? (John 21:22)

National Day of Prayer
Celebration of Praise – Part I

Today, in honor of the National Day of Prayer, I'd like to share a few thoughts from Dick Eastman, one of the leaders of the National Day of Prayer Committee. In his book, <u>Celebration</u> <u>of</u> <u>Praise</u>, Dick makes the point that the Hebrew word translated "triumph" in Psalm106:47 (Save us, O LORD our God, and gather us from among the heathen, to give thanks unto thy holy name, and to triumph in thy praise.) is generally translated "glory" and suggests an almost ecstatic shout of victory over a defeated foe. He then makes the observation that the essence of praise is to stand amazed at who God is!

His next thought is to understand how we can turn our knowledge <u>about</u> God into knowledge <u>of</u> God? The answer he gives is that we must turn each matter of truth that we learn <u>about</u> God into meditation <u>before</u> God, leading to prayer and praise <u>to</u> God. Notice the progression Dick Eastman gives as he leads us through the various dimensions of relationships we can have. Knowledge of something abstract (like a language) is acquired by learning. Knowledge of something inanimate (like the British Museum) is acquired by exploration. Knowledge of something animate (like a person or God) is acquired through relationship. Thus, we must never know God on the level of an abstraction or an inanimate reality – but only on the level of the animate through the living relationship that we can experience through prayer and meditation.

One powerful observation that Dick makes in terms of the relationship we can have with God is that God, the Master of the universe, is willing to have a relationship with us. He sums up the concept by saying, "It is a strange and beautiful eccentricity of the free God that He has allowed His heart to be emotionally identified with men." What a powerful thought! The God of the universe has made His very heart vulnerable by being willing to enter into a relationship with us! With this revelation in mind, we should respond with a new desire to have constant and consistent fellowship with Him through prayer and praise.

Celebration of Praise – Part II

In his book, Celebration of Praise, Dick Eastman makes the observation that we never find "His mighty name" or "His wise name" in the Bible. Instead, we find *His great name* and more frequently *His holy name.* Dick then goes on to observe that the word "holy" defies definition. In Hebrew, it only describes the act or character of something or someone that is holy. There is no definition, only a description. At this point, he makes a humorous observation that God is not considered holy because He does not smoke or drink – the criteria we often set for human holiness. He is holy because He has a totally different nature from that of mortals. Therefore, we should be cautious not to minimize the definition of "holiness" by associating it with abstaining from certain activities or habits.

At that point, he goes on to note that the wrath of God is actually the outflow of His holiness. His holiness, in a sense, necessitates His strong revulsion to sin. With the powerful sentence, "He is uniquely unique." Dick makes his point concerning the fact that God's holiness is what sets Him apart from man.

Dick follows up his observations with some very practical advice. First, he admonishes those who would be true worshipers to stay away from the love of money and to be satisfied with what we have. He reminds us that God has said, "I will never fail you. I will never forsake you." That is why we can say with confidence, *The Lord is my helper, so I will not be afraid. What can mere mortals do to me?* (Hebrews 13:5-6) Next, he encourages us to cry out for insight and understanding. He tells us to search for them as we would for lost money or hidden treasure so that we can gain the knowledge of God. Dick adds that God grants a treasure of good sense to the godly. Next, he encourages us to walk in integrity so that we can feel confident in God because He is a shield, protecting those who walk with integrity. (Proverbs 2:1-7) This kind of living shows forth praise to God in our everyday lives.

May 3
Celebration of Praise Part – III

A number of random thoughts from Dick Eastman's book <u>Celebration of Praise</u> are noteworthy on their own without comment or expansion.

Martin Luther said to Erasmus the monk, "Your thoughts of God are too human!"

To get a universe that has expanded as long as ours has without either collapsing or having its matter coast away would have required extraordinary fine-tuning. The odds of achieving that kind of precise expansion would be the same as throwing an imaginary microscopic dart across the universe to the most distant quasar and hitting a bull's-eye one millimeter in diameter.

If a man is justified, he does not need to be forgiven. If you are justified, there is nothing to forgive.

Anselm, archbishop of Canterbury, concluded that God is unitary rather than a composite of the number of parts working harmoniously. There is nothing in His justice that forbids the exercise of His mercy.

God is beautiful, meaning an appearance or perception that stirs a heightened response of the senses and of the mind at its highest level.

If God doesn't keep His word, His loss is greater than mine. I would lose my soul; He would lose His honor.

The communist, seeing the rich man and his fine house, said, "No man should have so much." The capitalist, seeing the rich man and his fine house, said, "Every man should have as much."

There are over seventeen thousand books in the Library of Congress on the person of Jesus.

Jesus Christ is like Humpty Dumpty – how many of us have a piece, but are not trying to put the whole back together?

How often do I hear the name of Jesus in Christian conversations and how many of those references are just passing comment versus the core of conversation?

May 4

Believe with Your Heart

A few years ago, I read an article about a doctor at an abortion clinic who was sentenced for murder because he killed a baby that was born alive during an abortion attempt. I couldn't help but think of the irony of the whole situation. Had the abortion procedure been successful, the doctor would have been within his legal rights and the "system" would have protected him as he destroyed the life of the fetus. However, the whole perspective changed because the baby that he was intending to kill somehow survived the saline injection and was actually still alive when it came out of the mother's body. At that point, the doctor simply completed his task by suffocating the baby. The murder that he began while the baby was still in the womb was legal; however, his completion of the task was illegal.

My thoughts for today are not about abortion per se, but about the mentality that would view the doctor's acts in such a way. How can two diametrically opposed opinions – killing a baby is legal and killing a baby is illegal – be held at the same time? It doesn't make any logical sense; however, this sort of inconsistency is tolerable in modern mentality. Unfortunately, this kind of counter-reality thinking exists in more than just the legal world. I see it on an almost daily basis in the lives of Christians I deal with. So many of us love to quote the Bible while continuing to live like the world – embracing two totally diametrically opposed opinions. One area I see this dramatic inconsistency is in the area of sickness. It never ceases to amaze me when I hear people talk about their healings and tell how they came through extensive surgery and prolonged hospital stays. If they were trusting God, why were they in the hospital? One lady told her doctor, "I'm here trusting God for my healing." If so, why was she in his office to begin with? Others go to a doctor and get his diagnosis only to respond with, "I'm not receiving that. I'm healed by Jesus' stripes!" If so, why waste the doctor's time and your money to get the examination? The same kind of inconsistency can be seen in all areas of life.

Temptation

Have you ever heard someone make the comment that there are so many more temptations today than there were when he or she was a kid? Maybe the temptations are more blatant or prevalent, but the truth is that there are no more temptations today than there have been since the day the earth was created. If the number of varieties of temptations has increased, then the Bible is untrue and God is unjust. Hebrews 4:15 declares that Jesus was tempted in all points just as we are. Therefore, if we have more temptations to face today than Jesus faced two thousand years ago, the Bible is in error. If there are more temptations for us to deal with in the world we live in today than there were in previous generations, then God is treating us unfairly. (I Corinthians 10:13) First John 2:16 defines the three areas of temptation that we all must face as the lust of the flesh, the lust of the eyes, and the pride of life. Did you ever stop to think that these were the same three areas in which Eve was tempted in the Garden of Eden? She saw the tree and thought that it was good for food – the lust of flesh. Next, she thought of the tree as a delight for her eye – the lust of eyes. Finally, she thought that it was desirable to make her wise – the pride of life. Jesus also confronted the same temptations in the desert. He was tempted to turn stones into bread to satisfy His hunger – the lust of the flesh. He was tempted with the kingdoms of the world – the lust of the eyes. He was tempted to jump from the pinnacle of the temple and let the angels miraculously rescue Him – the pride of life.

The same three temptations harass every one of us as well. Dr. Lester Sumrall used to sum up these various attacks as gold, gals, and glory. Gold represented all the things that money can buy. I always think of the expression of having one's eyes "pop out" over seeing something he really likes – the lust of the eyes. Obviously, gals (or guys) speaks of the sexual attractions that represent our fleshly desires – the lust of the flesh. Glory represents the things that stoke our egos and pump up our pride – the pride of life.

The Word of God

The Word of God is quick and powerful. (Hebrews 4:12) It is also sweet like honey and more precious than gold. (Psalm 19:10) It is pure and true and can cause us to rejoice like one who finds a great treasure. (Psalm 119:140, 151, 162)

The authors of the scriptures use a number of different symbols to help us envision the power of the words of God that they were recording:

> Fire (Jeremiah 23:29)
> Sword (Ephesians 4:12)
> Hammer (Jeremiah 23:29)
> Mirror (James 1:23-25)
> Lamp (Psalm 119:105)
> Seed (I Peter 1:23)
> Water (Ephesians 5:26)
> Milk (I Peter 2:2)
> Meat (Hebrews 5:14)
> Bread (Matthew 4:4)

Notice the wide spectrum of symbols used. They cover many different aspects of life, conveying to us how the Word of God relates to every area of our existence. Whether eating, farming, waging war, building, traveling, or taking care of personal hygiene, the Word of God proves to be the perfect tool for accomplishing the task before us. The Word of God can guide and guard us in every decision and choice. A gentleman once asked me how the Word of God could direct him in making a decision about buying a new car. I jokingly said that the Bible directed him to buy a Honda since all the apostles were with one accord on the day of Pentecost. I then seriously began to share with him what the Bible says about our responsibilities with our monetary resources: to tithe, to give offerings, to give alms, and to support our families. I told him that he could not purchase the car if his payments would interfere with any of these areas of his financial obligations. Once he assured me that there was no problem, I reminded him that the Bible says that God wants to bless His children and encouraged him to receive the new car as a blessing from God.

Leave the How to God

When Shadrach, Meshach, and Abednego were sentenced to be thrown into the fiery furnace, they answered the king, *If it be so, our God whom we serve is able to deliver us from the burning fiery furnace, and he will deliver us out of thine hand, O king.* (Daniel 3:17) They knew that God was able and willing to deliver them. Their only problem was that they didn't know how He would do it. They passed the test of faith that required them to trust in the character of God even when they couldn't see a logical or reasonable way out.

This was the same test presented to Abraham when he was asked to sacrifice his son. The amazing thing about this story is that it was more than the boy's life that was on the line. The credibility of God and the validity of His promise were also at stake. Abraham had waited all his adult life for the fulfillment of the promise of a son. When it seemed that there could not possibly be an answer to his prayers, Abraham took matters into his own hands because he simply could not see how God would uphold His promise. When God had miraculously upheld His end of the bargain, He punctuated the dialogue with a request to sacrifice the long-awaited son. Even though Abraham couldn't reason how God could fulfill His promises if the son were to die, the patriarch had learned enough about the character of God by now that he didn't hesitate to follow through with the request. Having seen how God had given new life to the "dead" bodies of both his wife and himself (Romans 4:19), Abraham was willing to wager his son on the proposition that God was able to raise him up, even from the dead. (Hebrews 11:19) With no idea that there was a ram caught in the thicket on top of the mountain, Abraham confidently climbed the hillside trusting that God was going to supply the sacrifice in one way or another (Genesis 22:8) and that he could come back down the mountain accompanied by the living son (verse 5).

If we leave the how to God, He will choose the option that would give Him the greatest glory.

Mother's Day
Spiritual Mothers

Many of the great ladies that we might call "spiritual mothers" were single and, therefore, not mothers. Should we strike them from the list of women for a Mother's Day message? If so, the first name to go would ironically be the woman known around the world as "Mother." Probably not since Mary, the mother of Jesus, has the title of "Mother" been so universally attributed to one woman. Mother Teresa may have been childless, but she certainly wasn't barren. The point here is that a mother is one who gives birth – and that birth is not necessarily restricted to the physical dimension; it can also include spiritual birthing. This nun gave spiritual life to millions who were pointed to the Lord Jesus through her life of kindness and sacrificial giving. She gave meaningful life to thousands of others who, touched by her example, gave up their self-centered existence to follow in her footsteps as caring, giving Christian servants.

In the story of Corrie ten Boom we see a great example of travail and spiritual birth. This brave young maiden willingly surrendered her own freedom and was hauled into the barbaric concentration camp where she saw her dearest family members die and where she too almost gave her own life. She did this, not because of any crime on her part, but in order to protect the lives of her Jewish countrymen who were destined for the Nazis' Final Solution in the German death camps. Though she never married nor had children of her own, she was mother to hundreds whose lives were physically saved by her actions and to thousands whose spiritual lives were saved through her testimony. By simply refusing to get involved, she could have easily saved herself from all the agony, torture, deprivation, cruelty, and despair which became her daily fare; but she courageously stood in the face of the Nazi invaders and cast her lot with those targeted for elimination. As a mother animal fiercely defends her young and puts her life in danger to protect them, Miss ten Boom threw herself between the German genocide machine and its victims.

Hurry

Several times in scripture, we find references to the need to hurry with the message we have. In Matthew 28:7-8, we read the story of Jesus sending the two Marys out to give the disciples the news about His resurrection.

And go quickly, and tell his disciples that he is risen from the dead; and, behold, he goeth before you into Galilee; there shall ye see him: lo, I have told you. And they departed quickly from the sepulchre with fear and great joy; and did run to bring his disciples word.

Paul speaks of having our feet shod with the preparation of the gospel of peace in Ephesians 6:15 – an expression which many interpret to be a reference to the need to be ready to go quickly with the gospel message.

In I Samuel 21:8, David misrepresents his need to hurry by telling Ahimelech, the priest, that he is on an errand for the king and that the king's business required haste.

Certainly, it is true that we must not be lethargic, lackadaisical, lazy, or unconcerned about the mission that the Lord has set before us; however, there is also another side to the coin. In Luke 24:49, Jesus adamantly insisted that we not hurry off to try to undertake the task until we are overtaken by the power of God to actually make the task possible. In the book of Acts, we see the story of how the disciples did indeed obey the Lord's directive to wait in Jerusalem until they had received the power of God; however, there is one additional detail I'd like to point out concerning this story. It is found in the message of the angels recorded in verse eleven of the first chapter as the disciples stared into the skies in amazement after the Lord's ascension, *Ye men of Galilee, why stand ye gazing up into heaven? this same Jesus, which is taken up from you into heaven, shall so come in like manner as ye have seen him go into heaven.* Here we see a paradox in that the disciples are commanded to hurry up to begin their wait.

The Spirit-dependent Life

Jesus Christ Himself was dependent upon the Holy Spirit to respond to His divine mission. Jesus was conceived by the Holy Spirit and was born supernaturally in that the Holy Spirit overshadowed Mary at His conception. Next, Jesus was filled with the Spirit at His baptism by John in the River Jordan. The gospels record that it was at this point that the Holy Spirit, having descended in the form of a dove, rested upon Jesus. John the Baptist confirmed that this experience with the Spirit of God was not just a temporary encounter but that the Holy Spirit remained, or took up residence, with Jesus. (John 1:33) Immediately after His baptism, Jesus was led by the Spirit into the desert for a period of temptation. However, Jesus' real key to a victorious ministry was yet a further relationship He had with the Holy Spirit. Luke 4:14 states that Jesus returned from the wilderness after His forty days of temptation *in the power of the Spirit.* The verse goes on to state that His fame went out through the entire region round about. This is perhaps where most of us fail to totally follow Jesus' pattern. Before Jesus could return to Galilee in the power of the Spirit, He first had to spend forty days and nights in the wilderness defying the world, the flesh, and the devil. Our Savior walked away from the comforts of life along the Galilean seashore and into the harshness of the Judean desert. Finally, He faced the devil head on. Refusing to budge an inch, He confronted Satan toenail-to-toenail and demanded that the prince of darkness yield to Him as He stood solidly on the promises of the Word of God. Here, we see the key to Jesus' victorious ministry: He was not only born of the Spirit, filled with the Spirit, and led by the Spirit; He was also empowered of the Spirit because He was willing to pay the price to walk on a different level from ordinary men. He had forsaken all the natural resources and moved into a realm where He was literally sustained by the Spirit.

We, too, can have the Spirit's anointing on every area of our lives if we come to a place of total dependence upon Him.

SHAPE

Rick Warren made a creative acrostic to help us understand the factors that shape our relationship with God.

S stands for our spiritual gifts. In his analysis, he was thinking more of the giftings listed in Romans chapter twelve where Paul analyzes our abilities and ministries as opposed to the supernatural charismatic gifts given in I Corinthians chapter twelve.

H stands for our hearts – the sensitivity we show toward others and toward God.

A stands for our abilities. Here, he is thinking of both the natural inherent abilities we have and the skills we learn through education and life experiences.

P denotes our personalities, those God-given qualities that make us uniquely ourselves – outgoing or reserved, task-oriented or people-oriented. None is better than the others, as long as they define who we really are as opposed to who we would pretend to be.

E, representing experience, wraps up the list. The more numerous and varied our experiences are, the fuller our lives will be.

These five elements do genuinely determine who we are and figure significantly into how we will live our lives. They shape our destinies and help set the course of service we will follow in the Body of Christ. In other words, God has placed within us qualities that determine our responses to the external situations He leads us into, then He leads us into external situations that reveal these internal qualities through the way we respond. We are shaped by what God put into us and by what He puts us into.

The Spirit of Error

When the Apostle John penned the verse referring to the spirit of error (I John 4:6), he was referring to the demonic seducing spirit that leads people into heresies; however, let me use the term totally out of context to introduce a few "gems" I've heard lately:

Paul wrote two thirds of the Bible. Actually, he didn't even write two thirds of the New Testament, although he was the major contributor.

Believers need to be baptized by immersion with evidence of speaking in tongues. Actually, they do need to be baptized by immersion, and they also need to be baptized with the Holy Spirit with the evidence of speaking in tongues; however, the two do not necessarily need to be simultaneous.

The ability to speak in tongues and pray in the Spirit is a sign of spiritual maturity. Actually, Paul made the exact opposite point in the first letter to the Corinthians. He acknowledged that they did not fall behind in any area of spiritual gifts, including the use of tongues (verses 1:4-7); however, he also emphasized that they were still carnal and immature believers (verse 3:1).

We need to pray earnestly. Actually, we do need to pray; and our prayers must be in earnest; however, the statement was made not in the context of facing a serious problem. It was intended to communicate a need for more intense prayer to get God's help through the situation. The whole mindset behind such a statement is that we have to impress and convince God. Quite the contrary is true. God is actually looking for ways to bless us. All we need is confident faith in Him.

We must fight the good fight. Although we must fight the good fight, we must remember that it is the fight of faith, not of our works. When we rely upon our ability to fight, we develop a conqueror mentality rather than the more-than-a-conqueror mentality that comes with realizing that the battle is the Lord's while the victory is ours.

In the Garden

The garden where He prayed was called "Gethsemane," named after an olive press that was there. How symbolic of the pressing, tearing, and grinding which Jesus endured there, resulting in the squeezing out of His life's blood just as the oil was squeezed out of the olives in the press. Knowing that the cup He was ordained to imbibe brimmed with the unmitigated wrath of God against the totality of past, present, and future sinfulness, transgression, and iniquity of the whole human race; it is no wonder that Jesus agonized before His Father, petitioning for an alternate plan. In the Garden of Gethsemane, our Savior went through what was certainly the three longest and most agonizing hours of history – foreshadowing the three longest, most agonizing hours of eternity which were to come the next day as Jesus' cross would be raised at noon and lowered again at three o'clock. The Garden of Gethsemane and the Rock of Agony themselves symbolized this epic event.

Since Jesus' prayer for the cup to pass from Him was outside God's will, it was not possible for God to answer the request. Even with three agonizing hours of prayer in the garden, Jesus did not get God to change His mind. At last, His moment of triumph came when Jesus could victoriously yield with the memorable words, *Not my will, but thine be done*. This total abandonment of His own will to the ultimate plan of God perfectly settled the matter. The whole idea that Jesus' prayer could have possibly been outside the will of God is a novel and foreign thought to most believers because we tend to have an image of Jesus as God walking around in human flesh. Although that idea is theologically true, the other side of the story is that He was a human walking around with a divine communication with the heavenly Father. Jesus repeatedly said that He did nothing without His Father's direction (John 5:19, 5:30, 8:28) and confessed that His wisdom was a result of seeking the will of God (John 5:30). In the garden, His human nature was put to the ultimate test – and won!

Details

When Peggy and I were in Africa last fall, we noticed a huge new sanctuary that had just been completed. When we asked about it, we learned that it was actually just ready to be dedicated and that the ceremony was actually to occur during our visit. We were holding a conference at a nearby church and were not able to attend the dedication service or even to take a tour of the new facility. We were at our meeting when a severe storm suddenly came up. Such storms with torrential rains are not unusual at that particular time of year in that particular climatic region. On previous trips, we had experienced such storms that hit with such violence that we had to stop our meetings because the sound of the rains pounding on the roof of the church would totally drown out our voices. However, this storm was accompanied with unusually strong winds that uprooted a couple huge trees near the church. But the tragic aspect of the storm was that it lifted the roof off the new church that was being dedicated and hurled pieces of the shattered roof inside the building. One of the projectiles of the roofing pieces struck the denominational president who was in the process of pronouncing the dedication. He was killed on the spot!

I do not know whether the building was in violation of building codes – or, for that matter, if there are even codes in place in that part of Africa. Occasionally, we do hear stories of freak accidents where many people were injured or even killed by some flaw in the design of a building or a shortcut on the part of the builder. One such incident occurred several years ago when the balcony of a building collapsed because of one bolt. What had happened is that the architectural design called for a separate bolt to suspend each level of the balcony; however, the construction team had used one bolt through two levels of balcony. When the bolt gave way from being overloaded, a number of people lost their lives.

The moral of the story is that we must pay attention to every detail – big <u>and</u> small – of the plans we are given if we are going to be successful in life.

May 15

The Unusual Funeral Procession

I recently heard a story about an unusual funeral procession. It seems that a man was raking the leaves in his yard when he looked up and noticed two hearses driving slowly through the neighborhood. Behind the second funeral vehicle was a man dressed in a black suit walking a dog. Behind him was a long line of men in various forms of attire. Some wore work clothes as if they had just come from their jobs in the factory. Others had on sports clothing as if they were on their way to the gym. One had on a referee's uniform as if he were ready to officiate at a soccer match. The gentleman who was raking his leaves was so overcome with curiosity at the unusual sight that he decided to ask the man with the dog what was going on. The man replied that it was his wife's funeral. At that, he expressed his remorse for the man's loss and asked why there were two hearses. The response was that the second one was for his mother-in-law. Really shocked by the fact that the man had lost his wife and mother-in-law at the same time, the onlooker asked how the wife had died. "My dog bit her" was the reply. The follow-up question was about the death of the mother-in-law. Again the answer was, "My dog bit her." After a moment to process what had happened, the next question was, "May I borrow your dog?" The reply, "Certainly, just join the line!"

I hope that this little story isn't too offensive to mothers-in-law and wives, but I just had to share it. Actually, I had a great mother-in-law, and I loved her very much; but mother-in-law jokes just have such a great flavor to them that it is hard to pass up a good one. I've even heard it said that some people are amazed that Peter stayed on good terms with Jesus even after He healed his mother-in-law. Others have suggested that the healing of Peter's mother-in-law may be the background cause as to why Peter eventually denied Jesus.

All joking aside, there is a serious role that mothers-in-law play in making life pleasant or miserable for the whole family. One biblical example is found in Genesis 27:46.

May 16
Men of Understanding

Several times, Jesus expressed His amazement that people didn't understand what He was saying to them. (Matthew 15:17, 16:9, 16:11; Mark 8:17, 8:21; John 8:43) Paul said that we become unworthy Christians if we do not understand the significance of communion. (I Corinthians 11:27-29) Other examples of men who lacked understanding can be seen throughout the scriptures. On the other hand, there was one group of people who were commended for their understanding of the times – the men of Issachar. (I Chronicles 12:32) Both Old and New Testament characters failed to understand the anointing: Nadab and Abihu (Leviticus 10:1-2), the sons of Eli (I Samuel 4:3), David (I Chronicles 13:7, 15:2), Uzzah (I Chronicles 13:9-10), and Simon the magician (Acts 8:18-23). There is also a list of individuals who failed to understand authority: Miriam and Aaron (Numbers 12:1-2), Korah (Numbers 16:1-3), Ananias and Sapphira (Acts 5:3). We can also find those individuals who did have a good understanding of authority: Elisha (II Kings 2:1-8), the centurion with a sick servant (Luke 7:6-8). We also see a number of biblical characters who lacked an understanding of money: the unworthy steward (Matthew 25:24-25), Judas (Matthew 26:14-15). On the other hand, there were those who truly understood finance: the disciples (Luke 10:4-7), Paul (Philippians 4:12), Gaius (III John 1-8). There were also those who lacked understanding of personal character: David and Bathsheba (II Samuel 12:7-9). Of course, there were those who did: Paul (I Thessalonians 5:1). We also find examples of men who lacked a spiritual understanding of succession: Eli and his sons (I Samuel 2:12), Samuel and his sons (I Samuel 8:1-3), David and his sons (II Samuel 13:13, 15:6; I Kings 1:5). Others, of course, understood the spiritual principles of succession: Elijah and Elisha (II Kings 2:9), Paul and Timothy (I Timothy 1:2).

> *Happy is the man that findeth wisdom, and the man that getteth understanding.*
> (Proverbs 3:13)

Rebuke

Paul wrote to his protégé Titus that he should speak the things that he had taught him and that he should exhort and rebuke with all authority. He added that he should be careful not to let anyone despise him. (verse 2:15) On first reading these directives, they seem rather harsh and dictatorial for a Christian minister. When we take a look at the meaning of the word "rebuke" and find that it means to sit at a judicial bench and look down to judge, there seems to be no room for the merciful, gracious nurturing image we have of a Christian pastor. However, if we take a little stroll through the scriptures, perhaps we'll see some important points to help us understand this passage. First of all, we might note that the King James Bible uses "charge" rather than "rebuke" in a number of the places where the Greek is used. Unfortunately, most translators don't see reason enough to soften the verse by using a milder English verb. Additionally, when we search the scriptures for the places where this verb appears, we find that it is often used to describe how Jesus spoke to demonic spirits, sicknesses, and the storm that threatened the lives of the disciples. (Matthew 8:26, 17:18; Mark 1:25, 4:39, 9:25; Luke 4:35, 4:39, 8:24, 9:42) However, Paul seemed fairly liberal with his direction that Christian ministers should stand in the position of rebuking those under their charge, telling Timothy twice that he should rebuke (I Timothy 5:20, II Timothy 4:2) and Titus twice (in the passage under consideration and in verse 1:13). Of course, even Jesus is "guilty" of rebuking and also directing His disciples to rebuke a brother if he transgresses. (Mark 8:33; Luke 9:55, 17:3)

It is not until the closing pages of the scripture that we get a real answer to why Christian ministers are expected to take such harsh measures. They are to do so in compliance with the nature of God that uses rebuke not as a means of intimidation or condemnation, but as a stern warning as a means toward repentance and restoration. (Revelation 3:19)

May 18
Meaning of a Name

I learned something very interesting about the culture in the African country of Burundi. Their names reflect the political condition at the time of the child's birth. If we were to do such a thing in the United States, there would be a whole shift in names each time the administration changed between the Democrats and the Republicans. A similar practice can be seen around the world as many people who are connected internationally give their children names that are easily pronounced by foreigners rather than traditionally nationalistic names that foreigners stumble over. This practice is especially common among Christians who want their children identified by biblical names rather than names that might have some background in the traditional religion of their homeland.

However, the idea of having names that reflect the times is nothing new. It was widely practiced in the Old Testament. We can see the name of God in many of the Old Testament characters in the use of the syllable "ah," which comes from the name of God YHWH, and the use of the syllable "el," which is also derived from the term for God. Let's take, for example, the three Hebrew companions of Daniel. Hananiah's name meant "YAHWEH is gracious." Azariah's name declared, "YAHWEH has helped." Mishael's name identified him as one who was borrowed from God. However, when they went into captivity in Babylon, their names were changed to represent their subjection in a pagan environment. Abednego meant "servant of Nebo," the Babylonian god of wisdom. Shadrach meant "command of Aku," the Babylonian god of the moon. Meshach meant, "Who is what Aku is?" – again referring to the Babylonian god of the moon. However, it wasn't only during the exile that the Israelites accepted other names. Even when in their own land, they shifted the names they gave to their children as they moved into pagan practices. For example, when Jeroboam ruled Israel and led them into paganism, he named his son Nadab (I Kings 14:20) which had no religious connotation at all.

Coincidences – Christ-ordained Incidents

Our recent mission to Zambia was birthed out of a phone call from a long-time friend to tell me that he felt that the Lord was speaking to him to actually go with me on a mission to "carry my bags" and experience life on the mission field. I gave him a list of countries that were on my heart and suggested that he would pray over the options. In his prayer time, my friend felt that he would get his answer that following Sunday at church. After the service, the pastor asked if he could talk to my friend privately for a few minutes. There was an exchange student from Zambia in the congregation who needed extra funds to get through his education. The minister was wondering if my friend might be willing to assist. Instantly, he knew that this request was an answer to his prayer since Zambia was one of the nations on the list I had given him. When they called me to tell me about what was happening on their end, I had some exciting news of a development on my end – the bishop who had invited me back to Zambia was coming to the United States for a ministry tour. One of the stops on his itinerary was to be in Phoenix. Although my friend lives in Indiana, he owns property in the Phoenix area and had to go there to check on things. The divine orchestration of the whole matter was that he was to be there the exact day that the bishop was to be arriving.

My friend's objective in going to Zambia was to look for possibilities where he could use his business expertise to bless the local Christians. On the way to an appointment, he asked a random question about the garbage that is piled along the roadsides everywhere. To his utter amazement, one of the gentlemen riding in the car with him turned out to be the director of sanitation in the capital city of Lusaka. Instantly, ideas about reclaiming energy from the mounds of trash were in motion. But that's not the end of the story. On the plane trip home, the gentleman in the seat next to my friend turned out to be an engineer who is working on exactly the same concept with Lusaka as one of his target areas – another divine connection.

They're Waiting for Us

Dick Eastman, President of Every Home for Christ, tells a story of meeting an elderly man in Africa who had a dream many years before about a man coming to share the gospel with him. When the man met Dick, he recognized him as the face in the dream he had had so many years before and was eager to hear everything that Dick had to share. When Dick began to inquire as to exactly how long the man had been waiting to meet the man in the dream, he discovered that the dream had occurred before Dick was even born! Only God could orchestrate such a thing as knowing that Dick would yield to the call into the ministry, that he would eventually wind up in the African village where the old man would be waiting to meet him, and how the individual who was not even conceived at the time would look as an adult.

Auntie Ruth, whom you've met in another Daily Ditty, was trekking into a very remote region of the Philippines when she met an elderly gentleman who had lived far beyond the life expectancy of the local people. When she shared the gospel with him, his immediate response was, "So, that's his name!" Even though the Christian faith had never been preached in his area, the man had had a revelation of Jesus and had his own personal understanding of the gospel; however, he didn't know who the Savior was. Very shortly after Auntie Ruth shared with him and led him to Christ, the elderly man passed away. God had kept him alive long enough to call on the one name in which there is salvation.

As a young evangelist, Lester Sumrall had a dramatic spiritual encounter in the form of a vision in which he saw the people of the world on a road that led them to a cliff. From that cliff, the individuals on the road tumbled into a lake of fire. Through that vision, God gave him the mandate to warn them about the damnation they were facing. As he traveled through a hundred nations of the earth over the next sixty years, he would often meet people whose very faces he had seen in that vision!

Planting and Harvesting

We were having some trouble with our heater control in our home. No matter what we tried, we simply could not control the heat. Even though a serviceman from the company that installed the system walked us through the process over the phone several times, we simply could not regulate the system. Finally, he agreed to come to the house to check out the problem. Within just a minute or two, he had the system working perfectly. Our problem was that we were pushing two buttons separately that should have been pushed at the same time. I have found that exactly the same thing is true in ministry – there are two different "buttons" that we must push simultaneously if we want to see results. These two buttons are evangelism and discipleship. Someone expressed it this way, "The harvest field is evangelism while the harvest yield is discipleship." The two must go hand-in-hand. Evangelism gets people into the kingdom of God while discipleship gets the kingdom into the people. Once the kingdom really becomes alive inside those we have reached through evangelism, they begin to perpetuate the evangelistic mission. Soon, we reach what is called the tipping point – where it is impossible to stop the momentum. At that point, the gospel will truly bring transformation to families, cities, and whole nations.

Amos 9:13 speaks prophetically of a day when the plowman will overtake the reaper, and the one who treads out the grapes will overtake the one who sowed seed. This prophecy foresees a time when world evangelism has reached that tipping point in that the harvest is coming as quickly as the planting of the seed of the gospel. Jesus also predicted this phenomenon in John 4:35 when He directed His disciples' attention to the men of Samaria coming to the well to see Him. When he said that the harvest wasn't really four months away, He was speaking of the full growing season. In other words, He was saying that it was really harvest time even though they were still in the planting season.

The Swim Meet

A good friend of mine recently shared a story that dated several decades back to his high school years. As a rookie member of the swim team, he was really surprised when the coach called him in as the anchor swimmer in a championship swim meet. Really eager to do his best for the team, he swam with all his might while totally focused on completing his laps. One of the rules that he knew that he had to adhere to was to keep his concentration on his own swimming, not on his competitors. In fact, he was so focused on his own strokes that he was oblivious to the other swimmers in the pool. As he tapped the end of the pool completing his leg of the relay, the whole team was jumping and shouting on the deck. Had he, as a freshman swimmer, actually won the meet for his team? It was unimaginable to him; but, from the team's elation, it seemed evident that he had! When the story was finally told, he hadn't come in anywhere near first place. Instead, he was in last place, and almost a full pool length behind the other swimmers. However, he had actually won by losing because the swimmers on the other teams had gotten so excited when they came in in the lead that they all jumped into the pool to celebrate their victory. They apparently were unaware or just too excited to remember that their interference with a swimmer still in motion would disqualify them. My friend was so focused on fulfilling his laps that he didn't even notice that he was trailing all the other swimmers or that the pool was now full of swimmers.

Because of his focus on finishing the race, he actually won by losing. Any other swimmer who had been paying attention to the swimmers on the other teams would have stopped swimming and lost the race.

Let us run with patience the race that is set before us looking unto Jesus the author and finisher of our faith. (Hebrews 12:1-2)

May 23

Ambassadors for Christ

In Ephesians 6:20, Paul referred to himself as an ambassador in bonds. In II Corinthians 5:20, he speaks of the whole Body of Christ when he used the plural form of the word to express that all of us are ambassadors for Christ. Ambassadors have special requirements and special privileges. The first requirement on the list of the ambassador's job description is to keep his own government well informed of all that may concern its interests in foreign countries. He is to be the eyes of the government he serves. His next duty is to protect and defend, if necessary, the persons and interests of his fellow countrymen abroad. A third, but not less important, duty of an ambassador is to maintain the most amicable relations with the government of the country to which he is assigned. As ambassadors of Christ, we are also charged with these same three responsibilities. The first, we fulfill in prayer as we keep our eyes and ears open to the needs in the world around us. The second, we accomplish in our care for the Body of Christ. The third, we can achieve by carefully guarding our lives as we interact with the unbelievers around us – cautiously walking the line between becoming friends with the world and isolating ourselves from them to the point that we do not let our light shine brightly before them. As ambassadors for Christ, we also have diplomatic privileges including diplomatic immunity. Immunity sets ambassadors apart from the citizens of the country where they live in that they are not subject to prosecution for certain laws of the local government. One of the laws of the government of the alien country in which we serve is the law of sin and death. As ambassadors of another kingdom, we have the privilege to refuse to be subjected to its penalties, including such things as sickness, poverty, and the fear of death. Many of us fail in our role as ambassadors because we allow ourselves to be subject to the fear of death; therefore, we don't want to go into certain areas for fear of disease or murder or we don't step out in faith for fear of starving to death.

May 24

Feasting and Fasting

The last time I was in St. Petersburg, Russia, they were preparing for their commemoration of their independence from the Nazi occupation. As I saw how they were to observe February 23, I couldn't help but contrast it with the way we celebrate our independence every July 4. In Russia, the holiday was to be essentially a day of fasting as the people would only eat rationed portions of food to remind themselves of how those who lived through the Nazi regime were deprived throughout the occupation. I couldn't help but compare this observance with the way we In America feast on all our holidays and make a focal point out of consuming massive amounts of hot dogs and hamburgers on summer holidays and turkey on winter holidays.

Please don't read anything unintentional into my musing today. I am not about to give up on the gastronomical aspects of any of our holidays; rather, I'm thinking about the different perspectives in which we can look at the same history. The Russians, in an effort to never take for granted the suffering that won them their independence, want to associate with the depravity of the occupation. We Americans, in celebration of the freedoms and abundance we have, want to "pull out all the stops" and revel in our blessings. There is something commendable to be said for both of these approaches to life.

Spiritually, we need to also balance these two focal points when commemorating the life, death, and resurrection of Christ. Some individuals and whole movements focus on the man of sorrows who was despised and smitten for us, while others revel in the fact that He has taken all such agony and depravity away from us. Very few of us know how to walk the fine line of balance between these two tensions so that we properly remember the cost of our liberty while also properly celebrating what that price has purchased for us. Perhaps that is why we are given only a small sip of wine and a mere crumb of bread in the communion – not enough to feast on but also just enough to remember the suffering without being gorged by it.

May 25

Christ is All in All

According to Hebrews 12:2, Jesus is the author and finisher of our faith. Philippians 1:6 records that He is the one who began a good work in us and the one who will bring it to completion. The book of Revelation repeatedly tells us that He is the Alpha and Omega, the beginning and the ending, and the first and the last. (verses 1:8, 1:11, 1:17, 2:8, 2:19, 21:6, 22:13). The point of these verses is not that Jesus is a set of bookends – at the front and at the rear. Rather, these verses declare that He is not just the starting point and the ending point; He is the whole – first, last, and all in between.

With this revelation in mind, let's take a fresh look at a verse that we may have somewhat glossed over in our previous readings. In I Corinthians 15:28, Paul said that there is to come a time when all things will be subdued unto God. At that point, Jesus will also subject Himself unto the Father who has put all things under Him. The Apostle then concluded the passage by saying, *That God may be all in all.*

The powerful revelation that this verse may have been holding back from many of us is that God the Father could not be the supreme of the universe without Jesus' voluntarily submitting to Him. Perhaps with our theological emphasis on the unity of the Trinity, many of us have never considered that Jesus could possibly function independently of the Father, taking all the authority He has gained through His sacrificial death and resurrection (Matthew 28:18) and establishing an independent kingdom separate from the Father's. In actuality, this is exactly what the devil tried to get Him to do during the temptation in the wilderness. Jesus resisted this enticement with the words, *Thou shalt worship the Lord thy God, and him only shalt thou serve.* (Matthew 4:10, Luke 4:8) Do you think that He was telling the devil to worship and serve the Father, or is it possible that He was reminding Himself that even though He was "all in all," He was destined to submit His authority to the Father and establish Him as the ultimate all in all?

Don't Read Your Bible

A wise man once advised me to stop reading my Bible. Now, before you panic, let me complete his instructions. Instead of reading the Bible, he suggested that I allow the Bible to read me. What a change that can make in one's private time with the Lord. Rather than coming to the Bible study session with the attitude of finding out some academic truth about the passage, if you come to the session with an openness to find out something about yourself, you actually have begun to live the way that God really expects you to. Notice how James tells us that, when we are exposed to the Word of God, it is supposed to give us an opportunity to see ourselves, not necessarily a history lesson about life hundreds of years ago.

> *But be ye doers of the word, and not hearers*
> *only, deceiving your own selves. For if any*
> *be a hearer of the word, and not a doer, he is*
> *like unto a man beholding his natural face in*
> *a glass: For he beholdeth himself, and goeth*
> *his way, and straightway forgetteth what*
> *manner of man he was. But whoso looketh*
> *into the perfect law of liberty, and continueth*
> *therein, he being not a forgetful hearer, but a*
> *doer of the work, this man shall be blessed in*
> *his deed.* (James 1:22-25)

Another wise man once confessed that the thing that bothers him about the Bible is not what he doesn't understand, but what he does understand. In other words, the things that are mysterious may remain mysterious without affecting his life. However, when there is something that he does understand, he knows that he is obligated to live by it else he be like the man who fails to comb his hair after looking at himself in the mirror. He had apparently begun to understand what it means to let the Bible read him rather than for him to read the Bible.

Finding Diamonds

When my middle son was about six years old, he was crawling around under the pew at church one Sunday evening. When he picked up a little jewel off the floor, and exclaimed to his mother, "Look, Mom, I found a diamond," his joy sounded like a child's dreams. He was insistent that it was really a diamond so we took it home with intentions of checking with a jeweler. A couple of days went by and the gem lay in Peggy's purse unnoticed. On Tuesday morning, I bumped into a lady at church carrying a flashlight. When I asked if she was "the light of the world," she responded that she wasn't a very bright light because she was worried sick about her missing $2,500 diamond setting. After having crawled all over her house, searched every inch of her car, and carefully examined her driveway and sidewalk, she had come to the church to look in the church carpet in case it had fallen out during the service the previous Sunday morning. She was praying the cleaning crew had not vacuumed it up.

When I told her that we had the diamond, she flatly refused to accept my statement and insisted that I stop joking with her. Finally, I convinced her that my story was true and that we would be very happy to return her diamond. I only asked that she wait until later in the afternoon so that Christopher could personally give it to her after he got home from school.

When I went home for lunch, I found that Peggy had taken the diamond out of her purse and had placed it in a little jewel box lined with a velvet cloth. What a contrast from the way it was carelessly tossed in her coin purse when she thought that it was a costume jewelry rhinestone. Once she realized that the stone had value, she began to treat it very differently. The moral of the story is that we are constantly surrounded by value that we simply do not recognize. If we could only get a glimpse of how the Lord has come to seek and save that which is lost, perhaps we will begin to see how valuable those around us are to Him and will begin to treat them with a new respect.

May 28

Twins

In Voorhees, New Jersey, twin sisters recently gave birth to their first babies, both boys, only thirteen minutes apart. The twenty-three-year-old sisters, who were born twelve minutes apart, claim that they had made no plans to try to get pregnant at the same time.

Twins seem to have an uncanny ability to communicate and function on the "same wavelength." When my wife and I were in the delivery room with our first son, her twin brother called from almost two thousand miles away to see if she was having the baby. Even though Peggy was two weeks late in delivering and there were two hospitals in our city but we had opted to go to a hospital in a neighboring town, her brother somehow sensed the exact moment the baby was coming and which hospital we had picked. My wife's identical twin uncles occasionally sent us identical Christmas cards and my identical twin aunts often showed up at events wearing identical dresses.

I have no way of explaining such phenomena except to look to the example of tuning forks. If you have two tuning forks set to the same pitch, when one vibrates, the other one will automatically respond by beginning to vibrate without ever being struck. This is the same physical principle that makes televisions and radios work. When things of identical focus are activated, they respond identically.

In the spiritual dimension, we should pray that our hearts could be so finely tuned to the heart of God that we will respond exactly as He does to every stimulus. The classic prayer that our hearts would be broken with the things that break the heart of God could also be expanded to include that our hearts be gladdened by the same things that gladden His heart. In essence, we should strive to become "twins" with the Spirit of God.

May 29

Raining Cats and Dogs

We've all heard the expression "raining cats and dogs"; however, I doubt that any of us have ever really imagined that such a thing could ever possibly happen. Actually, the city of Covington, England, recently experienced a fairly similar phenomenon when a whirlwind, spinning across the English Midlands, sucked up apples and later rained them from the sky on the city. At first, people thought that someone was playing a practical joke on them as the apples smashed into their backyards and onto the sidewalks. Realizing the force with which the fruit was striking the ground, they soon understood that it was coming from a height that ruled out the idea of a jokester at work. Actually, similar occurrences with frogs, fish, maggots, and other small objects have been recorded at various times throughout the world. However, the apples in England hold the record for being the heaviest such object to rain, ruling out the idea that it could ever rain dogs and cats.

On the other hand, the Bible prophesied of a time when it would be a relief if the falling objects could be limited to cats and dogs. Revelation 16:21 speaks of a judgment upon the wickedness of man in which hailstones weighing a talent will be hurled upon the earth. The biblical weight of a talent differed depending upon the material being weighed. The heavy common talent, used in New Testament times, was approximately one hundred thirty pounds. Imagine the impact of something that massive falling from the sky!

However, the thought in this verse that really catches my attention is not the massiveness of the hailstones, but the reaction of the people when the storm strikes: men blasphemed God because of the plague of the hail; for the plague thereof was exceedingly great. Rather than using this punishment as an occasion to repent, the victims used it to "dig their holes even deeper" by blaspheming the Lord.

Let us learn a lesson from this passage and learn to look to God for mercy and help when it starts to rain cats and dogs.

Fearful Father of Faith

Abraham is known as the father of faith (Romans 4:11); however, if we look at his life, we will see that he was actually characterized by fear rather than faith on a number of occasions. In the same chapter, where God gives him the magnificent promise that he will be led into a special place where that God will raise him up as a mighty nation that will bless all the families of the earth, we find Abraham hiding out in Egypt because he lacked the faith to stand against a famine. To compound the situation, he had to lie about his wife for fear of losing his life. (Genesis 12) Rather than following God's directive to go to the land that the Lord would show him, Abraham responded to the famine by making his own decision to move to Egypt. Rather than believing God's promise that he would be a blessing to the families of the earth, Abraham looked around and assumed that the Egyptians were going to be a detriment to him by taking his wife and possibly even his life.

If we continue reading to chapter fifteen, we see that God has to address the fear factor in Abraham's life, *Fear not, Abram: I am thy shield, and thy exceeding great reward.* At this point, Abraham was fearful that God was not going to honor His promise to give him an heir. What a contrast we see in the Old Testament record of Abraham's struggle between faith and fear and the New Testament's recollection of this patriarch.

> *And being not weak in faith, he considered not his own body now dead, when he was about an hundred years old, neither yet the deadness of Sara's womb: He staggered not at the promise of God through unbelief; but was strong in faith, giving glory to God; And being fully persuaded that, what he had promised, he was able also to perform. And therefore it was imputed to him for righteousness.* (Romans 4:19-22)

The beauty of this story is that it points out the way that God, once He has forgiven us, refuses to remember our faults.

Memorial Day
The Happy Meal
In a comment that at first seemed a little disrespectful, someone once referred to communion as a "happy meal." Because of the origin of the term as a children's meal at a fast-food restaurant, it seemed sacrilegious to give such a name to the most precious expression of our faith. However, after a bit of reflection, I was able to comprehend the message behind the reference. It was the same kind of revelation I came to as a child when I first heard the term "Good Friday." At first, I couldn't understand why we would call the day on which Jesus was crucified "good." It was only after my mother explained that we would never be able to go to heaven had Jesus not gone to the cross that I was able to see the day as a good day. With the communion – even though it is a remembrance of the sacrifice that Jesus made for us, it is also the remembrance of what that sacrifice purchased for us: entrance into heaven as well as joy, health, and prosperity as we make our journey toward our final heavenly home. Thus, it is a happy meal!

We will all celebrate Memorial Day today by gathering with friends and family to eat hot dogs, hamburgers, baked beans, cole slaw, and potato chips – a truly happy meal. But the whole reason for the holiday is that we are to take time to remember the brave men and women throughout the history of our country who have given so sacrificially that we could enjoy the freedom and freedoms that their lives and deaths purchased for us. Certainly, for those of us who have relatives and friends who have given their lives or who are presently serving in life-threatening assignments, the day has its somber side; however, the memory of sacrifice must never stop at the cost without also rejoicing over the rewards of that giving. On the other hand, we must never enjoy the happy meal without taking a serious moment to reflect and understand the price that was paid for it.

The Tower of Babel

When God confused the languages at the Tower of Babel, He did a great job of not only changing the words we use but also diversifying the way we use those words.

Some languages, like Matses in Peru, oblige their speakers, like the finickiest of lawyers, to specify exactly how they came to know about the facts they are reporting. You cannot simply say, as in English, "An animal passed here." You have to specify, using a different verbal form, whether this was directly experienced (you saw the animal passing), inferred (you saw footprints), conjectured (animals generally pass there that time of day), hearsay, or such. If a statement is reported with the incorrect "evidentiality," it is considered to be a lie. So if, for instance, you ask a Matses man how many wives he has, unless he can actually see his wives at that very moment, he would have to answer in the past tense and would say something like, "There were two last time I checked." After all, given that the wives are not present, he cannot be absolutely certain that one of them hasn't died or run off with another man since he last saw them. Even if he has seen them only five minutes ago, he cannot report it as a certain fact in the present tense.

The Guugu Yimithirr language is directional rather than relational as is the English language. For instance, we say that something is to our right, left, behind, or in front of us. The Guugu Yimithirr, on the other hand, seem to know intrinsically that things are actually to the east, west, north, or south of them. When Guugu Yimithirr speakers were asked how they knew where north is, they couldn't explain it any more than you can explain how you know where "behind" is.

Many languages assign a gender to every noun. In many cases, there seems to be no rhyme or reason as to why certain words are masculine or feminine. For example, why is Russian water a she, and why does she become a he once you have dipped a tea bag into her?

June 2
Fulfilled Prophecy
Many years ago – even before I was able to travel very much because I was still working at Indiana Christian University – someone prophesied over me that I would be traveling to so many countries that I would have to schedule my trips because there would be so many invitations to different places. It took a number of years before I would actually be traveling much to do the mission work I am called to do, but even then it didn't seem likely that I'd ever really be so busy that I'd have to juggle the trips in order to schedule my travels. But, the wonderful thing about a word from God is that it is true even if it may not be immediate. For a period of time in 2011, I had several obligations which overlapped: training national leaders for Every Home for Christ in Africa, Asia, and Latin America, leading their mission teams for Charis Bible college students, and the continually expanding ministry of Teach All Nations. In January of that year, I was requested by the college to take a team to the Dominican Republic, but I had to turn down the request because of an Every Home for Christ trip to Togo that I had already accepted. In April, the EHC director requested that I go to the Philippines but I had to turn down his request since I was already scheduled on a college trip to Ecuador.

> *For the vision is yet for an appointed time, but at the end it shall speak, and not lie: though it tarry, wait for it; because it will surely come, it will not tarry.* (Habakkuk 2:3)
> *For we are saved by hope: but hope that is seen is not hope: for what a man seeth, why doth he yet hope for? But if we hope for that we see not, then do we with patience wait for it.* (Romans 8:24-25)

Every word of the Lord shall surely come to pass (I Kings 13:32), and not one of His words will ever fall to the ground. (I Samuel 3:19)

June 3

Bear Claws and Stud Horses

Twice in the book of Proverbs (verses 18:8 and 26:22), King Solomon makes the same statement concerning gossip, *The words of a talebearer are as wounds, and they go down into the innermost parts of the belly.* When we first read these words, we can immediately envision someone planting a serious blow into another person's stomach, inflicting excruciating pain. And it is easy to relate such an image to gossip. We all know how much it hurts when we learn that others are talking about us behind our backs. However, if we read these verses in some other translations, we have to stop and scratch our heads when we see that the idea of wounds is rendered as sweet food (Bible Basic English), dainty morsels (Darby's Translation), tasty trifles (New King James Version), delicious morsels (Revised Standard Version), or dainty morsels (World English Bible). The explanation is that the Hebrew word "wound" in the time of Solomon was also the name for a pastry. Imagine our present-day word "bear claw," which could designate a dangerous weapon on the end of the arm of an angry bear or a tempting delicious pastry. Most translators prefer to use the latter option, giving the verse a totally different slant. In this case, it communicates to us how irresistible gossip is. No matter how disciplined we may be, our diets almost always fail when tempted with a doughnut. In fact, it has been proven that more break their diets over doughnuts than over any other food item. The same is true with gossip – even the most disciplined of us can't resist it.

In Esther 8:10, we read that King Ahasuerus' letters were sent out on horse, mules, camels, and dromedaries; however, other translations say that it was steeds that were sired by a royal stud. What happened to the camel? The simple explanation is that the original word was a Persian word that was not easily translated into Hebrew, resulting in an even more difficult task to translate it into English.

The point of these stories is that we need to read the Bible in several translations if we hope to really understand it.

Cuz

Not only were the lives of Jesus and John intertwined because they were cousins, they also shared a spiritual destiny of bringing the kingdom of God to earth. John's message was *Repent ye: for the kingdom of heaven is at hand.* (Matthew 3:1-2) After John was imprisoned, Jesus picked up the message that his cousin was preaching and began to proclaim the gospel of the kingdom of God (Mark 1:14) and to declare that, from the days of John the Baptist until His time, the kingdom of heaven had suffered violence and that violent men were taking it by force. (Matthew 11:12)

It was immediately after His baptism by John that Jesus went into the desert for His forty-day fast that ended with the dramatic encounter with Satan. Directly on the heels of this experience, Jesus entered the synagogue in Nazareth where He gave His first sermon. The major content of the message came from a reading from the book of Isaiah, *The Spirit of the Lord is upon me, because he hath anointed me to preach the gospel to the poor; he hath sent me to heal the brokenhearted, to preach deliverance to the captives, and recovering of sight to the blind, to set at liberty them that are bruised, To preach the acceptable year of the Lord.* (Luke 4:18-19) It would seem implausible that John did not somehow become aware of this sermon. After all, it was the inauguration of the ministry that he had come to introduce. Months later, while languishing in prison, John seemed to have second thoughts about his pronouncement that Jesus was the one who was to bring in the kingdom of God, so he called in two of his disciples and sent them to Jesus to ask Him if He was indeed the one they were looking for. (Luke 7:19)

Jesus' response was *Go your way, and tell John what things ye have seen and heard; how that the blind see, the lame walk, the lepers are cleansed, the deaf hear, the dead are raised, to the poor the gospel is preached.* (Luke 7:22) Notice how He deftly pointed out that He was actively fulfilling all the points He gave in that original sermon.

Jesus' ministry demonstrated that the kingdom that John had preached would come had actually arrived.

June 5

Least in the Kingdom

After John the Baptist sent his disciples to question Jesus if He really was the one who would bring in the kingdom of God, Jesus turned to the multitude around Him and made a startling statement about His imprisoned cousin, *Among those that are born of women there is not a greater prophet than John the Baptist: but he that is least in the kingdom of God is greater than he.* (Luke 7:28) It's not difficult at all to see why Jesus would say there has never been a greater prophet than John, but what could He mean by the statement that the least in the kingdom is greater than John? The extrapolation of that statement is that the least in the kingdom is, therefore, greater than all the prophets!

In his first epistle, the Apostle Peter makes a couple comments that might be helpful in understanding what Jesus was saying here. In verse ten, the apostle says that the prophets enquired and searched diligently to understand the salvation and grace that we so freely experience. In verse twelve, Peter goes on to say that this message of salvation through grace was revealed, but that it was not for them to experience. He makes mention that this whole experience of salvation is so intriguing that the very angels of heaven desire to look into it; they can investigate it, but they cannot experience it!

Even though, as we saw in yesterday's lesson, he saw the evidence that the kingdom was present in the ministry of Jesus, John would be executed before the crucifixion and resurrection of Jesus; therefore, he would not live to see the establishment of the kingdom of God. He could only be a prophet, just like the ancient prophets and the angelic hosts who point toward and proclaim the coming of the kingdom.

A simple analogy to help explain what Jesus was saying that day can be seen in the comparison of the travel agent who hands out beautiful color brochures about tropical cruises and the tourist who actually sets sail on the liner, even if he is in the least expensive cabin. Which is better – the one who talks about it or the one who experiences it? Even though we may be the least in the kingdom, we've got the better deal.

June 6

Vows

I was just a teenager at the time – so you know it was a long time ago – but I still remember the incident as vividly as if it were yesterday. There was a large group of us who wanted to go out for a pizza, but the whole thing "went down the tubes" because of one member of the group. He wouldn't go into the pizza parlor because they served beer and he had made a vow to God that he would never enter a place that served alcohol. Of course, we commended him for his integrity, but I simply could not excuse his stupidity for having made such a vow. The long-term implications of such a vow would be that he would never be able to do missionary work should the Lord call him to serve in a foreign country unless he could charter a private jet to get there because every ocean liner and commercial airplane serves alcohol. On a more practical level, just because he entered a building where others might be drinking didn't mean that he would also have to participate.

In Judges chapter eleven, we read the story of Jephthah who made a vow to sacrifice the first thing that met him when he returned home if the Lord would give him victory in battle. The tragedy of the story is that he was greeted by his beloved daughter! Of course, he honorably fulfilled his pledge, but I can't help but fault him for having made the pledge in the first place. If we examine the whole scenario of such pledges, I believe that we will see that they are built on a very faulty foundation to start with – the assumption that God is desperate for worship. We assume that He is so needy of having us do certain acts of reverence that He will enter into our little schemes and fulfill our requests just to get our devotion. The truth is that He can raise up praisers from the stones if need be. (Luke 19:40) The second faulty assumption is that we can change God's will by our little bargains. God has a master plan for running the universe, and He simply will not alter the course of nations simply in order to keep one person out of any pizza parlor that serves other patrons beer. In addition, we have to realize that many of our vows are simply contrary to His will – like sacrificing one's daughter.

June 7

The Cure

A man went to the doctor with a miserable cold. The physician prescribed some medicine, but it didn't help. The man went back, and the doctor gave him a shot, but that didn't do any good. He called the doctor and asked what else he could try. The doctor advised him to take a hot bath, then without drying off, to open all his windows and stand in the draft. "But if I do that, I'll get pneumonia." "Yeah," the doctor sighed, "but I can cure pneumonia."

"I don't know what it is," the young man said. "I just don't feel good." The doctor examined him and ran some tests. Then she talked to her nurse and came into the examination room with three bottles of different-colored pills. "OK," the doctor said, "I want you to take one blue pill with a large glass of water every two hours. I want you to take a green pill with a large glass of water every three hours. And then take one of the yellow pills, with a large glass of water, every four hours." "Geez, that's a lot of pills," the patient said, "What's the matter with me?" "You're not drinking enough water."

These two humorous stories point out a really important life lesson – the symptoms that we treat may not be the real problem that we are experiencing. This can be especially true on the spiritual level. Many times, the physical ailments we encounter are actually just the byproducts of spiritual deficiencies. One woman I know suffered from rheumatoid arthritis so severe that it doomed her to a wheelchair. It was only after she discovered that her external debilitation was only a physical manifestation of the spiritually crippling condition of unforgiveness that she was healed. Not only did she get up out of her wheelchair, she began a ministry based on Jesus' command to forgive seventy times seven (Matthew 18:22) and taught others how to be healed through forgiving those who had offended them.

June 8

The Irony of it All

Does the thought of lobster make you salivate? Lobsters have been an important menu item in fine restaurants for years. But the pricey crustacean wasn't always so upper crust. Up until the 1800s, lobster was chiefly consumed by the lower classes – the poor, indentured servants, and people in prisons and mental institutions. In colonial America, there were even laws against feeding lobster to inmates more than once a week, and employment agreements often specified that servants would not have to eat lobster more than twice a week. One reason was probably because lobsters were so abundant on the East Coast. The Plymouth pilgrims, according to some stories, could wade into the water and capture by hand more than they wanted. After great storms, so much lobster washed ashore that it was ground up and used as fertilizer. It wasn't until the mid-nineteenth century that New Yorkers and Bostonians developed a taste for lobsters, and commercial lobster fisheries flourished only after the development of the lobster smack, a boat with a large open holding well on deck that allowed live lobsters to be shipped.

The most expensive meal that I have ever paid for was a sixty-ounce lobster dinner that my sons consumed at a resort on St. Thomas. When I learned this fascinating tidbit of culinary history, my first thought was that I should have lived a century or so earlier so that I could have fed them for pennies! Of course, the real message here is in the irony of how something that had been considered essentially worthless could become a valuable commodity.

> *The stone which the builders rejected, the same is become the head of the corner: this is the Lord's doing, and it is marvellous in our eyes?* (Matthew 21:42)
> *He is despised and rejected of men; a man of sorrows, and acquainted with grief: and we hid as it were our faces from him; he was despised, and we esteemed him not.* (Isaiah 53:3)

June 9

Hostage

In his book <u>The</u> <u>Believer's</u> <u>Authority</u>, Andrew Wommack made an interesting statement about the devil's strategy. Giving the illustration of how a lone bank robber with one gun and a hostage can outweigh the police force with a whole arsenal of weapons, he suggested that Satan took Adam and Eve hostage and was able to hold the entire human race captive through these same tactics.

The base line is that the devil does have power (Ephesians 6:12), just like the lone bank robber has a gun. On the other hand, God has exceedingly great power (Ephesians 1:19), just like the police force has a full arsenal of weapons. The problem with the whole scenario is that the enemy also has a hostage. In our individual cases, the hostage that he is holding is our thought processes. As long as we allow him to grip our minds, all the powerful tools of God cannot set us free.

I recently talked with a young man who was held captive to debilitating habits and a self-destructive lifestyle. At the root of all his problems was a simple incident that had happened to him many years before. Rather than simply forgiving the individuals who had injured him, he held on to the humiliation of the event and allowed the resulting anger to totally devastate his life. No matter what anyone could say or do, he could not be free and find fulfillment in life. That one incident was the devil's single handgun against a full stockpile of military-grade weapons in the hands of the Christian believers who would try to help him. Until the young man's mental processes can be released, there is nothing that can be done for him.

When a bandit is holding a hostage, the approach that must be taken is not an aggressive attack but a process of negotiation, trying to get the captive released. Spiritually, it is only the Word of God that can release such hostage minds. This is the powerful weapon that Paul described in II Corinthians 10:4 that pulls down the strongholds over our minds and brings our thoughts and imaginations into obedience to Christ.

June 10
There's a House Waiting for You

Before moving to Colorado, we made arrangements for Peggy to fly out and spend a few days looking for a house. Since we had planned to make the move in July, we scheduled her trip in May, thinking that that would give us plenty of time to negotiate the purchase and wait for the closing. We figured that if all went well, we would be able to move in immediately upon our arrival in the city. In February, I was speaking in Atlanta where I shared the platform with Dick Mills, a remarkable prophet who has memorized thousands of Bible promises. When he meets a person, the Lord quickens a topic to him and he is able to draw upon his repertoire of verses to give the individual a series of verses related to his current need. When Peggy and I met Dick in the lobby of the hotel where we were staying, he said to us that the Lord showed him that we were in transition. We shared with him the story of our upcoming move and thought that was the end of the conversation. But God was not finished talking. That evening, Dick was ministering to a couple on the other side of the auditorium where the conference was being held. Suddenly, he stopped in the middle of ministering to the couple and pointed to us all the way across the room, "God says that He has a house waiting for you."

By April, we were seriously into our house hunt, looking at internet listings and dealing long distance with an agent. We were beginning to realize that anything we would be happy with was far outside our price range. Suddenly, our agent called us to say that she had found something that she was sure we would like and that it was priced far below market value. She encouraged us to come out right away to see the house because she was certain it would not be on the market in May. Reminded of the word from God, we decided that it would still be available if it really was the one God had for us. In the time between April and our visit, the sellers turned down two offers. However, they accepted ours even though we offered less than the asking price.

Murphy's Law

Murphy's Law states, "What can go wrong will." It somewhat reminds me of the pessimistic attitude that some people express by saying that they can't win for losing. But there is a biblical precedent for Murphy's Law – in fact, it appears in scripture twice!

Isaiah 24:17-18 says, *Fear, and the pit, and the snare, are upon thee, O inhabitant of the earth. And it shall come to pass, that he who fleeth from the noise of the fear shall fall into the pit; and he that cometh up out of the midst of the pit shall be taken in the snare.* The prophet Amos tells us the story about a man who fled from a lion only to be met by a bear from which he escaped by running into a house where he was bitten by a serpent. (verse 5:19)

These passages give us the image of a man with a dark cloud following him around. Even when others are basking in the sunshine, he is continually having his parade rained on. Why would the Bible portray such a life for some people? These passages are in context of the judgment of God upon those who have rebelled against His ordinances. In Deuteronomy chapter twenty-eight, we see that we can make the choice to live under Murphy's Law or to live free of it.

> *It shall come to pass, if thou shalt hearken diligently unto the voice of the LORD thy God, to observe and to do all his commandments which I command thee this day,...all these blessings shall come on thee, and overtake thee, if thou shalt hearken unto the voice of the LORD thy God.,,But it shall come to pass, if thou wilt not hearken unto the voice of the LORD thy God, to observe to do all his commandments and his statutes which I command thee this day; that all these curses shall come upon thee, and overtake thee.* (verses 1, 2, 15)

June 12
Do It Anyway

A pastor who had a strong ministry teaching that we are living in the last days was raising money for a big new sanctuary for his church when someone from the congregation challenged him that it was illogical to build a new building if he really believed that the end of the world was coming soon. His answer was that the building would be left behind for people to use during the Millennium. His logic was similar to the contemporary Christian song that teaches us that we might spend our whole lives building something from nothing just to see a storm come and wash it all away, but that we should build it anyway. The point is that nothing has to be permanent as long as God has a purpose in what we are doing.

Mother Teresa wrote the following poem, entitled "Do It Anyway," on the wall of her room:

People are often unreasonable, irrational, and self-centered. Forgive them anyway.

If you are kind, people may accuse you of selfish, ulterior motives. Be kind anyway.
If you are successful, you will win some unfaithful friends and some genuine enemies. Succeed anyway.

If you are honest and sincere people may deceive you. Be honest and sincere anyway.

What you spend years creating, others could destroy overnight. Create anyway.

If you find serenity and happiness, some may be jealous. Be happy anyway.

The good you do today, will often be forgotten. Do good anyway.

Give the best you have, and it will never be enough. Give your best anyway.

In the final analysis, it is between you and God. It was never between you and them anyway.

June 13

Doers of the Word

When James told us to be doers of the word rather than simply hearers of it (verse 1:22), he was likely trying to communicate a deeper meaning than we usually read into it. Although everything that we always think of in this passage is certainly true, it would seem that we could find a new idea if we were to "peel back" the surface layer.

When the apostle spoke of being a doer of the word, he used a term that comes from the Greek word for writing poetry. It implies creativity and is the same word that Paul used in Ephesians 2:10 when he said that we are the workmanship of God, created in Christ Jesus unto good works, which God hath before ordained that we should walk in them. What Paul was trying to say about our new lives in Christ is that we are like Michelangelo's <u>David</u> or Sistine Chapel – the masterpiece of God's creation. I would think that James was intending for us to have the same understanding about the way we live our Christian lives. When we read the truths of the Word of God, we are to implement them in such an exquisite way that our lives become masterpieces for God.

His wording for simply being a hearer refers to someone who is listening for philosophical concepts, not necessarily to find life principles. This person, the apostle says, is deceiving himself by feeling that he has done his duty in reading his allotted number of chapters for the day or attending his assigned quota of church services, even though he has not allowed the message of the scripture to change his life into a masterpiece of God's redemptive work.

Flag Day
Terrible with Banners

The other day during worship, I caught a glimpse of a lady on the periphery of the congregation jubilantly waving two large banners. Just the sight of her flags fluttering in the breeze that was created as she danced and twirled "kicked me up a notch" in my own praise. After the worship time was over, I stopped to reflect on what had just happened and remembered how the old-time Pentecostal church where I grew up would occasionally have a "wave offering" in which the folk would pull out their handkerchiefs and whirl them above in the air. Then I remembered one really exuberant young worship leader in Sikkim, India, who ripped off his necktie and, dancing around the church in what we all hoped was not the first stage of a striptease, waving his tie above his head. It was at that moment that I realized that there is a powerful energy that is somehow released by a flag.

Flags seem to somehow have a life of their own that goes far beyond the fact that they are symbols of countries or organizations. Just think of the times when you have seen the American flag draped over a casket, burned in a newsreel taken in one of our enemy countries, presented at the beginning of a ceremony such as a graduation, raised over the camp at the beginning of the day, or unfurled before a marching band in a parade. The emotion evoked at such a moment can actually defy verbal description, but the amazing thing is that we can't actually describe why or how it happens. It's because the flag has a life force of its own – a life force that brings meaning to the event just as much as the event brings meaning to the symbolic piece of cloth being displayed. No wonder we set aside a special day in our year to honor the national flag.

The title for today's reflections comes from the Song of Solomon (verses 6:4, 6:10) that speaks of the lover as being terrible as an army with banners. The original Hebrew wording does not mention the army; it simply attributes the awesome force directly to the flags. Wave your flag and release its power.

Father's Day
Fathers, Sons, and Money
The national news services recently carried the story of a man who, while rushing through an airport to catch a flight, noticed an envelope on the floor. He picked up the unmarked packet and thrust it into his pocket. When he got onto the plane, he had a moment to open the envelope only to discover that it was full of cash – lots of cash. When he got home, he counted it all out to find that it was ten thousand dollars! He immediately called the airport to report his finding. The airport authorities did know about the missing envelope and were able to connect the gentleman with the rightful owner. When the reporters asked the man why he had returned the money since there was no way he could have ever been traced, his reply was, "I wanted to set a good example for my children."

A similar story, though not on the same scale, has to do with the gentleman who took his twin sons to the amusement park for their tenth birthday. When they reached the ticket counter, the attendant started to ring up the charges for one adult and two children's tickets. Just then, the father noticed that the adult fare began at ten years old. He stopped the cashier and said that he needed to pay for three adults. Again, the dad knew that the lesson he was teaching his boys was far more valuable than the half-price admission to the park.

Basketball star David Robinson feeds the homeless through his Feed My Sheep program and he helps needy families get diapers and baby food through a charity called The Ruth Project. Here's what he says about such giving: "These aren't sacrifices for me. If I'm clutching on to my money with both hands, how can I be free to hug my wife and kids?"

Unfriended

The other day, I heard someone mention that he was going to unfriend a certain individual from his Facebook page. Even though it seems like a rather strange word and rather unfriendly act, I assume it is a common practice among those who are into such social networking. Well, as soon as I heard the term, my mind rushed to Hebrews 13:5 where it is said of the Lord that He will never leave us or forsake us. In twenty-first-century lingo, Jesus will not "unfriend" us!

Actually, that verse goes much further than to say that He will not allow us to continue with His social network. The original wording in the passage comes from the term for orphan, meaning that God will never abandon us like parents leaving a baby wrapped in a blanket on the orphanage steps – or, even worse, wrapped in a newspaper tossed into a dumpster.

But there is even more to be seen in this passage in that it uses a triple negative to emphatically communicate the point. A few translators try to capture the power of this verse by repeating the negative wording. For example, Young's Literal Translation renders this verse as, *No, I will not leave, no, nor forsake thee.* Yet it is probably the Amplified Bible that comes the closest to communicating what the first-century readers would have understood when they read this passage, *I will not in any way fail you nor give you up nor leave you without support. [I will] not, [I will] not, [I will] not in any degree leave you helpless nor forsake nor let [you] down (relax My hold on you)! Assuredly not!*

Friendships and relationships among humans may come and go, but the love of the Lord is steadfast. He will not ever unfriend us. He's the friend who sticks closer than a brother (Proverbs 18:24), and He is the one who loved us even when we were His enemies and will care for us even more now that we are reconciled to Him (Romans 5:10).

June 17
The Great Race

You've probably seen the television show about people who have to go all over the world to find clues in the most unusual places. I can understand why they call it the Great Race because it is a race on the grandest scale imaginable. However, there is an even greater race – the race of faith that we are called to.

Of course, as soon as we make mention of the race of faith, there are certain biblical passages that instantly come to mind. However, there are a couple different aspects of the race that I'd like to consider today. One is found in a verse that doesn't even mention a race in so many words. In I Thessalonians 2:18, Paul wrote that Satan had hindered him. The term that he used referred to a runner elbowing his competition out of the track. If the great Apostle Paul had to deal with being forced off course by the enemy, we certainly need to be aware to keep our guard up so that we aren't also hindered by his tactics. The next thought comes from what is possibly the most obvious verse on running the race; yet, its message is one that we don't see so readily. When the author of Hebrews 12:2 tells us to lay aside the weights and sins that beset us, he is referring to things that stand around us comfortably. In other words, it is the ordinary, the commonplace, and the familiar issues of life that hinder us. His term for "lay aside" implies to diet. Ouch, that actually hurts, doesn't it? It's not just the devil that can stop us in our race, it's also the things that we need to resist like a dieter resisting high-calorie snacks. One last thought comes from Ephesians 2:2 where Paul talks, not about running, but about walking and saying that we have been walking according to the course of this world. The terminology here implies that we were in a rut that we couldn't deviate from. We can't win the race because we are running on the wrong track.

Notice our three enemies: the world, the flesh, and the devil. We can outrun them all if we fix our eyes on Jesus and run with diligence.

June 18

Walking on Water

Let's notice several details about the story of Peter's little stroll on the Sea of Galilee, found in Matthew 14:25-31.

1) Peter never asked if it was the will of God for him to walk on the water; he essentially made the decision for Jesus. We must be careful what we ask for when we pray.

2) When Peter got out of the boat, it was in jeopardy of sinking. Had he stayed in the boat, he would have likely been faced with the same ultimate disaster of being out in the stormy sea without a life preserver. What may seem like a leap of faith is simply the only logical alternative to drowning.

3) Apparently, Peter sank when he was already at Jesus because the scripture says that Jesus reached out his hand to him. There is no mention that Jesus had to walk to where Peter was flailing in the water. Apparently, Peter relaxed his faith when he came to what he thought was the end of his task. Just because we have experienced Christ doesn't mean that we've arrived.

4) Peter's failure was when he looked at the wind and the waves. He was not doing anything sinful such as looking at pornography. Failure may not necessarily come from sin; it may simply be living in the natural element.

5) Peter didn't sink all at once; he began to sink. Failure is rarely instantaneous.

6) Peter's problems began to manifest when he looked at the stormy sea. The reality is that it is no more difficult to walk on troubled waters than on calm water. Both are equally impossible! It takes the same faith to trust Jesus in good times as in bad ones.

7) When Jesus asked Peter why he doubted, His question was in relationship to Peter's doubt about his continued ability to walk on the water. Peter continued to believe that Jesus could walk on water, but he doubted that he could. Faith isn't just faith in Christ, but faith in what Christ is doing in and through us.

Ten Plagues

When Pharaoh resisted Moses' demand that the people of Israel be freed to go worship their God, God sent a series of ten plagues upon him and his people. Each plague became more serious and the devastation more severe: the plague of blood (Exodus 7:14-25), the plague of frogs (verses 7:25-8:11), the plague of lice (verses 8:12-15), the plague of flies (verses 8:20-32), the plague of pestilence (verses 9:1-7), the plague of boils (verses 9:8-12), the plague of hail (verses 9:13-35), the plague of locusts (verses 10:1-20), the plague of darkness (verses 10:21-29), and finally the death of the firstborn (verses 11:1-12:36). However, there is a little-known message that underlies the story of these calamities. From the first day that God spoke to Moses to go challenge Pharaoh, He had determined that His final hand was to kill the firstborn.

> *And I say unto thee, Let my son go, that he*
> *may serve me: and if thou refuse to let him*
> *go, behold, I will slay thy son, even thy*
> *firstborn.* (Exodus 4:23)

Each one of the plagues was an expression of God's mercy in that it was another chance to divert the extreme penalty of the death of the firstborn. Had the king been willing to submit to God, the whole scenario could have been over as soon as Moses appeared in the palace and did a few parlor tricks. Oh, please forgive me for that. I don't mean to say that Moses was practicing sleight of hand. I'm just using the idea to express that the signs and wonders he performed were almost like entertainment compared to the judgments he had to invoke because of the hardness of Pharaoh's heart. If Pharaoh had yielded to the first plague, there would have been no death or devastation, just polluted water. But at each level of Pharaoh's resistance, God had to up the ante; however, He didn't jump straight to the ultimate judgment. In His merciful graciousness, He turned up the heat slowly. At any point that Pharaoh would have chosen, God would have diverted His predetermined plan.

Spirit and Soul

When I was still single, I was ministering at a church service when a young lady about my age came up for prayer. Her issue was that she had just been jilted by her fiancé and was suffering from a serious depression as a result. I ministered to her and broke the spirit of depression off of her. She was instantly free and began to rejoice in her deliverance. However, there was a second part to the story. Her boyfriend was a minister, and she was really disappointed not only about the loss of her boyfriend but also about the loss of the avenue she would have taken into the ministry. Almost as if I could read her mind, I was able to see exactly what was going on inside her head. She could see that I was single and in the ministry – a great substitute for what she had just lost. Discerning what was going on, I immediately called one of the ladies of the church over to continue praying for her while I went to another person in the prayer line. When I had ministered to the young lady, she had received a deliverance in her spirit, but she had responded in her soulical nature.

Unfortunately, it is far too easy to mix up the two parts of our personalities and make the mistake of making soulical decisions, thinking that we are acting in the spirit. In chapter twenty-one of the book of Acts, we see two examples of believers who did just that by trying to discourage Paul from going to Jerusalem because danger awaited him there. (verses 4, 12) They accurately heard God's direction in their spirits but responded in the soulical dimension, giving him advice based on their emotions rather than on what God had said.

> *For the word of God is quick, and powerful, and sharper than any twoedged sword, piercing even to the dividing asunder of soul and spirit, and of the joints and marrow, and is a discerner of the thoughts and intents of the heart.* (Hebrews 4:12)

Codependency

A friend of mine had been through some "serious stuff" and needed some personal one-on-one ministry. After a while of meeting with a counselor, she became aware that the sessions were "going nowhere" and that she wasn't getting any better. Instead, it just seemed that she and the counselor had developed a mutual dependency that fed the need to continue meeting without really making progress toward a cure. Eventually, she came to me with the question, "How do you balance between seeking counsel and being co-dependent?"

First of all, we have to understand codependency. This would occur in a counseling situation only when the counselor feels a need to give advice <u>and</u> the counselee feels a need to receive advice. If you are ever in a situation where the counselor gets his fulfillment in life by meddling in other people's lives – run like your pants are on fire! If you ever get into a situation where you feel that you can't survive without the other person's input – run to Jesus as fast as you can. A healthy counselor-counselee relationship would be one in which the counselee is seriously seeking God's help but is looking for a guide to hold his hand as he walks through the fog. Godly counselors can see clearly where our vision is foggy. They can sense danger in places where we are not looking.

> *Where no counsel is, the people fall: but in the multitude of counsellors there is safety.* (Proverbs 11:14)
> *There are many devices in a man's heart; nevertheless the counsel of the LORD, that shall stand.* (Proverbs 19:21)

Notice that, even though Solomon emphatically stresses the need for counsel from wise men, he is even more insistent that the only unquestionable counsel comes from God. If there is to be genuine healing in a counseling session, both counselor and counselee must be dependent – not upon one another, but upon the wisdom of God.

June 22

Totally Saved

In II Corinthians 1:10, Paul makes an interesting statement in which he refers to the past, present, and future aspects of salvation all in one verse, *Who delivered us from so great a death, and doth deliver: in whom we trust that he will yet deliver us.* Not only does this process of various steps of deliverance refer to the totality of the three dimensions of time, it also expresses that His redemptive work is in operation in the totality of our three-part personality. God has already delivered us in that we were saved in our spirits the day we got born again. He is in the process of delivering us in that we are being saved in our souls on a daily basis if we allow Him to take us through the process of renewing our minds. He will deliver us in that we will be saved in our bodies when we receive our glorified bodies – either at the rapture or in the resurrection.

> *And the very God of peace sanctify you wholly; and I pray God your whole spirit and soul and body be preserved blameless unto the coming of our Lord Jesus Christ.* (I Thessalonians 5:23)
>
> *By grace are ye saved through faith; and that not of yourselves: it is the gift of God.* (Ephesians 2:8)
>
> *He that shall endure unto the end, the same shall be saved.* (Matthew 24:13)
>
> *For if, when we were enemies, we were reconciled to God by the death of his Son, much more, being reconciled, we shall be saved by his life.* (Romans 5:10)
>
> *Much more then, being now justified by his blood, we shall be saved from wrath through him.* (Romans 5:9)
>
> *Who will have all men to be saved, and to come unto the knowledge of the truth.* (I Timothy 2:4)

Blessed Hope

For the grace of God that bringeth salvation hath appeared to all men, Teaching us that, denying ungodliness and worldly lusts, we should live soberly, righteously, and godly, in this present world; Looking for that blessed hope, and the glorious appearing of the great God and our Saviour Jesus Christ; Who gave himself for us, that he might redeem us from all iniquity, and purify unto himself a peculiar people, zealous of good works. (Titus 2:11-14)

Paul wrote to Titus, making reference to the Second Coming of Christ as the "blessed hope." Indeed, the return of the Lord is something that we should certainly hope for. However, many Christians seem to have an unhealthy concept of what that hope really should mean for them. One Christian sister I know often exclaims after she encounters any difficulty – even minor setbacks in her finances or family life – that she wants the Lord to come back and rapture her out of all her problems. It is healthy to long for the return of the Lord – after all, he is the bridegroom and we should be in eager anticipation for our wedding date. When we want to run away from the world we were left in with the command that we occupy until He comes back, we have totally missed the point of what our faith is all about. Notice the context of what Paul wrote to Titus. First, he mentioned that the grace of God brings salvation to all men. Until every man has had an exposure to this saving grace, we shouldn't anticipate the fulfillment of the blessed hope. We can't abandon this world until we complete the task of evangelizing all of it. Next, Paul addresses the issue of establishing a godly presence in the present society through rejecting ungodliness and worldly lusts while embracing a sober, righteous, and godly lifestyle. We can't look for our blessed hope until we infuse hope into the society around us. When we do that, we will be free to go!

June 24

Increasing in the Knowledge of God

The more we know about God, the more grace and peace we can live in. For example: if we don't know that He is a healer, we will not live in grace and peace when the doctor says that we have some terrible disease. The more we know about God as our healer, the less disturbed we become when we get a negative report from the doctor. The fullness of grace and peace is constantly with us, but we don't know how to appropriate it unless we know the One from whom it originates. We will never be able to live in full grace and peace unless we know everything about God.

> *Grace and peace be multiplied unto you through the knowledge of God, and of Jesus our Lord, According as his divine power hath given unto us all things that pertain unto life and godliness, through the knowledge of him that hath called us to glory and virtue: Whereby are given unto us exceeding great and precious promises: that by these ye might be partakers of the divine nature, having escaped the corruption that is in the world through lust...For if these things be in you, and abound, they make you that ye shall neither be barren nor unfruitful in the knowledge of our Lord Jesus Christ. But he that lacketh these things is blind, and cannot see afar off, and hath forgotten that he was purged from his old sins...For if ye do these things, ye shall never fall: For so an entrance shall be ministered unto you abundantly into the everlasting kingdom of our Lord and Saviour Jesus Christ. Wherefore I will not be negligent to put you always in remembrance of these things, though ye know them, and be established in the present truth.* (II Peter 2:2-12)

June 25
Balancing Persecution and Miraculous Deliverance

In the great "roll call of faith" in chapter eleven of Hebrews, those who had to endure suffering and loss were no less men of faith than those who were listed as ones who saw miraculous deliverances. In verses thirty-two through thirty-eight we learn something about the differences between them. Notice that some of them were delivered <u>from</u> their persecution. This was a deliverance of the body.

> *And what shall I more say? for the time would fail me to tell of Gedeon, and of Barak, and of Samson, and of Jephthae; of David also, and Samuel, and of the prophets: Who through faith subdued kingdoms, wrought righteousness, obtained promises, stopped the mouths of lions, Quenched the violence of fire, escaped the edge of the sword.*

Others were delivered <u>in</u> their persecution. This deliverance was of the soul.

> *out of weakness were made strong, waxed valiant in fight, turned to flight the armies of the aliens. Women received their dead raised to life again.*

Still others were delivered <u>through</u> their persecution. These experienced deliverance in the spirit.

> *and others were tortured, not accepting deliverance; that they might obtain a better resurrection: And others had trial of cruel mockings and scourgings, yea, moreover of bonds and imprisonment: They were stoned, they were sawn asunder, were tempted, were slain with the sword: they wandered about in sheepskins and goatskins; being destitute, afflicted, tormented; (Of whom the world was not worthy) they wandered in deserts, and in mountains, and in dens and caves of the earth*

June 26
Diligently Harkening
A prophetic word came forth in which the Spirit reiterated three times that the Lord is God and that His people should kneel before Him in worship. As soon as the prophecy had ended, the moderator of the meeting took the podium, "Let's stand up and praise the Lord." The Holy Spirit had directed us to kneel – not stand – and to worship – not praise. No matter how sincere he may have been, he was wrong and would have led the people astray because he did not hearken diligently to the voice of the Lord in the prophetic message.

Deuteronomy chapter twenty-eight paints a stark contrast between two different possibilities for our lives. Verses one and two say that blessings will come upon us, and overtake us if we will hearken diligently unto the voice of the Lord and observe all His commandments. On the other end of the spectrum, verse fifteen says that curses shall come upon us and overtake us if we do not hearken unto the voice of the Lord and do all His commandments and his statutes. Wow – total blessing or total cursing! The one thing that makes the difference is our diligence to hear and obey the Lord's directions.

Suppose I tell you that there is a bank downtown that is giving one hundred percent interest on savings deposits. You have some money to save, so you head out to make a deposit. Along the way, you stop and buy shoes and then go to the coffee shop. Now you have only a few dollars to deposit and don't want to go all the way to town for such a small investment, so you stop and deposit it in a bank in the mall that is giving two percent interest. At that point, you have not hearkened diligently to my directions to follow them and you will not get the benefit that I had offered you. You are not being punished with curses; you are simply not walking in the blessings that would have been available.

God is not in the habit of giving suggestions, but direct commands that must be followed explicitly. However, we will never be able to follow them without learning to listen diligently.

June 27
Stigmata
A number of years ago, a female evangelist began to rise to prominence in the ranks of the Charismatic Movement because of unusual manifestations that would occur in her meetings. Stigmata, the marks of the crucifixion would appear in her hands and drops of blood would ooze from them. Later, other supernatural signs such as oil and feathers, supposedly representing the presence of the Holy Spirit, would miraculously appear. When I first heard of Lucy Rael and her unusual manifestations, my immediate reaction was, "We Protestants have condemned this sort of thing among Catholics for centuries as demonic; but now that it's happening among us, how can we embrace it as a move of the Holy Spirit?" Then it got a little closer to home when she was invited into a church of a close friend of ours and the students from the Bible school where I was dean began to make the several-hour drive to the church to see her. It seemed as if I was the only one who didn't believe, and I had to take a lot of flak because of my stance. I even pointed out that Jesus must have gotten terribly confused during the two thousand years since His crucifixion in order to allow Lucy to get her marks in the palms of her hands since the nails went through His wrists rather than His palms. Only after Dr. Lester Sumrall sent a television crew to one of her meetings with the instructions to use their telephoto lenses and get a high quality close-up shot that revealed how she was doing her trickery was her ministry debunked. Well, so much for one particular charlatan, but what about the whole Body of Christ that was so easily taken in? So many are trapped by false prophets because they are looking horizontally at experiences of the supernatural rather than vertically at the source of the supernatural. The author of Hebrews gives us a great lesson on focus in the first two verses of chapter twelve when he says that we can see the cloud of witnesses referred to in chapter eleven but that we must look unto Jesus as the source of our faith. We can notice others, but we must focus on Jesus.

June 28

Grieve Not the Holy Spirit

And grieve not the holy Spirit of God, whereby ye are sealed unto the day of redemption. (Ephesians 4:30)

When the Apostle Paul warned us against grieving the Holy Spirit, he used a Greek term that takes us far beyond what most of us have likely ever considered. His wording here speaks of a deep emotional wound like that inflicted when jilted by a lover. First of all, many of us never stop to think that the Holy Spirit is a personality with all the same qualities that we humans share. He has emotions and can be insulted and offended by our actions just as another human can. When we disregard an impression He has placed in our hearts, it is not just a nebulous, impersonal impulse that we are dealing with – it is a living, emotional personality that has been rejected. Even when we do realize that our ignoring or contradicting the wooing and prompting of the Holy Spirit is a personal offense against a living personality, we generally fail to understand the intensity of our actions. Just think how deep the wound and how long the healing process associated with the breakup of lovers or a divorce. Now, take that to the infinite level on which God lives. This is the picture Paul was trying to paint for us to understand how significant our response to the Holy Spirit can be.

Notice that he also intensifies the passage by adding that the Holy Spirit's work is to seal us unto the day of redemption. The message that Paul is trying to communicate here is that our responses to the Holy Spirit's directions are not just for the moment, but they have eternal consequences, effecting our eternal destinies.

Balaam – Man of Intrigue – Part I

We find the story of Balaam in Numbers chapters twenty-two through twenty-four. The Moabite king Balak was frightened by the multitude of Israelites headed toward his country and decided that, rather than doing physical battle against them, he would fight them spiritually by hiring Balaam to curse them. Although the prophet Balaam heard God and was determined to follow the voice of God, he was also perverse in his actions. Balaam initially refused the request because he obeyed the direction from God that he should not go; however, he eventually received permission from the Lord upon a second inquiry. The scripture offers no explanation concerning why God seemed to have changed His mind about the matter; however, it is clear that God was not pleased with Balaam's decision to accompany the Moabites. It was only after a dramatic encounter with an angel that Balaam was able to recognize his sinfulness and was willing to forego the mission. Upon meeting with Balak, Balaam reiterated that he could not speak beyond what God would speak through him. In the heated discussion between Balak and Balaam that followed Balaam's failure to curse Israel, Balaam reminded the king that he had warned him from the beginning that he would not say anything beyond the words that the Lord showed him to say. In Revelation 2:14, we find what seems to be a missing portion to this story; since Balaam could not curse the people, he apparently told Balak how to get the people to bring a curse upon themselves by breaking the Ten Commandments. The New Testament passage says that Balaam showed Balak how to get the people to sacrifice to idols and commit sexual immorality – exactly what happened, resulting in a plague that killed twenty-four thousand. Numbers 31:8 records what seems to be a judgment from God upon this mystery man. I don't think that God would have judged him if he had truly done the will of God. Even though he came with God's permission and he didn't curse Israel, he was still outside the will of God.

Balaam – Man of Intrigue – Part II

In yesterday's lesson, we learned a little about the intriguing individual, Balaam. Today, I'd like to look at a few more verses that relate to this mysterious character. In Deuteronomy 23:5, Moses said, *Nevertheless the LORD thy God would not hearken unto Balaam; but the LORD thy God turned the curse into a blessing unto thee, because the LORD thy God loved thee.* Notice the wording here, "turned the curse into a blessing," implying that Balaam had originally attempted to speak a curse over the people. Although the account in Numbers seems to say that Balaam was neutral – ready to speak out anything, whether good or evil, that the Lord would give him – when he opened his mouth, this passage seems to imply that he did come with the intent of speaking out a curse. Even though the story as told in Numbers says that Balaam was in communication with God, Joshua calls him a soothsayer (verse 13:22), a pagan practice that is repeatedly forbidden among the people of God (Deuteronomy 18:10, 18:14; I Samuel 6:2, 28:8; II Kings 17:17; Isaiah 3:2, 44:25; Jeremiah 27:9, 29:8; Ezekiel 13:9, 13:23, 21:21, 21:23, 21:29, 22:28; Micah 3:6, 3:7, 3:11; Zechariah 10:2). When we come to the New Testament, we find that Balaam is never presented in a favorable light. Peter says that he forsook the right way and went astray because he loved the wages of unrighteousness (II Peter 2:15), and the reference in Revelation that we looked at yesterday says that he taught Balak how to make the people of Israel sin.

So, how are we to understand this man? Perhaps we can get a clue by looking at another biblical character with a similar background. In Acts chapter eight, we meet Simon the Great, who was a magician (the New Testament counterpart to a soothsayer). He was a baptized believer (verse 13), yet Peter declared that he would perish because he had no part or lot with the true believers because his heart was not right in the sight of God (verse 21). We have to truly know our hearts or else we can be seriously deceived by outward actions.

July 1

God's Looking Upon Sin

I'm not exactly sure where the whole idea came from, but all my life I have heard the explanation given for Jesus' cry from the cross, *My God, My God, Why have you forsaken me?* that the Father did, in deed, turn His back upon the Son because God cannot look upon sin. To get the full explanation of what this verse is all about, you'll have to read my book The Last Enemy, but I do want to say one thing about the passage in today's meditation – God has never been known to overlook or turn His back on my sins. On the contrary, I've found Him to always be quite observant every time I've disobeyed His commandments! In fact, it is His ability to look upon our sins that actually gives us hope that we can escape our sinfulness. As He sees our desperate condition, He is able to intervene and help us. Rather than turning His back on sinful men, He tunes His ear to them, listening for their cry for help. Rather than rejecting men because of their flaws, He is drawn to them even more strongly than a nurse is drawn to an ailing patient.

In Ephesians 2:13, Paul said that we are brought near through the blood of Christ. It is not God that is able to get close to fallen humanity because of the blood; it is the sinner who is brought near to Him through the blood. In other words, the problem is on our end, not God's. In other words, God has always been drawn to us – no matter how sinful we have been. The problem was that we were distanced from Him. The solution to this separation is found only in the blood of Christ. The moment we allow the blood of Christ to cover our sins, we are no longer divorced from the presence of God.

But now in Christ Jesus ye who sometimes were far off are made nigh by the blood of Christ.

July 2

Jonah and the God of Nineveh

According to the earliest records we have, the very beginning of civilization in Chaldea and Babylonia was under the direction of a person, part man and part fish, who came up out of the sea. During Jonah's time, the people of Nineveh believed in a divinity who sent messages to them by a person who rose out of the sea, as part fish and part man.

Berosus, a Babylonian historian from the fourth century BC, mentions "Oannes," as an avatar of this fish-god. Interestingly, the name "Oannes" is used in the Septuagint (the Greek version of the Old Testament) for Jonah. It also appears in the New Testament with the addition of "I" (Ioannes).

The preservation of the name "Yunas" or "Jonah" at the ruins of Nineveh also confirms the historicity of the story of Jonah. As soon as modern discoverers unearthed the mound that had been known for centuries by the name of "Neby Yunas," they found beneath it the ruined palaces of the kings of Nineveh.

I find it to be just another matter of the cleverness of our God that He would use a fish to bring Jonah to Nineveh. By doing so, He made their god into a messenger boy for the God that Jonah proclaimed. What better heralding, as a divinely sent messenger to Nineveh, could Jonah have had, than to be thrown up out of the mouth of a great fish, in the presence of witnesses, say, on the coast of Phoenicia, where the fish-god was a favorite object of worship? The recorded sudden and profound alarm of the people of an entire city at his warning was most natural as a result of the coincidence of this miracle with their religious beliefs and expectations.

Was the Old Testament Law Taken Away by Jesus?

Christ hath redeemed us from the curse of the law, being made a curse for us: for it is written, Cursed is every one that hangeth on a tree.

Many Christians look to Galatians 3:13 as proof that we are no longer under any of the obligations of the Old Testament. When presented with this idea, I ask these believers to reread the passage for themselves – this time starting with verse ten.

Cursed is every one that continueth not in all things which are written in the book of the law to do them. But that no man is justified by the law in the sight of God, it is evident: for, The just shall live by faith. And the law is not of faith: but, The man that doeth them shall live in them. Christ hath redeemed us from the curse of the law, being made a curse for us.

The curse of the law is expecting that you can obtain God's promises by doing the works of the law. The freedom of the new covenant is that we can live by faith that Jesus inside us (Galatians 2:20) fulfills the requirements. This does not negate the conditional nature of some of the Old Testament promises. It simply gives us faith that we really can obtain the promises connected to the conditions.

Perhaps the best way to understand how we have been liberated from the law is to turn to the words of the Apostle James where he tells us that our liberty actually becomes a law to us. In other words, the freedom that we have actually becomes a motivational force to direct us to keep God's standards.

Whoso looketh into the perfect law of liberty, and continueth therein, he being not a forgetful hearer, but a doer of the work, this man shall be blessed in his deed. (verse 1:25) So speak ye, and so do, as they that shall be judged by the law of liberty. (verse 2:12)

Independence Day
Mr. President

As we celebrate our great country today, it is important to remember exactly what made it great and keeps it so. The following are direct quotes from our former presidents on the topic:

It is no slight testimonial, both to the merit and worth of Christianity, that in all ages since its promulgation the great mass of those who have risen to eminence by their profound wisdom and integrity have recognized and reverenced Jesus of Nazareth as the Son of the living God...The highest glory of the American Revolution was this: it connected in one indissoluble bond the principles of civil government with the principles of Christianity. – John Quincy Adams

The only assurance of our nation's safety is to lay our foundation in morality and religion. – Abraham Lincoln

All must admit that the reception of the teachings of Christ results in the purest patriotism, in the most scrupulous fidelity to public trust, and in the best type of citizenship. – Grover Cleveland

The foundations of our society and our government rest so much on the teachings of the Bible that it would be difficult to support them if faith in these teachings would cease to be practically universal in our country. – Calvin Coolidge

The rights of man come not from the generosity of the state but from the hand of God. – John F. Kennedy

Of the many influences that have shaped the United States into a distinctive nation and people, none may be said to be more fundamental and enduring than the Bible...Without God, there is no virtue, because there's no prompting of the conscience. Without God, we're mired in the material, that flat world that tells us only what the senses perceive. Without God, there is a coarsening of the society. And without God, democracy will not and cannot long endure. – Ronald Reagan

Four Categories of People

Someone recently explained to me that all humans fall into one of four different financial categories. As I thought about the breakdown, I could see that it made some good sense that might be helpful to understand.

Category one is "breadwinners," those of us who work and earn our way through life. Whether factory workers, salaried positions, commission-based employees, or self-employed individuals – these people make up the bulk of workers. This category even includes most ministers because they receive a salary from the church.

The next category can be labeled "the poor and needy" because they have no income of their own, or if they do have income, it is so limited that they are still dependent upon assistance from others. This group includes those physically and mentally challenged individuals who are not able to earn a living for themselves as well as those who, for one unfortunate situation or another, simply cannot find employment even though they are physically and mentally capable of making their own way. It also includes those who lack the skill or motivation to make a place for themselves in the marketplace. The interesting observation about this category is that Jesus did not tell us to give only to deserving poor; He simply and directly instructed us to care for the widows, orphans, and other special needs cases by giving generously of our alms.

"Sent ones," the third category, are the ones whose mission in life calls them to forgo earning a salary for themselves and must rely upon others to bless them and send them on their way through freewill donations.

He labeled the final category as "manna people," those individuals who, because of special purposes and callings of God, are directly supported by God. Usually, God uses people to meet the needs of His ministers because He wants to bring people together into relationship; however, He does have His miraculous ways of getting funds to His servants.

The one thing required no matter which category we find ourselves in is faithfulness in handling our position properly.

July 6
Your Bible Versus Your Pastor

I really hated to be caught in the middle, but it was just one of those things that couldn't be avoided. I suppose that it was inevitable, but I had hoped that somehow I just wouldn't ever have to "go there." The problem was how to honestly answer a biblical question without showing disrespect for the ministry I was submitted to.

Dr. Sumrall had a teaching about sending the curse back to its originator. In fact, he even emphasized the point by saying that we should send the curse back with double of its original intensity. He often talked about using this tactic to stop witches in their tracks when they would try to cast spells and curses on him while on the mission field. He would describe how that he would boldly confront these witchdoctors and mediums with, "Well, I don't believe in your curse, but since you do – take it back, DOUBLE!" The approach was always effective in getting these occultists to leave him alone.

Several years after Brother Sumrall's death, a member from the church who felt that someone was trying to curse him called me to ask where the verse was in the Bible that Dr. Sumrall used to validate this practice so that he could get back at his antagonist. Of course, I was able to cite the passages that he used (Isaiah 40:2, 61:7; Jeremiah 16:18, 17:18; Zechariah 9:12; Revelation 18:6); yet, I also felt it necessary to point out that each of these verses spoke of God's initiative, not man's. I simply asked him, "Do you want Dr. Sumrall's answer or Jesus' answer?" I then quoted Mathew 5:44:

> But I say unto you, Love your enemies, bless them that curse you, do good to them that hate you, and pray for them which despitefully use you, and persecute you.

When in such a dilemma, always go with the Bible. Remember that all your teachers are also earthen vessels. By the way, some of the greatest men of God became that way because they dared to challenge traditional teachings when they saw something different in the scripture.

Mentoring

In the mentoring process, a mature (or at least, maturing) person takes a developing individual "under his wing" to help him grow in the Lord. This must be a trust relationship in which both parties are willing to be totally transparent. There must not be any secret areas which are forbidden, so that the mentor has full freedom to ask any question about any area of his disciple's life – and vice versa. Now, that's a big one to swallow. Most people who are willing to be mentors would fail this transparency test. However, it is necessary for the person being mentored to learn to be genuinely transparent himself. Take a look at Paul and Timothy. Paul had total access to Timothy's life because he had given the young man total access to his.

Over the years, I've seen several waves of emphasis on mentoring sweep through the church. However, I've yet to see anyone really present a true biblical model. I remember when a young man consulted me about wanting to find a Christian role model to whom he could submit himself as a son. I answered that such an act would certainly be powerfully significant if he could find a "father in the Lord" who would really be just that. You see, fathers essentially give their lives for their sons. They work extra long hours at extra hard tasks in order to be able to send their sons to school, cover their medical bills, pay for their insatiable appetites, and clothe their constantly growing bodies. They reorganize their entire lives around Little League and PTA. They strain and sprain their aging muscles to help their sons learn how to handle baseballs, footballs, basketballs, and soccer balls. And they do all this without a second thought! The problem with the church is that we have a whole army of men who are willing to "mentor" younger men by simply expecting these disciples to submit themselves in a unilateral relationship. On the other hand, true mentoring requires more giving on the end of the mentor than on the end of the one being mentored. The end result is a loyal and trusting sonship relationship birthed out of the sacrifice and loyalty of the spiritual father.

July 8

Knowing Jesus

Wherefore henceforth know we no man after the flesh: yea, though we have known Christ after the flesh, yet now henceforth know we him no more. (II Corinthians 5:16)

This passage speaks of no longer knowing others after the flesh, referring to having a new viewpoint from which to see them. I once saw this principle dramatically displayed in a simple skit where the main character changed glasses in order to truly see the people around him. No longer were they drug addicts, prostitutes, and thieves; suddenly, they were hurting individuals in need of a Savior's love. Paul then goes on to say that we must no longer see Jesus through our own human viewpoint that we have used in the past. What he is trying to say is that we must no longer allow our own colored glasses to taint or distort our true vision of Him. I remember hearing a "prosperity gospel" preacher on the radio preaching about how Jesus was so wealthy that He had to have a treasurer to keep all His money. Just one quick twist of the dial found me at another station where another preacher was expounding on the poverty-stricken Jesus who didn't even know where He would lay His head that night. Obviously, both of these men could not be right. The background for such a dilemma was not in the scriptures that they were reading but in the mindset they already had before they read the scriptures. Because one wanted to see a wealthy Jesus, he did. Because the other wanted to see a meek and lowly Jesus, that is exactly what he found. The answer is to ask the Holy Spirit to totally renew our minds so that we can approach the scriptures with an unbiased mind and an open heart. When we do, we will see a whole new world of revelation about the Jesus that we think we already know!

We spend millions of dollars building libraries to maintain the notes, letters, and documents of the Presidents because those original source materials will help researchers know the man who was in the office. Remember how the Nixon Tapes showed us a whole new man from the one we thought we knew!

July 9

Earthen Vessels

But we have this treasure in earthen vessels,
that the excellency of the power may be of
God, and not of us. (II Corinthians 5:7)

One of my students remarked about the fact that it seemed that it was taking her years to become usable in the kingdom of God even though she knew that Christ did the complete work in her the moment she was born again. She was having a really difficult time reconciling the fact of who she was in Christ versus who she was in everyday life. I had to remind her that we have a heavenly treasure inside an earthen vessel. We need to focus on the treasure, not the vessel. On the other hand, the verse suggests that it is actually God's plan that our lives continue to be the flawed earthen vessels that we are. It is the very fact that we are imperfect packages that makes the gift that we contain stand out so much.

Just imagine the surprise you would experience if you opened a package wrapped in a plain brown wrapper, or even in a newspaper, to discover a diamond ring inside. Now, compare that experience with finding the ring in a gem box that clearly proclaimed that it was from one of the most expensive jewelry shops in the country. The package would have given every clue away to the point that there would be no surprise when the diamond sparkled as the lid was opened. Even though the ring would still be breathtaking, it would have been expected.

God loves to put His wonderful gifts into flawed human wrappers so that there is never a question that the gift is really from Him rather than just the efforts of the vessel. My student was apparently focusing too much on her wrapper and not enough on the gift hidden inside. She knew theologically that Jesus had done a perfect and complete work inside her, yet she still felt that she could not be usable in the kingdom as long as her vessel was still imperfect and incomplete.

Someone once said that God uses flawed servants because that's all there is.

July 10

God's Chosen Fast

*Is not this the fast that I have chosen? to
loose the bands of wickedness, to undo the
heavy burdens, and to let the oppressed go
free, and that ye break every yoke? Is it not
to deal thy bread to the hungry, and that thou
bring the poor that are cast out to thy house?
when thou seest the naked, that thou cover
him; and that thou hide not thyself from thine
own flesh?* (Isaiah 58:6-7)

Most of us have a very limited understanding of fasting. We generally think of a fast more along the lines of a hunger strike. If we want something from God, we think that our skipping a few meals and suffering a little discomfort will attract God's attention and invoke His pity enough that we can "force His hand" to act on our behalf. That is a very immature approach to God, not unlike a little child threatening to hold his breath unless his parent gives him what he wants. It also demonstrates a very faulty image of God as an unconcerned deity who has to be tricked or pressured into benevolence. Quite the contrary, God is our loving Father who is always looking for a way to bless us and who initiates these blessings even before we realize that we need His help. (Matthew 6:8)

True fasting is to come to the place that we are so concerned for the needs of others (not our own needs) that we are willing to give up our own nourishment in order to have extra resources to help meet their needs. One friend of mine demonstrated this kind of fasting when he gave up eating out at restaurants for a month to have extra money to give to missions. Another aspect of true fasting is that we get to the place where we are so occupied with the needs around us that we actually lose our appetites because our focus has shifted from ourselves to the needs of others. One final implication of true fasting is that it motivates us to go beyond ourselves to breaking bands of injustice. It may motivate us to sacrifice not only a few meals, but our whole focus in life, to become politically and socially active on the behalf of those who have no voice of their own.

July 11

Creation

Today I want to share a few random thoughts from the biblical account of the creation of the universe.

Have you ever thought about the fact that the Bible begins with a wedding and also ends with a wedding? The actual climax of the creation story was the creation of Eve and the anticipated climax of the book of Revelation will be the manifestation of the Bride of Christ. The thing that brought fulfillment and completion to man will also bring fulfillment and completion to God Himself.

In the creation story, we read that God used words to create the universe. In the rest of the Bible, we learn that we can use words to create <u>our</u> universe as well.

> *Thou art snared with the words of thy mouth, thou art taken with the words of thy mouth.* (Proverbs 6:2)
>
> *A man's belly shall be satisfied with the fruit of his mouth; and with the increase of his lips shall he be filled. Death and life are in the power of the tongue: and they that love it shall eat the fruit thereof.* (Proverbs 18:20-21)

Man was made in the image of God, meaning that we are to be like Him in every way. (Genesis 1:26) If the very first thing we learn about God is that He is a creator, then we should anticipate that one of the major similarities we share with Him would be to be creative. (Exodus 31:2-6, Proverbs 8:12)

When God planted a garden for Adam, He caused it to produce every tree that is pleasant to the sight and good for food. (Genesis 2:8) I think we all have the idealistic image of the utopia that the Garden of Eden was. Everything that Adam needed was in abundant supply, simply for the taking. In essence, poverty was not the way of life that He created for Eden. In fact, even outside the Garden, it was still not the norm. Even though Adam had to work for what he needed, there didn't seem to be a shortage. (Genesis 3:19) Lack and shortage are still not God's plan for man. (Ephesians 3:20)

July 12

Discipling Nations

Jesus gave the church the responsibility of discipling the nations. Unfortunately, we have spent most of the last two thousand years clueless as to exactly what that means. During much of the church's history, we have assumed that this task is something that could be accomplished by force. History books are filled with examples of how the cross and the canon have been wielded together in the conquest of the new territories. One major justification used during the periods of great exploration was that the expeditions were actually spiritual campaigns to win the heathen to Christianity. One tragic error of such "discipling" was that the conversions were superficial. In essence, the "converts" simply baptized their paganism into the church and named it Christianity while it still was paganism underneath the surface. The result has been that all over the world the church looks, acts, and believes just what the local people were already – only with a Christian façade. For example, in Haiti, much of what happens in the churches is simply a Christianized voodoo culture. In more recent history, there has been a realization that force is not the way to spread the faith, and there has been a shift to gentler forms of persuasion. Even though the process is radically different, the result has not been much different. By trying to put the gospel into the existing context through "the seeker sensitive approach," the church has again produced a "Christianized" version of the general secular perspective with new Christian titles for an unconverted worldview.

Our secular guide on a recent trip in Africa, trying to set the region's history into perspective, pointed out a powerful example of a time when the church actually did fulfill the Lord's command. He explained that the area was once inhabited by very hostile and warring tribes; however, everything changed when the missionaries came. The local people began to see that they didn't need to fight and kill and that they could all live together in peace and build a productive society. It wasn't by force or philosophy – but by example – that the tribes were discipled and a nation built.

Nabal

*Let not my lord, I pray thee, regard this man
of Belial, even Nabal: for as his name is, so
is he; Nabal is his name, and folly is with
him.* (I Samuel 25:25)

The quote in today's meditation is from the story of
David, Abigail, and Nabal. David's men had served as a
protective shield keeping down looting, marauding, and theft in
the area. One of the local residents who had greatly benefited
from the presence of David's encampment was Nabal because
none of his flocks or herds had been confiscated by bandits as
in the previous years. When David asked that Nabal show his
appreciation by sending a gift to the men who had kept the
peace in the region, Nabal refused. Abigail, his wife, realized
the insensitivity of this rude response and took it upon herself
to rectify the situation by sending a generous gift to David's
men. When she tried to explain to David why her husband had
acted so inappropriately, she referenced his very name. The
Hebrew word *nabal* actually means stupid, wicked, impious,
foolish, or vile. I can only imagine what must have been going
through the minds of his mom and dad when they named him.
But, be that as it may, we have to realize that his name actually
did become a reality, defining his personality and actions.

Of course, we can see a number of examples in the
scripture where God actually changed people's names when He
did a redemptive work in their lives, changing their
personalities and destinies: in Genesis 17:15, Abram (high
father) became Abraham (father of a multitude); in Genesis
32:28, Jacob (the cheater) became Israel (the ruler); in Genesis
17:15, Sarai (domineering) became Sarah (lady, princess,
queen); and in Matthew 16:17-18, Simon (hearer) became
Peter (rock). The interesting thing about how God changes
people's names is that it is prophetic – He calls us things that
we have not yet become. (Romans 4:17) One other aspect of
this whole matter is that He gives us humans the ability to also
speak prophetically into the future through our proclamations.
(Genesis 2:19) Therefore, we must be very cautious as to how
we address ourselves and others.

July 14

Biblical Misconceptions

The Lord is one, but He looks much older.

Adam and Eve were not ashamed about being naked because mirrors weren't invented yet.

It's a mystery how they were driven out of the Garden since cars had not been invented.

God was the first to split the atom when He made Eve.

When Noah invited people onto the ark, they took a rain check.

Cain's brother was in trouble because he was Able.

Moses' real name was Charlton Heston.

"Manna" was the Jewish way of pronouncing "manicotti."

Humor thy father and thy mother.

Joshua fought the Battle of Geritol.

There are twelve Minor League prophets.

When Jesus forgot to close the door, His mom asked, "Were you born in a barn?" Of course, He was.

We read a lot about the sinners and Republicans, but what about the Democrats?

Jesus was betrayed by Judas Asparagus.

Jesus had a long talk with the Germans on the Mount.

He had twelve opossums.

Of course, all these misconceptions are just humorous plays on words; however, we often make just as silly mistakes about things that are really serious business: who God is, that Jesus is the only way to Him, the power of prayer, exactly how our good works fit into the plan of salvation, the work of the Holy Spirit, the power of the devil, what exactly faith is, and much, much more. We all should make a fresh commitment to purposefully, honestly, and regularly study the Word of God, allowing it to speak to us directly rather than through the filters of our denominational, cultural, or personal prejudices.

> *Sanctify them through thy truth: thy word is truth.* (John 17:17)
>
> *Thy word is true from the beginning: and every one of thy righteous judgments endureth for ever.* (Psalm 119:160)

Palindromes

Palindromes are clever arrangements of words so that they can be read backwards to spell exactly the same message. In fact, it is likely that the very first sentence spoken between two humans was a palindrome: "Madam, I'm Adam." Of course that was after the first emotional response when Adam first laid eyes on Eve also came out as a palindrome: "Wow!"

The following is a list of a few humorous palindromes, concluding with one serious one to make sure that we have dealt with:

Don't nod.

Dogma: I am God.

Never odd or even.

Too bad – I hid a boot.

Rats live on no evil star.

No trace; not one carton.

Was it Eliot's toilet I saw?

Murder for a jar of red rum.

May a moody baby doom a yam?

Go hang a salami; I'm a lasagna hog!

A Toyota! Race fast... safe car: a Toyota.

Straw? No, too stupid a fad; I put soot on warts.

Are we not drawn onward, we few, drawn onward to new era?

No, it never propagates if I set a gap or prevention.

Anne, I vote more cars race Rome to Vienna.

Sums are not set as a test on Erasmus.

Some men interpret nine memos.

Campus Motto: Bottoms up, Mac.

Lewd I did live & evil did I dwel.

Go deliver a dare, vile dog!

Oozy rat in a sanitary zoo.

Ah, Satan sees Natasha.

Lisa Bonet ate no basil

Do geese see God?

God saw I was dog.

Dennis sinned.

WWJD

I recently received the following email from a friend:
One of the great challenges of the life of faith is to bring the truth and principles of the Word of God to bear on our own lives. We tend to excuse ourselves with lines like, "That was then," or "We know different now." And I am as guilty as anyone. I have never worn a "WWJD" bracelet because I can excuse myself from the question. Jesus did not have my boss, spouse, children or mortgage. What I really need is a "WWMWS" bracelet. "What Will My Wife Say?" is the question I should ask regarding my own conduct.

I, of course, thought that he had a rather insightful point. However, there is one even more significant set of letters that I would like to suggest for a Christian bracelet: WWIDIIRTIWJ, "What would I do if I realized that it was Jesus?" The idea comes from the story that Jesus told in Matthew chapter twenty-five about a shepherd in the process of separating his sheep and goats. The ultimate criteria set for separating those who will inherit the kingdom prepared for them from the foundation of the world and those who will be cast into the everlasting fire prepared for the devil and his angels is whether they fed Jesus when He was hungry, gave Him something to drink when He was thirsty, took Him in when He was a stranger, clothed Him when He was naked, visited Him when He was sick, and came to see Him when He was in prison. Neither the sheep nor the goats remembered ever having seen Jesus hungry, thirsty, as a stranger, naked, sick, or in prison. Of course, Jesus answered that they had seen Him every time they had seen the least of His brethren in any of those hurting conditions.

The real identifying characteristic of a Christ-motivated believer is that he sees Jesus in everyone he meets and treats them as if they really were Jesus right in front of him.

Why Tongues?

Over the years, I've heard the issue debated many times why God instituted the gift of speaking in tongues. One of the standard answers is that tongues is a secret code language between man and God that allows them to communicate without the devil's being able to decode their private messages. I have never accepted that argument on a couple points.

First, such an explanation would undermine the power of prayer in the known language. If the fact that Satan can understand what you are saying gives him some sort of advantage, then praying in our understanding is detrimental. However, we are repeatedly commanded to pray using our normal vocabulary. (I Corinthians 14:15) Additionally, just because the devil understands what is being said doesn't necessarily give him an advantage. He could read every prophecy in the Old Testament predicting the coming of Christ and His redemptive death; however, just because He could read the words did not mean that he could understand the message. First Corinthians 2:8 explains that had he understood what he was doing, he would never have inspired men to crucify Jesus. He instituted his own undoing by not being able to interpret Isaiah chapter fifty-three and Psalm twenty-two.

The second reason that I have rejected this explanation is that I'm not convinced that Satan cannot understand tongues. I Corinthians 13:1 explains that tongues are the languages of men and angels. Satan was originally an angel; therefore, he spoke the language of angels. I really doubt that he forgot his original tongue just because he was cast out of heaven. He also understands every language of men; otherwise, how would he be able to tempt them and put wrong thoughts into their minds?

I believe that the real reason God instituted the gift of tongues is that it requires men to trust Him in a totally new and radical way. When we speak in tongues, we are no longer in control of the words that are coming out of our mouths – a totally new, foreign experience. If we can't trust God that what we are saying is really of Him, we fail the faith test.

July 18
In the Movies
Maybe you saw the movie <u>2012</u>, based on the Mayan legend that the world would end in 2012. If not, don't worry. It would have been a waste of your money. The movie opened with some impressive cosmic activity that promised more than the rest of the film delivered. But the real clincher was that when the climactic devastation does sweep across the earth, it is in the form of a flood. Now, the average moviegoer may not have seen the significance in this, but anyone who is even vaguely familiar with the scriptures should have realized that a flood is exactly the one thing that God said won't happen again. When Noah came out of the ark, God placed a rainbow in the sky as a confirmation of His promise to never again use water to destroy the earth. (Genesis 9:11-17) If the script writers had wanted to have anything realistic in their description of the end of the earth, they could have simply looked into the scriptures and found explicit details that the planet is destined to go up in flames, not under floodwaters. (II Peter 3:10-12) The significance of this movie is that it depicts the spirit of the age that deliberately denies anything that the Bible proclaims as truth. It demonstrates the humanistic viewpoint that anything other than the Word of God – even ancient Mayan calendars – is a viable source of truth.

Another movie that was making the circuit at roughly the same time made the point even more blatantly. <u>Invention of Lying</u> depicted lying as a good thing to help people suffering from depression, and other ills. The biggest lie presented in the movie was the story of God and heaven. The film portrayed religion as the presentation of a false hope that helped people overcome their fears, worries, and disappointments. There was not even the slightest camouflage of the humanistic idea that religion is a total farce and, as the Communist would say, "the opiate of the people."

They are the enemies of the cross of Christ:
Whose end is destruction. (Philippians 3:18-19)

July 19

Compassion

We live in a hurting world. Bob Moffitt of Disciple Nations Alliance collected the following statistics by evangelists and then made the following observations and analyses concerning the present human condition.

The Bible is not available in sixty percent of the world's languages. Of one hundred ninety-three national governments, one hundred sixteen are considered corrupt. One billion people live on less than one dollar per day. Racial and religious hatred are the top reason for crimes in the United States. Worldwide, sixteen thousand children die of hunger-related diseases each day. Forty million people are living with AIDS/HIV. Each year, one million children are sold into the sex trade. Only nine percent of born-again Christians in America are considered to have a biblical worldview. Six million children are injured in armed conflicts each decade. One hundred million children of primary-school age are not in school. There are three thousand six hundred people groups categorized as least-reached by the gospel. Worldwide, a suicide is committed every forty seconds. There are over eleven thousand reported terrorist attacks annually. Annually, two hundred million people use illicit drugs.

The church has had two distinct responses to the rise of secularism in the West – the liberal church has embraced it, and the evangelical church adopted a dualistic view that set spiritual ministry apart from the rest of life. In general, the church has misunderstood how God expects us to respond to the human dilemma. If compassion means what most Christians understand it today, Jesus would have been in line for a Nobel prize, not a cross. An individual gospel without a social gospel is a soul without a body. A social gospel without an individual gospel is a body without a soul. One is a ghost; the other is a corpse. We must save men's souls from hell by presenting the gospel of personal salvation; however, we must be socially active at the same time to save those same men from their present hell by actively attacking social injustice and abuse.

July 20

What the Church Should Be
and What It Should Be Doing

In this generation, we are seeing the highest level of new converts and church plants in world history; however, the countries where we are seeing the most growth continue to be the most broken, politically unstable, corrupt, impoverished, and diseased.

The church is not called to survive history but to serve humanity.

Of all the things Paul did, he was most eager to preach the gospel and remember the poor (Acts 26:28-29, 24:14).

The current problem in the church world is not the lack of evangelism, but that of immature believers and weak churches. We have babies giving birth to babies.

The primary reason people do not act like Jesus is that they do not think like Him. – George Barna

Social action is not just an implication of the gospel or an addendum to it; it is an intrinsic part of it.

Nearly ninety percent of children raised in evangelical homes abandon the church after high school. They feel that their parents' practice of going to church was a habit or a hobby without authentically living the principles of Christ.

We must fulfill not only the Great Commission but also the cultural commission to create a culture under His lordship.

We are called to be agents of His common grace as well as of His saving grace. – Chuck Colson

If knowledge and truth form the foundation of a nation's development, then ignorance and lies form the foundation of its destruction. Satan is the father of lies, not only to individuals, but also to whole nations.

There is not a square inch in the whole domain of humans over which Jesus does not cry out, "Mine!"

The point of church growth is not to collect new people and cage them with church programs. The church exists to equip them and release them back into the world – dangerous for the gospel.

Every square inch and every split second is claimed by God and counterclaimed by Satan. – CS Lewis

July 21
Christianity Must Affect Culture

Thirty percent of the aborted babies in America had mothers who claimed to be Christians. In Kenya, eighty percent of the people claim to be Christians, but its government has been ranked as one of the three most corrupt in the world. Rwanda claimed to be eighty percent Christian, but one million of its seven million population were killed in the genocide.

Unless the gospel is preached in a way to cause a nation to change its culturally held ideas, there will be no real change in the people's consequences. Just like the DNA that is in the seed is what is in the mature plant, it is the root ideas in the people's hearts that determines the fruit (consequences) of their lives. God sent His son to not only redeem us but to redeem the effects of our sinfulness in society, and then Jesus sent His church as not only couriers to proclaim the message of redemption but also as agents to help bring about change. Most of us in the church have become disengaged from effective connection with society; we are in church and out of the world. The truth is that the church doesn't have the luxury of withdrawing from the community. We are commanded to be connected in meaningful and influential ways.

One significant arena of connection is that we are to teach the truth in a way that dispels ignorance and demonic strongholds. For example, since poverty of the mind is worse than poverty of circumstances, we need to be able to not just hand out loaves of bread but to also give out the Bread of Life that breaks the poverty mentality off the lives of the people. We must break the mind-set of scarcity in every area, including the way people think about their own abilities, as well as how they think about their physical lack of funds and resources. Until we break that mental stronghold, a poverty mentality will short-circuit all the divine creativity that God is trying to release in the people's lives. In reality, the whole thought process is actually a mind-set about God and His involvement in the human condition. Poverty and lack are simply manifestations of doubt and unbelief: thinking that God isn't able to intervene – or even worse, that that He is unconcerned about intervening – in our needs.

July 22

Adegboyega Ilori

No, that's not a message in unknown tongues. It's the name of a young man I met in Africa. One of the fringe benefits to traveling and ministering all over the world is that I have the opportunity to meet and get to know so many interesting members of the family of God. Adegboyega is a promising young author from Lagos, Nigeria, who asked me to review a couple of his books.

A few of his points in a book he did on marriage were so poignant that I felt it worthwhile to share them in today's meditation:

Anyone who knows how to eat should know how to cook.

It is better to seek the God of men than the men of God.

Six of seven barren women in the Bible had outstanding children. Michal was barren to death because she ridiculed David, God's anointed servant.

Paradise is between your ears.

What lies within determines what lies ahead.

The way you dress is the way you will be addressed.

Marriage is for people who believe in tomorrow.

Don't eat the honey before the moon.

In Nigeria, seven of ten men and two of ten women are guilty of adultery; also, nine out of ten armed robberies are committed by children out of broken homes.

Divorce is the end of a wife – not of a life.

I have to admit that his one-liners really "pack a punch." I especially like the one about knowing how to cook if you know how to eat. I'm sure that he was meaning more than just in the kitchen. To be successful in marriage – and in any arena of life – we must know how to be givers, not just takers.

I was also impressed with the statement that marriage is for people who believe in tomorrow. So many people today live simply for the now and never build for the future. They spend all that they have and all that they can get on credit without a thought about what they will need later on. They live on today's excitements without a concern for future security. But marriage is a genuine commitment to building for the future.

July 23

In the Original Greek

We so often hear Bible teachers make reference to words and phrases that are more vivid or meaningful when read directly from the Greek as opposed to any of the published translations. In today's ditty, I'd like to share a few insights I've gleaned from the writings of the excellent Greek scholar and Bible teacher, Rick Renner.

The word "devil," *diabolos* in Greek, means one who throws through. The devil is the one who throws his accusations and lies totally through us and penetrates us with them.

The thorn in the flesh that Paul referred to in II Corinthians 12:7 is literally a stake upon which decapitated heads were displayed. In other words, the devil was using the harassment that he was bringing against Paul as a trophy case to exhibit the seeming defeat of a Christian leader. Praise God, Paul had the grace to deal with it! The Greek word for "sufficient" that Paul used when he said that the grace of God was sufficient to deal with this thorn means much more than what we might think at first. It literally means "to be more than enough" or "to display abundance." Wow, Paul wasn't just going to barely crawl out of the ring with the devil. He was able to knock him out! And so are we!

Although the words are similar, "weakness" is <u>not</u> the word for "sickness." Even though we may have physical infirmities, we don't have to be weak and powerless.

When Paul said that a great door had been opened for him (I Corinthians 16:9), he explained that it was <u>uniquely</u> opened. God has a way of doing things on our behalf that just won't happen without His intervention.

"I am persuaded" (Romans 8:38) implies that he had changed his mind. Apparently, there was a time when he – like all of us – wasn't convinced. But, praise God, he got past that point – and so can we!

When Paul said that the Macedonians were ready to give in the offering for the needy saints (II Corinthians 9:2), he said that they were euphoric about every opportunity. Can we say the same thing about our willingness to bless others?

July 24

Digging a Little Deeper

By looking just a little deeper into the meaning of the words in a verse, we can see so much more meaning in most of the passages in the Bible. Here are just a few examples:

In Matthew 27:4, Mark 15:31, and Acts 2:13, we read that the high priest and bystanders mocked the disciples on the Day of Pentecost. The term used here actually means to play charades. In other words, they were acting out a script handed to them. Obviously, the author of that script was the devil.

In II Thessalonians 2:3, we learn that the day of the Lord will not come unless there is first a falling away. The term for "falling away" means that an anti-God attitude will develop. The context of the verse suggests that this will be prevalent in society in the last days. Many evangelical preachers have used this verse to promote the idea that there is to be a time when the church will dwindle in numbers and force, but this verse does not speak of the condition within the church. It dramatically paints the picture of the condition that the Body of Christ will have to confront – and, in fact. is already confronting.

In James 5:13, those who are merry are asked to sing and those who are afflicted are directed to call for the elders to pray for them. The Greek term used to describe the merry person literally means that he is about to explode with joy. Wow! What a wonderful description of the joy of the Lord! When the physically frail or feeble are commanded to call for the elders, the terminology depicts an urgent plea, and the response of the eldership is that they are to offer urgent and passionate petitions. Physical infirmity is nothing to be taken lightly on the part of the infirm or the eldership. The prayers in the name of the Lord speak of exerting the full authority of Christ that will result in deliverance of the sick person. Interestingly enough, a new word for "sick" is introduced at this point in the verse. Here, James refers to those who have suffered a long time and have become extremely weakened. The point is that we can call for prayer when we are first afflicted, but we can still be healed even if the situation is severe and long-standing.

July 25
More Than Meets the Eye

Sometimes, there are great treasures buried just beneath the surface. Let's peel back a layer of translation to see what we can find buried in some rather familiar scripture passages.

In Romans 12:13, we are commanded to distribute to the necessity of the saints and to be given to hospitality. The word that Paul used for hospitality in this verse is *philoxenia*, which can be literally translated to mean to love strangers. The term he used for "given" means to pursue and is actually translated "persecute" in some cases. In essence, what Paul was requiring in this passage is that, in addition to helping out our fellow believers who have needs, we are to pursue every opportunity to bless anyone in need with the same aggressive attitude that we would if going after an opponent.

When we are commanded to bless those who persecute us (Matthew 5:44, Romans 12:14), the Greek word is *eulogia*, meaning to say something good. It is from this exact term that we get the modern word "eulogy" for a speech that is given at a funeral. Perhaps there are two underlying messages here – to be as nice as we would in honoring a departed loved one, and to expect that our blessing will put an end to their persecution just as a funeral brings closure to the life of the friend.

When Jesus said that we could command a sycamine tree to be plucked up and to be planted in the sea (Luke 17:6), he was referring to planting the tree in a saltwater environment that would kill it. Since this parable is actually in context of unforgiveness, there is a powerful message to be understood. We are to toss all our grudges into an environment where they will not have the nutrients to flourish.

There are several individuals in the New Testament who are called "laborers" for the gospel. (Mary in Romans 16:6, Tryphena, Tryphosa, and Persis in Romans 16:12, Paul in I Timothy 4:10, the elders in Titus 5:17) The Greek term applied to them refers to a person who is completely exhausted due to non-stop work – sacrificial love for the Lord, the gospel, and the Body of Christ.

July 26

Principles to Live By

The difference between coaching and fathering is that the coach will yell at you from the sidelines while a father will weep with you in the locker room.

The biggest tragedy in life is not death but life without a purpose.

Without a strategy, your dream will die with you.

Unity is "U" and "I" ty (you and I tied together).

Success in the business world is usually built on networking; in the kingdom of God, it is based on "knitworking." Believers must all be knit together to do the work. (Colossians 2:2, 19)

The kingdom of God depends on three lines:

The prayer warriors, our lifeline
The ministers who go, the frontline
The giver, the supply line

Mission is the essence of our faith. Notice how the key words to Christianity are built on the word "go": God, gospel, good news. If you take the "go" out, you have "spel" (the people are under Satan's spell) and "od news."

The theme of Acts is "up, down, and out": Jesus went up, the Spirit came down, and the people went out.

Humility isn't beating yourself down, but lifting others up.

Humility isn't thinking less of yourself but thinking of yourself less.

God didn't call you to be a success, just faithful. – Mother Teresa

Where there is no vision, you bump into things and get bruises.

Vision without a strategy is at best, a dream and at worst, a nightmare.

Turn your life into a FEAST:

Focus on God's plan.
Establish your ways in His Word.
Assess if what you believe agrees with God?
Supply – God will supply your every need.
Tie – Unite with other believers.

July 27
Sharp Tools

The early days of the nation of Israel occurred just as the human race was moving from the Bronze Age into the Iron Age. Unfortunately, the Philistines developed the technology of working with iron before the Israelites did and were careful to keep these skills to themselves because they understood that the Israelites would be a threat to them once they were able to sharpen their implements.

> *Now there was no smith found throughout all the land of Israel: for the Philistines said, Lest the Hebrews make them swords or spears: But all the Israelites went down to the Philistines, to sharpen every man his share, and his coulter, and his axe, and his mattock. Yet they had a file for the mattocks, and for the coulters, and for the forks, and for the axes, and to sharpen the goads. So it came to pass in the day of battle, that there was neither sword nor spear found in the hand of any of the people that were with Saul and Jonathan: but with Saul and with Jonathan his son was there found. (I Samuel 13:19-22)*

The devil is still using this same tactic on believers today, except he has added a new twist. He doesn't prohibit us from the ability to sharpen our tools; he simply makes us think that it is unnecessary.

A man felt that he didn't have time to sharpen his axe because he was too busy cutting trees. On the first day, he cut eighteen trees. On the second day, his productivity dropped to fifteen. By the third day, he could only fell ten trees. The lesson to be learned is that time in preparation is never wasted time. Prayer, study, and planning are essential to keeping our axes sharp to do the work of the Lord. Time invested in these activities is not lost time; on the contrary, the productivity we gain by having our spiritual weapons at their sharpest far outweighs any "jumpstart" that we have by simply taking on the challenges of life in our own strength and wisdom.

Be Careful, Little Eyes

In the story of the healing of the lame man at the Gate Beautiful in Acts chapter three, there is an interesting mix of terms. In verse three, we learn that the lame man saw Peter and John. In verse four, we are told that Peter fastened his eyes on the lame man and then commanded the man to look on him and John. Notice the progression in the words used to speak of sight: see, fasten eyes, look. It was through the deliberate focusing of attention that the miracle occurred. It is likely that Peter and John had seen the man many times before, but on this one day, they focused on him. They then directed him to do the same. When there was deliberate attention by all parties, the healing was possible. The author of Hebrews gives us a similar message when he tells us that we can see the witnesses around us, but we must look to Jesus. It is the deliberate, focused attention that brings us victory. Peter learned the same lesson when he stopped looking at Jesus and started focusing on the waves and wind around him.

We are given several explicit instructions in the scripture as to where we are to focus our eyes:

On the Lord – *Wherefore seeing we also are compassed about with so great a cloud of witnesses, let us lay aside every weight, and the sin which doth so easily beset us, and let us run with patience the race that is set before us, Looking unto Jesus the author and finisher of our faith; who for the joy that was set before him endured the cross, despising the shame, and is set down at the right hand of the throne of God.* (Hebrews 12:1-2)

On the Word – *Open thou mine eyes, that I may behold wondrous things out of thy law.* (Psalm 119:18)

On the harvest – *Say not ye, There are yet four months, and then cometh harvest? behold, I say unto you, Lift up your eyes, and look on the fields; for they are white already to harvest.* (John 4:35)

On the prize before us – *I press toward the mark for the prize of the high calling of God in Christ Jesus.* (Philippians 3:14)

Satan's Twelve-step Program

We have all heard of the twelve-step programs used to get free from alcohol and drug addictions. However, I was intrigued to see the following twelve-step program that leads us into bondage. The thing that I was so impressed by when I ran across this was that it was comprised by a friend of mine who spent a number of years in severe depression and bondage from the devil. After many prayers and counseling sessions and much spiritual warfare, he was finally set free. When I saw this analysis of the devil's tactics, I realized that even though my friend had suffered immeasurably during his bout with the enemy, he had come out victorious and had even found out how to expose the enemy's tactics.

> *Lest Satan should get an advantage of us: for we are not ignorant of his devices.* (II Corinthians 2:11)
> *Put on the whole armour of God, that ye may be able to stand against the wiles of the devil.* (Ephesians 6:11)

1) Disguise (Counterfeit)
2) Deception
3) Disappointment
4) Discouragement
5) Displeasure
6) Distraction and entanglement
7) Detour
8) Displacement
9) Discontentment
10) Disgust
11) Disillusionment
12) Despair, hopelessness, severe depression, being at your wit's end

July 30

Is Heaven Worth It?

I'm sure that the title of today's ditty caught your attention. Of course, heaven is worth whatever it might take to get there. After all, it has streets of gold, walls of diamonds, eternal happiness in the presence of God and all the saints plus all our departed loved ones – and not even to mention what the alternative is! But I guess my question is not really if heaven is worth it; maybe it is more like, "Do we perceive heaven as being worth it?"

Before we tackle that question, maybe we should do a little background preparation to understand human nature in general. Since heaven is where we go (or at least we hope we are going to go) at the end of our lives, let's back up just one step and take a look at retirement, the step just before death. In preparing for retirement, we have to make sacrifices during our working years. If a worker begins saving just one hundred dollars per month at age twenty, he will have over half a million dollars in his retirement fund by age sixty-five. However, if he waits just ten years to start his savings, he will have less than half that amount in his retirement fund. It's not magic or rocket science – just simple math. But the vast majority of wage earners just don't get it. Why? Because of the emotional component in the human makeup that enjoys the present "kick" more than the future security and payoff. Even the promise of a million dollars thirty years away is not as effective as the immediate gratification that the hundred dollars in the hand rather than in the bank can bring.

Now let's get back to the original question. Yes, heaven is worth it – BUT – no, we don't perceive it as so. Just think about the constant parade of opportunities we have to invest in heaven but chose rather to invest in our immediate pleasure, comfort, or gratification instead. Certainly, the Christian life is a both-and rather than an either-or situation. God wants us to have pleasure, comfort, and gratification now as well as heaven in the future. He just doesn't want us to lose the perspective of building our heavenly retirement fund. (Matthew 6:19-21)

July 31
Kingdom Seeds

Jesus said that the kingdom of God is like a tiny seed that will develop into a great tree that provides food and shelter for many. (Matthew 13:31-32) The following thoughts are kingdom truths that if allowed, like tiny seeds, to get into your heart and germinate there can produce wisdom that will nourish and protect your own life and many others to whom you will minister:

Christians are seed throwers, fire starters, hope peddlers, grace-givers, and risk takers.

Sweat intellectually. Have a purpose for what you invest your energy in and a well thought-through plan for accomplishing that purpose with the efforts you are investing.

Jesus was not crucified in a cathedral between two candles but in a garbage dump between two thieves.

There are many ways in which the nature of God is manifest in humans. The most significant is sacrificial and voluntary servanthood.

We must see the difference between serving (activity) and servanthood (lifestyle). When we simply serve, we are still in charge.

Every day He keeps us alive is an opportunity to give Him delight or disappointment.

The electric company has the power, but we have the authority of turning on the switch. The same is true in the spiritual dimension. God has the power, but we have the authority through faith and prayer to release it into the world we live in.

We can forget what we are taught, but we will always remember what we discover. That's why it is so important to study the scriptures on our own rather than to simply attend church and Bible classes where others teach us what they know.

Sin has created a wall between God and man; the church is a window in that wall. Therefore, we need to always have the window washers actively at work.

August 1
In the Image of God
     I grew up in the Old South when segregation was still very much a part of the culture. I remember three restrooms at the gas stations (men's, women's, and colored's), two water fountains in the department stores (one with a cooler for whites and one that was just a faucet on the pipe for coloreds), "separate but equal" schools, an occasional Ku Klux Klan cross burning, and a special meeting of the church leadership to discuss a plan of action just in case a colored person were to attempt to exercise his civil rights by attending a Sunday service. Even when I was old enough to enter college, I had to answer questions on my admission application about my willingness to share a dorm room with a classmate of a different race or ethnic background. When I was in seminary, one of the professors had a foreign student visit him for lunch, sparking quite a stir in his neighborhood about having a black guest in his home. His response was, "Oh, he isn't a Negro; he's an African." But prejudice is not only limited to race. It is just as prevalent with gender. In fact, sexism may actually be more persistent than racism. Even in today's society where the racial barriers have pretty well been broken down, we still find strong bastions of male domination. This is especially true in the church world, the one arena that we would think should be the first place to practice liberation and equality.

     I once heard a story of a man who went to heaven and had a personal visit with God. When he returned to earth, everyone wanted to know about his audience. He was reluctant to talk about the Almighty; however, he eventually decided to share his story. He began, "Now, first of all, you have to understand that many of us haven't really understood what God is actually like, so please don't be surprised with what I have to say. She's black." I doubt that this is true, but all of us – male, female, black, white – are all created in His image. (Genesis 1:27)

> *If a man say, I love God, and hateth his brother, he is a liar: for he that loveth not his brother whom he hath seen, how can he love God whom he hath not seen?* (I John 4:20)

August 2
Thought Gods
It was a rather stark and to-the-point statement, but it rang out with a genuine sense of truth, "What occupies your thoughts is your god." As I thought about it, I realized that there was significant truth in that abrupt, terse little sentence. Whether it is something that we worry about, something that we are really interested in, or something that we just seem to obsess over – that thing has taken control of our minds and has pushed God out of first place. It could be sex, sports, money, a job, or even something as noble as working for the Lord; but – whatever it is – it has taken a seat on the throne of the mind and has, therefore, taken control. It is a thought god.

Another poignant statement that I heard on the same day, but from another source in an unrelated situation, really hammered the point home. This quote from a book on finances read, "if you have missed my love for God, you will not understand this book and none of these economic principles will work for you." His point was that even though he was talking about finances, money was not the thing that occupied the throne of his mind. Those individuals who were focused on the prosperity that God could give them rather than the God who could give them prosperity were serving the wrong god and would, therefore, fail to receive blessings from the one true God.

> *And be not conformed to this world: but be ye transformed by the renewing of your mind, that ye may prove what is that good, and acceptable, and perfect, will of God.* (Romans 12:2)
> *For though we walk in the flesh, we do not war after the flesh: (For the weapons of our warfare are not carnal, but mighty through God to the pulling down of strong holds;) Casting down imaginations, and every high thing that exalteth itself against the knowledge of God, and bringing into captivity every thought to the obedience of Christ.* (II Corinthians 10:3-5)

August 3

The Mountain Ahead

Looking at the mountain ahead may cause you to stumble on the present level road. We may not think this way very often, but the message is actually very pertinent for everyday life.

Isn't it just too easy to become so focused on the big challenges that lie ahead of us that we fail to pay close attention to the details of our present situation? There may be a big project due a few days down the road, but thinking about it right now distracts us so much that it interferes with taking care of the present assignments. Now, don't get me wrong – I'm in no way advocating shirking future responsibilities or failing to plan ahead for upcoming tasks. My point is that we shouldn't focus on the future to the point where it becomes a detriment to our present lives. Who knows? The road you are on may take a turn and not even go to the mountain. If that turns out to be the case, just think of all that you missed while focusing on something that never even came about.

Jesus corrected this overly anxious attitude toward the mountains before us in the Sermon on the Mount by stating thal we must replace our concern for future needs and responsibilities with a conscious awareness of the kingdom oi God. When the kingdom is in proper focus, everything else seems to naturally fall into place.

> *Therefore take no thought, saying, What shall we eat? or, What shall we drink? or, Wherewithal shall we be clothed? (For after all these things do the Gentiles seek:) for your heavenly Father knoweth that ye have need of all these things. But seek ye first the kingdom of God, and his righteousness; and all these things shall be added unto you. Take therefore no thought for the morrow: for the morrow shall take thought for the things of itself. Sufficient unto the day is the evil thereof.* (Matthew 6:31-34)

August 4
Don't Be Afraid of Men's Doctrines

When I was mid-way through graduate school, the Lord directed me to switch from my chemical engineering career plans to teach in a Bible school. I knew that I would have to have a degree from an accredited theological school in order to fulfill this directive; however, there were no recognized Full Gospel schools back then. Because Southeastern Baptist Seminary was just a few miles from my home and their tuition was incredibly reasonable for off-campus students, I decided to check them out. I applied and was accepted; however, I never told anyone about what I was up to. About this time, I was invited to be interviewed on a Christian talk show. After the interview, we went to the chapel to pray over the prayer requests which had been called in during the program. One of the engineers from the studio joined us, but instead of praying over the call-ins, he wanted to pray over me. He began to prophesy and spoke out, "Do what's in your heart and don't be afraid of the doctrines of men." Well, this was a real word from God because – as a tongue-talking, devil chasing fanatic – I was concerned about sitting under Baptist doctrines for the next several years. Southeastern was the most liberal seminary among the most conservative Southern Baptist schools – a perfect setting for me because they were open to new ideas even though they held to biblical foundations.

On the orientation day at campus, I sat in the balcony of the chapel and counted a dozen students whom I had led to the Lord, prayed for to receive the baptism in the Holy Spirit, or discipled through the ministry I had done on the secular college campuses in the area before making the move to go to seminary. Long story short – I was able to initiate a charismatic movement on campus that even involved some of the faculty by the time I finished my degree. During my final year, we were able to arrange a campus meeting with a leading Baptist minister who was also a well-known charismatic figure. It was the largest attended meeting on campus that year short of the graduation!

August 5
Europe, Here We Come!

We serve a wonderful God who wants to bless us with the desires of our hearts – and He has the most unusual ways of doing so! A number of years ago, I had a desire to take my family on a vacation to Europe, but such a trip was nothing more than a "pipe dream" on our budget. However, we could afford a trip to Florida because my mother-in-law had a home there; so, all we had to pay for was the airline ticket, which I was able to get at an almost unbelievable discount. We made it as far as Atlanta, but were told that the flight from there was overbooked by five seats – just the number in our party. When I offered up our seats in exchange for a later flight and compensation toward future travel, the airline agent went to work to rebook us. After a good while at her computer, she looked up and explained that the other flights she wanted to get us on were also overbooked. My response was, "Well, just bump us off of those flights too." Before we left her desk, we had free dinner vouchers, a hotel room in Atlanta for the night, free breakfast vouchers, and three thousand dollars worth of free airline travel! When we added in the mileage points we had earned for the trip and the points we earned from buying the tickets on our credit card, we were able to fly to Europe for free!

Now, to put this miracle in perspective, the airline statistics for that particular year showed that only one out of every five thousand travelers was bumped off a flight. Of course, we have to remember that there were five of us bumped off of two consecutive flights, making the probability more like one in fifty thousand! Imagine that! Our God certainly knows how to work the odds in favor of His kids!

When we started working on our plans for the dream vacation to Europe, we decided to travel through Switzerland, Italy, and Greece on the Eurorail because they offer a pass that allows the passenger to go anywhere the trains travel, boarding and disembarking as often as he wishes. As you might expect, the train system was offering a special for the exact dates that we were to be traveling. We wound up traveling for sixteen days for less than the normal ten-day fare!

August 6

Europe, We're Still Coming!

In yesterday's ditty, I shared the story of how the Lord miraculously provided for my family to go on a European vacation. But, I also have to share with you, as Paul Harvey would have said, "the rest of the story." Just about three weeks before the trip, I was helping my boys build a jumping ramp for their bikes. Once we finished it, I decided to test it out with them. The result was a broken shoulder blade, a trip to the emergency room, and an immovable arm. Since we had decided that we were only taking backpacks on the trip because we didn't want to haul suitcases on and off of the trains, I was in a terrible predicament. There was no way that I could get a backpack over my immovable arm, and carrying a backpack on a broken shoulder was totally out of the question!

The week before our trip, Rev. R. W. Schambach, a renowned healing evangelist, was to hold several days of meetings at our church. Brother Schamach had a rather unusual ministry in that he did not exercise any gentleness when dealing with problems. To watch him minister, you might wonder if he was intending to heal you or kill you – and that is exactly the approach he took with me. After I explained why my arm was in a sling, he asked me to show him how far I could move the arm. Pulling it about six or eight inches from my side, I explained that it was excruciatingly painful to move it any further. Taking my hand, he gently moved my arm a bit and asked if that was about as far as I could move it. When I answered in the affirmative, he looked me directly in the eyes in what I assume was an attempt to get my attention off my injury. Suddenly, he jerked my arm totally above my head, and I was instantly healed!

The next morning, I went back to the doctor who had examined me after the fall to ask him if I needed to continue with the follow-up visits he had scheduled. He took one look at my shoulder and confirmed that it was totally healed! So off to Europe I went – backpack and all!

August 7
Negative Parenting

And Jabez was more honourable than his brethren: and his mother called his name Jabez, saying, Because I bare him with sorrow. And Jabez called on the God of Israel, saying, Oh that thou wouldest bless me indeed, and enlarge my coast, and that thine hand might be with me, and that thou wouldest keep me from evil, that it may not grieve me! And God granted him that which he requested. (I Chronicles 4:9-10)

Several years ago, praying the prayer of Jabez became essentially a fad in Christian circles. Books, magazine articles and sermons in almost every pulpit encouraged believers to ask God to increase their capacity for blessing and to keep them from evil while not allowing grief to invade their lives. It was, of course, a very positive message with some very positive results; however, I don't remember anyone ever addressing the whole story of the character of Jabez. Notice in the first part of the passage that Jabez got his name because his mother gave birth to him in sorrow. There is no explanation as to what sorrow she had experienced; but, whatever it was, she passed it along to her son by giving him a name meaning "sorrowful." You have to wonder how intense her anguish must have been for her to hang this moniker on her son, knowing that he would have to answer to it for his entire life.

Understanding the negative influence that his mother had exerted upon the poor boy helps set the stage for digging ever more meaning out of this passage. The point of the story is that we are not limited by negative parenting. We each have the choice to use the bad influences our parents have had on us as an excuse for not succeeding in life or for not accomplishing more. On the other hand, we can "reverse the curse" and declare an end to any harm done, whether intentionally or unintentionally. After all, the most influential parent we have is our Heavenly Father, not our earthly mom or dad!

August 8

Challenging Thoughts

When you are down to nothing, God is up to something.

A true Christian can stand persecution, but not being ignored.

Don't spend your life shooting at nothing because you'll hit your target every time.

We need a holy dissatisfaction with being normal.

When the disciples saw Jesus walking on the water, one out of twelve (about eight percent) got out of the boat to walk on the water themselves. It's about the same ratio today of people who genuinely walk by faith.

If you aren't supernatural, you are superficial. Being normal is grossly overrated.

You can't keep from being melted, but you can decide which mold you will be poured into.

If you aren't living on the edge, you are taking up too much space.

We must grow in grace because you can't really grow any other way.

All of us can do something, even if it is nothing more than serving as a bad example.

Plan to live by faith and then have faith to live by your plan.

If your vision doesn't embarrass you when you share it, it's probably not from God.

Many Christians fear that prosperity would make them backslide. If that were true, the devil would see to it that your salary would double tomorrow.

There are things in life that we consider to be fiery trials, but, if we look closely enough, we may discover that they are just the flambé on the cherries jubilee that God is making out of our lives.

Don't eat your seed, but also be careful not to plant your bread. He gives seed to sowers; therefore, if you are short on finances, it is probably because He doesn't see you as a sower.

The followers of Jesus often missed the point because they were the "duh-ciples."

August 9

Bells and Gongs

Now concerning spiritual gifts, brethren, I would not have you ignorant. Ye know that ye were Gentiles, carried away unto these dumb idols, even as ye were led. Wherefore I give you to understand, that no man speaking by the Spirit of God calleth Jesus accursed: and that no man can say that Jesus is the Lord, but by the Holy Ghost. (I Corinthians 12:1-3)

When Paul introduced his discussion on the gifts of the Holy Spirit, he took what seems like a really abrupt detour by discussing the pagan practices that the people once participated in. It is not until we get to the famous love chapter (thirteen) that we are able to begin to piece together what must have been in his mind as he penned these words. Paul says that practicing the gifts of the Spirit without the motivation of love is like a tinkling cymbal or a sounding brass. To understand what he meant, we need to be aware of the pagan practices familiar to the Corinthian believers. The pagan temples of the time had bells that served the same function as the bells in Hindu temples today. They were essentially doorbells to announce the arrival of a devotee to the demon spirits that inhabited the shrine. They also contained gongs much like the gongs found in present-day Buddhist temples, which also serve the purpose of awakening the demonic presence. Paul's evaluation of speaking in tongues outside the divine control of love was that it was nothing more than a demonic practice arousing evil spirits. It is because of the possibility of activating the wrong spiritual powers that the apostle felt it important to lay a foundation of understanding the difference between the demonic and the Holy Spirit.

It doesn't take too much experience in Pentecostal and Charismatic circles for one to encounter those who are doing things that certainly seem to be miraculous, but are actually motivated by demonic spirits rather than the Holy Spirit. Jesus Himself said that there will be those who will do miracles in His name without ever having known Him. (Matthew 7:22-23)

August 10

Underlings

When I was a brand new employee in Dr. Lester Sumrall's ministry, Brother Sumrall asked me to help him remember a rather important issue that he needed to discuss with one of his other employees. Since he knew that he would be with the other gentleman the following day at a specific time of the day, Dr. Sumrall asked me to arrange to come by that specific place at that specific time to remind him about the matter that needed to be handled. When I stopped in to bring up the topic, the gentleman became rather indignant because he was a long-standing employee and I was essentially still "wet behind the ears" within the ministry. He confronted Dr. Sumrall directly as to why he had asked an underling to bring the message. Being the great statesman of the kingdom of God that he was, Brother Sumrall responded without a second's hesitation, "I don't have any underlings."

It was a wonderfully affirming moment as Brother Sumrall demonstrated the nature of God Himself who sees each of us as of ultimate worth. After all, didn't Jesus compare Himself to the very least of His brethren? (Matthew 25:40) Didn't he also say that if we desired to be of any significance in the kingdom we would have to become the servant (underling) of everyone else? (Mark 10:44) Of course, Jesus proved that this principle was more than just a great philosophy lesson when He took the towel and basin of water and washed the disciples' feet – a job that was universally reserved for the lowest servant "on the totem pole." (John 13:4-5)

> Let this mind be in you, which was also in Christ Jesus: Who, being in the form of God, thought it not robbery to be equal with God: But made himself of no reputation, and took upon him the form of a servant, and was made in the likeness of men: And being found in fashion as a man, he humbled himself, and became obedient unto death, even the death of the cross. (Philippians 2:3-8)

August 11

Sources of Happiness

I recently read an article in a secular publication on the sources of happiness in life. The article listed three significant ways to ensure joy and satisfaction:

Get connected to others

Give

Invest in experiences rather than things

As I read through the article, I wondered if the author had any relationship to church or the Christian faith because every principle he was suggesting is definitely part of the practice and lifestyle of a good Christian believer.

We understand that fulfillment in life has to do with being part of community and that we all find our significance as we take our place in the Body of Christ.

That there should be no schism in the body; but that the members should have the same care one for another. And whether one member suffer, all the members suffer with it; or one member be honoured, all the members rejoice with it. Now ye are the body of Christ, and members in particular. (I Corinthians 12:25-27)

We also realize that true happiness is not in what we can obtain for ourselves but in what we can bless others with.

I have shewed you all things, how that so labouring ye ought to support the weak, and to remember the words of the Lord Jesus, how he said, It is more blessed to give than to receive. (Acts 20:35)

Finally, we know that it is not what we have, but what we build into others' lives that gives us lasting satisfaction.

Lay not up for yourselves treasures upon earth, where moth and rust doth corrupt, and where thieves break through and steal: But lay up for yourselves treasures in heaven, where neither moth nor rust doth corrupt, and where thieves do not break through nor steal. (Matthew 6:19-20)

August 12

Both-And

As the evangelist reached across the table to take a roll from the breadbasket, one of the other preachers at the table commented about the expensive watch he was wearing, "Just think how many hungry children we could feed with the money you spent on that watch." Without even pausing to think of a response, the evangelist answered, "You don't know how many children I fed before I bought this watch!" Hopefully, their bantering was all good natured rather than a malicious attack and a hostile response, but the conversation points out a mentality that often hinders us from seeing the full picture: our "either-or" mentality. It is purely human reasoning that thinks that we must have either one thing or the other one. In God's wisdom, there is room for both the humanitarian outreach and the generous blessing on the evangelist. Jehovah is big enough to be a "both-and" rather than an "either-or" deity.

I was a guest speaker at a church that had two services each Sunday morning. The early service was more upbeat with guitars, drums, and contemporary music. The second service was more traditional with hymnals and organ music. It seemed like a perfect solution to the fact that this was a denominational church that had just begun to experience the charismatic move of the Spirit. It welcomed everyone at the place he was, not inhibiting the ones who wanted a more open worship experience or forcing out those who were a little slower to welcome the change. After the second service, one of the older gentlemen in the congregation asked to talk with me about the set up. His question was, "Where is unity?" He didn't understand how one church could welcome two different expressions of worship. I answered that the unity was in the fact that the same pastor preached the same message in both services and that the church was built on the undivided truth of the Word of God. Unfortunately, the "either-or" mentality soon won out, and the church went through a painful split over the music in the two services.

Let's expand to the God-sized mentality that has room for everyone and all of God's plans and purposes.

August 13

Africa

We have long operated under the impression that Africa is a "Dark Continent," home of Tarzan, elephants, monkeys, and savages. In fact, most of the rest of the world would be greatly surprised to discover exactly how wrong we are in our opinion of this great land. Actually, the African continent is richly blessed by God and is the world's most abundant source of uranium, tantalum, manganese, potash, cobalt, platinum, oil, gas, gold, and diamonds. In addition to the natural resources that the Lord planted in the soil, He also planted wisdom and skill in the hearts of the people of the continent. Picasso was at the end of his creativity until he discovered African art and began to draw from its inspiration. The singular little country of Kenya has produced more Olympic medalists in long- and medium-distance running than any other country in the world. The largest church in the world is Winners' Chapel in Nigeria with an inside seating capacity of fifty thousand and an outside overflow capacity of a quarter million. Some of the most in-depth biblical teaching I have ever heard has come from the lips of African pastors. Many of the greatest miracles of our time have taken place through African believers.

Certainly, much of Africa is still bound in superstition, ignorance, and poverty. In many areas, only about two percent of the pastors have any formal training at all – a wide-open door for false doctrine and superstition. But Africa is a continent on the move and is an awaking giant. Presently, the new birth rate is outpacing the birth rate with more people being born again each day than are being physically born. However, there is a powerful struggle going on for the souls of men in the continent of Africa. In the spiritual dimension, Islam is aggressively invading nation after nation bringing the hearts and minds of men under its influence. In the economic realm, despots have found ways to capture the control of nation after nation and suck their wealth from the people. In the physical arena, AIDS, cholera, and malaria are running rampant throughout the land. Africa is a jewel planted by God, but it needs our love and prayers to prevent it from being pawned to the devil.

August 14
Where the Rubber Meets the Road in Africa

In yesterday's ditty, I shared a little about Africa. Today, I'd like to follow through with just a few comments about what I've seen in my numerous trips to the various corners of the continent. I mentioned yesterday that in many parts of Africa, only about two percent of the ministers have any formal training. But there is also another problem that faces those who do have the opportunity to get a formal Bible education. I have found that there are many Bible schools where students can study for three years but not learn the practical aspects of ministry. They can graduate without knowing how to preach in their native language because they are only quoting what they read in their English textbooks. They may talk about the omnipotence of God to show off how much they know, but the village people they are preaching to have no idea what they are talking about. The people in the churches and in leadership all agree that they need more practical training in how to evangelize, lead people to Christ, and disciple them. In response to such a need, I have helped with the development of a simple and easily implemented discipleship curriculum and training program that can be presented without the need for a formal educational institution. The program gets the students directly into the Bible itself rather than into a set of theological books, and it stresses practical application of the biblical principles and immediate application of the truths taught. One young man who went through just one week of this training said that he gained more useful knowledge and hands-on application in that one week than he had learned in three full years at his church's Bible college. Most of the African pastors will never be able to attend a formal Bible school, so we need to bring the training to them. Even the ones who do attend a traditional college may still need to augment that formal training with a more practical and hands-on approach as presented in this discipleship curriculum.

The title of our course is "Be Fruitful and Multiply" – a great slogan and life approach for all of us, even if we never touch African soil.

August 15
What is Discipleship?

We shortchange the flock if all we do is take them through a discipleship program whereby they master a number of Christian precepts but miss the most important issue of intimacy with God. Discipleship is learning to walk with God and finding the path of life. (Psalm 16:11) A true discipleship program will teach the congregation how to follow the pastor in his walk with God rather than to simply follow his program. (I Corinthians 11:1) Such a personal walk with God will begin with wisdom and revelation. (Ephesians 1:17) This spiritual wisdom is not cramming the follower's heads with knowledge; rather, it is developing their hearts to know God. (I Kings 3:12)

Notice that Solomon had a wise and discerning heart, meaning that he had revelation as well as intelligence. The example that the Bible gives to demonstrate how Solomon had such wisdom is the story of Solomon's idea to cut a baby in half so as to settle the argument between the two women who claimed it. (I Kings 3:16-27) However, it is likely that he actually took the idea from the scripture where Moses instructed an ox be cut in half to settle a dispute between two men. (Exodus 21:35) If this is the case, then we see how true discipleship and wisdom work. Scriptural knowledge was the foundation, but insight and application made the teaching come alive in the specific situation he was facing.

True discipleship will lead the disciples to do what you do, but even better. (John 14:12) David killed one giant, but his disciples killed four. (II Samuel 21:22)

True discipleship will leave the mark of the master on the lives of the disciples. (Acts 4:13) Peter and John did things that made people recognize that they had been with Jesus.

> *Then said Jesus to those Jews which believed on him, If ye continue in my word, then are ye my disciples indeed.* (John 8:31)
> *By this shall all men know that ye are my disciples, if ye have love one to another.* (John 13:35)

August 16

Dislocated

Last winter, my youngest son took a serious fall while snowboarding at the Colorado ski resort. Fortunately, no bones were broken, but he did dislocate his shoulder, resulting in the loss of the use of his arm and a whole lot of pain. His arm didn't leave his body, but it became useless and the source of extreme discomfort for the rest of his body.

In the first chapter of I Timothy, Paul made reference to some individuals within the Body of Christ who had become just like my son's damaged shoulder.

> *Now the end of the commandment is charity out of a pure heart, and of a good conscience, and of faith unfeigned: From which some having swerved have turned aside unto vain jangling; Desiring to be teachers of the law; understanding neither what they say, nor whereof they affirm.*
> (verses 5-7)

The term that the apostle used for "turned aside" literally refers to a bone that is out of joint. That dislocated bone is still in the body, but it is dislocated or pulled away from where it ought to be so that it can no longer function as it was designed to. Although the dislocated member is not broken, it is definitely very painful and actually hampers the functioning of the undamaged parts of the body.

We should learn a lesson from the out-of-joint members and always strive to maintain our proper position and function with the Body of Christ.

> *But speaking the truth in love, may grow up into him in all things, which is the head, even Christ: From whom the whole body fitly joined together and compacted by that which every joint supplieth, according to the effectual working in the measure of every part, maketh increase of the body unto the edifying of itself in love.* (Ephesians 4:15-16)

August 17

Patience

I've always thought of patience as a rather passive attitude like sitting patiently for the waiter to serve your table or standing passively outside the ladies' room door at the mall while your wife takes her "sweet bippy time" inside. However, the other day, I ran across the actual Greek definition of the word – and it totally revamped my thinking! The Greek word for "patience" literally means to dig in your heels and refuse to budge. Wow! The word that I always assumed to be just a passive acceptance of things that you can't change suddenly became a very active word, demonstrating genuine fortitude! Reread the following verses with this new understanding and see how your faith will be lifted.

> *In your patience possess ye your souls.* (Luke 21:19)
>
> *And not only so, but we glory in tribulations also: knowing that tribulation worketh patience; And patience, experience; and experience, hope.* (Romans 5:3-4)
>
> *In all things approving ourselves as the ministers of God, in much patience, in afflictions, in necessities, in distresses,* (II Corinthians 6:4)
>
> *Strengthened with all might, according to his glorious power, unto all patience and longsuffering with joyfulness.* (Colossians 1:11)
>
> *The Lord direct your hearts into the love of God, and into the patient waiting for Christ.* (II Thessalonians 3:5)
>
> *Ye have need of patience, that, after ye have done the will of God, ye might receive the promise.* (Hebrews 10:36)
>
> *Seeing we also are compassed about with so great a cloud of witnesses, let us lay aside every weight, and the sin which doth so easily beset us, and let us run with patience the race that is set before us.* (Hebrews 12:1)
>
> *Knowing this, that the trying of your faith worketh patience. But let patience have her perfect work, that ye may be perfect and entire, wanting nothing.* (James 1:3-4)

August 18

Ministers of Christ

Let a man so account of us, as of the
ministers of Christ, and stewards of the
mysteries of God. (I Corinthians 4:1)

In this verse, Paul used a different word for "minister" from his normal vocabulary. In fact, this is one of only five times in the Bible where this term is used to speak of ministers. (Luke 1:2, 4:20; Acts 13:5, 26:16; I Corinthians 4:1) Generally, the term is translated as "officer," referring to a subordinate official. (Matthew 5:25; John 7:32, 7:45, 7:46, 18:3, 18:12, 18:18, 18:22, 18:36, 19:6; Acts 5:22, 5:26) On three occasions, it is translated with its most basic meaning of "servant." (Matthew 26:58; Mark 14:54, 14:65) It is from this servanthood definition that we are able to see the true intent of the statement about being the minister of Christ. The origin of the term he used can be found in the seafaring galleons of the Roman armada. The oarsmen, those assigned to row the boats, were called by this term, and this position was generally filled only by the lowest criminals.

Paul was making two points by his careful wording in this verse. The first, and most obvious, point was made by paralleling himself to the oarsmen who were treated as if they were the engine of the vessel. Such men were essentially no longer considered as being humans but simply a piece of machinery to power the boat. By using this term, Paul was declaring that he didn't consider his position as one of prestige, but one of extreme servanthood. The second point that he was communicating was that he did see his position as one of importance in that it was his place to see to it that the ship did remain in motion; therefore he would strive with everything within himself to accomplish the task given to him.

And I will very gladly spend and be spent for
you; though the more abundantly I love you,
the less I be loved. (II Corinthians 12:15)

We should all strive to have the same attitude of servanthood in whatever ministry the Lord has placed us.

August 19

Your Burden to Bear

I'm sure that we've all heard people talk about unfortunate or painful things in their lives and conclude the discussion with the resignation, "Well, I guess it is just my burden to bear." We can gain some interesting and helpful insights by flipping to Galatians chapter six to see what the Apostle Paul had to say about the topic.

> *Bear ye one another's burdens, and so fulfil the law of Christ. For if a man think himself to be something, when he is nothing, he deceiveth himself. But let every man prove his own work, and then shall he have rejoicing in himself alone, and not in another. For every man shall bear his own burden.* (verses 2-5)

In verse two, he directs us to help one another with our burdens; but in verse five, he commands each of us to carry our own burden. Is he contradicting himself? No! And the explanation is simple. Although we see only one term in English, there are two different Greek words used in this passage. The word for burden in verse two is *bastazo*, meaning a crushing load. In verse five, the word is *phortion*, meaning an expected allotment to carry. In essence, Paul was saying that we should jump in and assist when we see a brother struggling under an unusually heavy situation. On the other hand, we need to "buck up" and readily accept the normal challenges of life. The burdens that are a challenge to bear are mentioned several times in scripture, generally with the negative connotation of unrealistic expectations (Acts 15:28, II Corinthians 12:16, I Thessalonians 2:6, Revelation 2:24) However, there is one significant use of the term in II Corinthians 4:17 where Paul speaks of the "weight of glory" in reference to the presence of God in our lives. Wow! What a descriptive idea – the presence of God is the burden we are to bear, and God will give it to us in such liberality that it will become almost more than we can hold up under! In terms of the burden referred to in verse five, this is the burden that Jesus promised to be light. (Matthew 11:30)

August 20

Outer Darkness

Many shall come from the east and west, and shall sit down with Abraham, and Isaac, and Jacob, in the kingdom of heaven. But the children of the kingdom shall be cast out into outer darkness: there shall be weeping and gnashing of teeth. (Matthew 8:11-12)

And he saith unto him, Friend, how camest thou in hither not having a wedding garment? And he was speechless. Then said the king to the servants, Bind him hand and foot, and take him away, and cast him into outer darkness; there shall be weeping and gnashing of teeth. (Matthew 22:12-13)

His lord answered and said unto him, Thou wicked and slothful servant...And cast ye the unprofitable servant into outer darkness: there shall be weeping and gnashing of teeth. (Matthew 25:26-30)

All the above references mention the horrible punishment of casting a victim into outer darkness where there is weeping and gnashing of teeth. From the history of the time of the New Testament, we understand that these are references to the practice of tossing suspected criminals out on the garbage heap to be eaten by lions that scavenged in the dump at night. When a victim was eaten alive, it was considered proof positive of his guilt. If he was not eaten, he would bear the emotional and physical scars of the ordeal for the rest of his life. The trauma of hearing the sounds of animals prowling in the darkness and the cuts and bruises he would inflict upon himself in his desperate attempt to free himself from his fetters would leave their indelible marks on his psyche and body. The reference to gnashing teeth speaks of the fact that the victims would often literally wear down their teeth from terror of the experience.

These terms are also used to give us a glimpse at the anguish of those who will spend their eternities in hell.

August 21

Quick Insights from the Greek – Part I

In I Corinthians 10:13, Paul said, *There hath no temptation taken you but such as is common to man: but God is faithful, who will not suffer you to be tempted above that ye are able; but will with the temptation also make a way to escape, that ye may be able to bear it.* The term he used for "way of escape" literally means a way to walk out. Most of us feel that we have to struggle to get out of temptation. But the truth is that we can simply walk away from it if we determine to do so. In the Lord's Prayer, Jesus taught us to pray that we not be led into temptation because He knew that our feet can go both directions – into temptation and out of it.

Colossians 3:15-16 reads, *And let the peace of God rule in your hearts, to the which also ye are called in one body; and be ye thankful. Let the word of Christ dwell in you richly in all wisdom; teaching and admonishing one another in psalms and hymns and spiritual songs, singing with grace in your hearts to the Lord.* There are several significant truths we can glean from looking at the Greek wording of these verses. The term "rule" means to call the shots like an umpire in a ball game. The term for "richly" speaks of giving a lavish welcome similar to "rolling out the red carpet." If the Word of God dwells in us with this kind of exuberant welcome, it will umpire our thoughts to help us win the game.

Paul's choice of words in Philippians 3:12-13, *Not as though I had already attained, either were already perfect: but I follow after, if that I may apprehend that for which also I am apprehended of Christ Jesus. Brethren, I count not myself to have apprehended: but this one thing I do, forgetting those things which are behind, and reaching forth unto those things which are before,* comes from the business world. When he says that he counts himself not to have apprehended, the word he uses is an accounting term meaning to make an accurate assessment. He didn't leave his destiny to chance; instead, he took careful examination of every detail in order to ensure that he was totally accountable.

August 22
Quick Insights from the Greek – Part II

Ephesians 6:16, *Above all, taking the shield of faith, wherewith ye shall be able to quench all the fiery darts of the wicked,* holds some revealing insights when studied in the original language. The shield referred to here was one that was covered with leather. In order to keep this leather from becoming dried out and brittle, it had to be regularly rubbed with oil. The Greek term for this application of oil is the source of our term "anointed." In order for our shield of faith to be effective, we must remain anointed. Another step in preparation for battle was that the shield would be soaked with water so that it would extinguish the flaming arrows fired at it rather than catching fire when struck by them. Using the symbolism of the water of the Word (Ephesians 5:26), we can readily see the significance of being immersed in the truth of the Word of God for our shields to be effective. One other truth we can pick up from the Greek wording here is found in the phrase "be able," which literally means to be dynamically empowered. Wow! What a promise of victory if we properly use our shield of faith.

The perilous times referred to in II Timothy 3:1, *This know also, that in the last days perilous times shall come,* speak of a fierceness like a demon-possessed man. The end times are not just difficult; they are deranged and out of control. Just one simple indicator can be seen in the fact that the world has seen twenty-nine million Christians martyred since the beginning of the Twentieth Century.

When Paul wrote to his protégé, *Thou therefore, my son, be strong in the grace that is in Christ Jesus* (II Timothy 2:1), his wording was that he should be strong <u>by means</u> of the grace that is in Christ Jesus. Unfortunately, many Christians use the grace of God as an excuse to be weak, saying that the grace of God will cover their failures. On the contrary, the grace of God is intended to make us able to overcome our propensity for failing.

First Corinthians 14:40 tells us that all things should be done decently and in order, meaning with honest motives and courteously waiting for our turn, not thrown together.

August 23
Quick Insights from the Greek – Part III

In II Timothy 4:2, Paul left the commandment that we should *Preach the word; be instant in season, out of season; reprove, rebuke, exhort with all longsuffering and doctrine.* When he said to be ready *in season and out of season,* his choice of words spoke of good times and bad times.

The Greek wording for the statement that grace abounds speaks of a river overflowing its banks. Notice how much more clarity this idea adds to the following verses:

Moreover the law entered, that the offence might abound. But where sin abounded, grace did much more abound. (Romans 5:20)

Therefore, as ye abound in every thing, in faith, and utterance, and knowledge, and in all diligence, and in your love to us, see that ye abound in this grace also. (II Corinthians 8:7)

And God is able to make all grace abound toward you; that ye, always having all sufficiency in all things, may abound to every good work. (II Corinthians 9:8)

The Greek word for "intercession" implies a rescue operation like the Coast Guard's response to a sinking ship or the fire department's heroic attempt to pluck stranded children from a flame-engulfed building. Read the following verses with this new insight:

Likewise the Spirit also helpeth our infirmities: for we know not what we should pray for as we ought: but the Spirit itself maketh intercession for us with groanings which cannot be uttered. (Romans 8:26)

And he that searcheth the hearts knoweth what is the mind of the Spirit, because he maketh intercession for the saints according to the will of God. (Romans 8:27)

Who is he that condemneth? It is Christ that died, yea rather, that is risen again, who is even at the right hand of God, who also maketh intercession for us. (Romans 8:34)

Wherefore he is able also to save them to the uttermost that come unto God by him, seeing he ever liveth to make intercession for them. (Hebrews 7:25)

Quick Insights from the Greek – Part IV

In the Sermon on the Mount, Jesus gave us some important instructions about prayer, *But thou, when thou prayest, enter into thy closet, and when thou hast shut thy door, pray to thy Father which is in secret; and thy Father which seeth in secret shall reward thee openly.* (Matthew 6:6) However, in addition to everything that we can understand from the English version, we can gain at least one new level of insight by studying the Greek wording. The closet referred to here is not just a private area; it is the secret place where you hide your most valuable possessions – essentially a safe. It may also refer to the bedroom, your place of private intimacy. In other words, it is a place reserved for the most valuable and private things in life. This is where our prayers should be prayed because they are definitely our most treasured and intimate times.

Second Timothy 2:11-13, *It is a faithful saying: For if we be dead with him, we shall also live with him: If we suffer, we shall also reign with him: if we deny him, he also will deny us: If we believe not, yet he abideth faithful: he cannot deny himself,* is written with the cadence of a song. It is likely that it was actually a pre-existing song that Paul incorporated into his epistle. If so, it was probably a hymn sung by the early Christians encouraging one another not to give up the faith, even in the face of martyrdom.

In John 16:8, Jesus told us about the work of the Holy Spirit, *And when he is come, he will reprove the world of sin, and of righteousness, and of judgment.* It's interesting to note that He said that His role was just as significant in reproving the world of righteousness as in reproving it of sin. The Holy Spirit examines all our actions – good and bad – to determine the motivation through which we are doing them. Paul explained in the thirteenth chapter of I Corinthians that all our good deeds are profitless unless done through the motivation of love and Jesus blatantly said that He will reject even those who were able to prophesy and cast out devils if they are not operating with the proper relationship to Him.

August 25
Quick Insights from the Greek – Part V

Philippians 4:7 tells us, *And the peace of God, which passeth all understanding, shall keep your hearts and minds through Christ Jesus.* The word for "keep," means to fortify or protect, comes from the idea of the gate monitor at a city gate. His responsibility, not unlike the TSA agents in an airport or the security personnel at any building, was to make sure that dangerous people did not gain access to the city. God gives us peace that serves in the same role for our minds and hearts. When we get an uneasy feeling about something, it may be just the peace of God identifying a potential threat.

Reading the Greek wording of John 1:5, *And the light shineth in darkness; and the darkness comprehended it not,* adds a whole new dimension to the verse because the statement that the darkness did not comprehend the light can be interpreted to say that the darkness was not able to suppress the light.

The Greek term for "bears" in I Corinthians 13:7, *Beareth all things, believeth all things, hopeth all things, endureth all things,* means to cover a problem like a roof covers a house. In other words, love will make sure that others' faults and weaknesses are not exposed and vulnerable.

In Philippians 1:23, Paul discusses the dilemma he faced wishing that he could go ahead to heaven and the need to stay on earth to continue his ministry, *For I am in a strait betwixt two, having a desire to depart, and to be with Christ; which is far better.* The terminology he used to speak of his desire to depart and be with the Lord literally means that he had passionate enthusiasm about the matter. When he said that he was considering departing, he used a military term describing a ship setting sail or an army breaking camp to start on an expedition. Sailing is the purpose that the ship was built for, and expeditions are why an army exists. What Paul was saying is that dying is the whole purpose for living. Unfortunately, we fail to see this and wind up living our lives with a distorted view of the balance between life and death.

Quick Insights from the Greek – Part VI

Most of us can readily quote Hebrews 11:6, *But without faith it is impossible to please him: for he that cometh to God must believe that he is, and that he is a rewarder of them that diligently seek him.* However, until we recognize the meaning of the wording "without faith," we won't grasp the full intent of the verse. The terminology used here means outside of faith, not being devoid of faith as we generally think. What the author was trying to communicate isn't that we might not have faith but that we might actually have it and still live our lives without incorporating it. Just like you might own a house but get soaked to the bone in the rain because you were standing in the yard when the storm came up. So it is with our faith, we must not only have faith, we must live and function in that faith.

James 5:16 directs us, *Confess your faults one to another, and pray one for another, that ye may be healed. The effectual fervent prayer of a righteous man availeth much.* That's good advice, and it carries a great promise; however, there's still a bit more to be mined out of the passage. The word for "confess" literally means to blurt out our faults. In other words, not to bashfully try to hide them. Faults, by the way are the times when we accidentally bumped into something – not just deliberate sins and rebellion.

The Greek term translated "take no thought" and "the cares of life" is the same word also translated as "anxious." See how this truth changes your view of these verses:

> *Be careful for nothing; but in every thing by prayer and supplication with thanksgiving let your requests be made known unto God.* (Philippians 4:6)
> *And that which fell among thorns are they, which, when they have heard, go forth, and are choked with cares and riches and pleasures of this life, and bring no fruit to perfection.* (Luke 8:14)
> *Therefore I say unto you, Take no thought for your life, what ye shall eat, or what ye shall drink; nor yet for your body, what ye shall put on. Is not the life more than meat, and the body than raiment?* (Matthew 6:25)

August 27
Quick Insights from the Greek – Part VII
Paul wrote in II Timothy 1:3, *I thank God, whom I serve from my forefathers with pure conscience, that without ceasing I have remembrance of thee in my prayers night and day.* His word for "remembrance" implied a physical reminder such as a written note or a statue. Today, we might think of having a prayer list or a visual image such as a picture of the people we want to remember in prayer.

In II Timothy 2:2, *And the things that thou hast heard of me among many witnesses, the same commit thou to faithful men, who shall be able to teach others also*, Paul stressed that the gospel message be entrusted to faithful men because this book was written just after the persecution under Nero had caused many church leaders to abandon the faith. The gospel must be planted in the hearts of those who will never swerve, no matter how bad the situation may become.

The due season spoken of in Galatians 6:9, *And let us not be weary in well doing: for in due season we shall reap, if we faint not*, is not a set time. It is a time of reaping that depends upon the maturity of the crop, which in turn depends on the climate conditions. The underlying message here is that we can actually pray for favorable conditions so that the seed we have planted can ripen to a full and bountiful harvest.

Our salvation is referred to as a helmet in at least two New Testament passages. However, we generally overlook much of the significance of these references because we think of the helmets we are familiar with today – a construction worker's hardhat, a football player's helmet, or a combat soldier's headgear. These all serve totally functional roles as protection for the wearer. However, the helmet referenced in these passages was the soldier's identity in that it displayed the colors of his regiment and his position within the troop:

> *Take the helmet of salvation...* (Ephesians 6:17)
>
> *Let us...be sober, putting on the breastplate of faith and love; and for an helmet, the hope of salvation.* (I Thessalonians 5:8)

August 28
Quick Insights from the Greek – Part VIII
We all know the words of Jesus, *Blessed are the meek: for they shall inherit the earth.* (Matthew 5:5) However, most of us associate meekness with weakness. In reality, the Greek term for "meek" refers to strength under control like a tamed animal. A scene in the movie <u>Water for Elephants</u> depicted this image so clearly when the elephant wanted a drink of lemonade from the nearby lemonade stand. When she thought no one was looking, she simply pulled up the stake that she was chained to, walked over to the lemonade stand, helped herself to the refreshment, walked back to her position, and reinserted the stake into its original hole. We, as Christians, have immeasurable strength just like that pachyderm; however, we must also learn to control our strength and use it only when appropriate. It is this kind of strength under control that will guarantee our inheritance.

In Matthew 11:28, Jesus invited, *Come unto me, all ye that labour and are heavy laden, and I will give you rest.* His term for "heavy laden" refers to having a heavy backpack for a <u>long</u> journey. His term for the easy yoke refers to a delightful journey. In other words, our lives without Jesus will be a long, arduous haul, but we will find joy in working with Jesus.

John 10:10 is a popular verse, *The thief cometh not, but for to steal, and to kill, and to destroy: I am come that they might have life, and that they might have it more abundantly.* However, when we dig a little beneath the surface, we find some intriguing concepts. The word Jesus uses to speak of the thief refers to a kleptomaniac, an individual who can't resist the impulse to steal. The word for "kill" means to sacrifice something that is precious. The word for "destroy" is from the word *Apollyon*, the title for the devil in Revelation 9:11.

In II Corinthians 5:17, *Therefore if any man be in Christ, he is a new creature: old things are passed away; behold, all things are become new*, the concept of being a new creature is that of being an original creation, unlike anything that has ever existed before. It is similar to the original creation of the world when everything was created from nothing already in existence.

August 29

Quick Insights from the Greek – Part IX

Most of us know that the word for "transformed" in Romans 12:2, *And be not conformed to this world: but be ye transformed by the renewing of your mind, that ye may prove what is that good, and acceptable, and perfect, will of God*, is the Greek word *metomorhpus* from which we get the English term "metamorphosis." However, most of us would be surprised to find that this word is used only four times in the New Testament. Twice it refers to the transfiguration of Christ when the glory of God shone through Him so brightly that He actually emitted light. (Matthew 17:2, Mark 9:2) The other occurrence of this term is in II Corinthians 3:18, *But we all, with open face beholding as in a glass the glory of the Lord, are changed into the same image from glory to glory, even as by the Spirit of the Lord.* Taking all these references into account, we can understand that the ultimate goal of a Christian is to be so filled with the glory of God that it will show right through our faces as well.

First Peter 5:8 warns us, *Be sober, be vigilant; because your adversary the devil, as a roaring lion, walketh about, seeking whom he may devour.* The expression applied to the devil, calling him our adversary, is a legal term used to refer to a lawyer who accuses you in court. Thank God that we have the Holy Spirit as our advocate (John 14:16) to stand up as a defense on our side. Our adversary is bloodthirsty in his attacks upon us in that the term for "devour" literally means to consume to the point of even drinking the blood. Thank God that we have our victory through the blood of the Lamb. (Revelation 12:11)

The word for "guide" in John 16:13, *When he, the Spirit of truth, is come, he will guide you into all truth: for he shall not speak of himself; but whatsoever he shall hear, that shall he speak: and he will shew you things to come*, means that the Holy Spirit will take us on the shortest and safest route.

When Paul, in II Timothy 3:17, declared, *The man of God may be perfect, throughly furnished unto all good works*, he used a nautical word that refers to a ship that is so well equipped that it can sail any place, not just in the safe harbors.

August 30
Quick Insights from the Greek – Part X

The "wiles" of the devil in Ephesians 6:11, *Put on the whole armour of God, that ye may be able to stand against the wiles of the devil,* is the Greek word *methodos.* It doesn't take a scholar to recognize the fact that this word is the source of our English word "methods." But the thing that we don't recognize immediately is that the term literally means "with a road, not driving aimlessly." In other words, the enemy's attacks against us are well thought through. Because they are so well masterminded, we could never be able to stand up against them without the special help and protection we gain through the armor of God.

When Paul wrote to us about *casting down imaginations, and every high thing that exalteth itself against the knowledge of God, and bringing into captivity every thought to the obedience of Christ* in II Corinthians 10:5, he used a carefully selected term to express the idea of bringing thoughts into captivity. The term specifically means to arrest with a sharp sword pressed into the back. Of course, we know that the sharp sword we have as Christians is the Word of God. (Ephesians 6:17, Hebrews 4:12) To take control of our thoughts, we must aggressively and forcibly "press" the Word of God against each thought until it is afraid to squirm.

The Greek words used in Hebrews 12:15, *Looking diligently lest any man fail of the grace of God; lest any root of bitterness springing up trouble you, and thereby many be defiled,* give us insights into two different areas of truth. The word used to communicate "looking diligently" is the same word used for "bishop" in other passages. With this in mind, we can gain a better understanding of the role of a bishop. He is one who looks diligently over the souls of the people and the affairs of the church. The second truth revealed in this verse comes from the Greek word for "trouble." Literally translated, it means to stalk like a prowler stalking our property or a predator stalking its prey. If we allow a root of bitterness to spring up due to a lack of diligent oversight, it will hound, haunt, menace, and lurk after us until it captures and defiles us.

August 31
Quick Insights from the Greek – Part XI

In Mark 16:15 when Jesus told His disciples to go into all the world and preach the gospel to every creature, He used the word *kerusso* to express the concept of preaching. This term is the origin of our English word "crux," meaning the essence of a matter. The background of this word has to do with the king's messenger who knows the king's message, personality, lifestyle, and can be his <u>total</u> representative. We are to do more than just deliver sermons; we are to deliver a total representation of the Lord.

The Greek wording of Acts 2:6 indicates that the audience on the Day of Pentecost heard the disciples speaking in their very dialects, not just in their national languages. There were one hundred twenty believers in the Upper Room and sixteen languages being spoken. It is likely that each of these believers was speaking a distinct dialect so that every person present was able to identify with the speaker as easily as if they were from the same village.

Acts 2:7 says that the hearers were amazed and marveled at the phenomenon of hearing the disciples speaking in tongues. The wording of the sentence actually says that they were "beside themselves" with amazement at what they heard.

First John 3:9 declares that anyone who is born of God will not commit sin because the seed of God remains in him, and that he actually cannot sin because he is born of God. Since everything reproduces after its own kind, the DNA of God will produce a life inside of the believer that looks like the sinless life of God. Just as we look like our earthly parents without even trying, we will effortlessly take on the nature of our Heavenly Father. However, if we have an habitual lifestyle of sinning, the issue is that we have deliberately overruled the power of the seed.

The Greek word for "longsuffering" in the New Testament is derived from *makrothumia*, which is used in reference to a candle with a long wick to keep on burning. The word "macaroni" (long noodle) is derived from this term.

Labor Day

In honor of the fact that today is set aside as a special time to appreciate the great working class that makes society run, I'd like to look at a few verses that help us understand the divine perspective on work.

First of all, let's remember that Ephesians 2:9 clearly teaches us that our salvation is not through works, *lest any man should boast.* However, once we have attained salvation, there is work that is expected of us in the kingdom of God. Just a couple chapters later in the same book, Paul makes it clear that work is involved in being a part of the kingdom. (Ephesians 4:12) Jesus Himself said that He was expecting us to work as part of our role as believers:

> *Verily, verily, I say unto you, He that believeth on me, the works that I do shall he do also; and greater works than these shall he do; because I go unto my Father.* (John 14:12)

However, in John 5:17, we get a glimpse at what is really expected when Jesus said, *My Father worketh hitherto, and I work.* Jesus made this statement in answer to the accusations that He had violated the Law by healing the lame man at the Pool of Bethesda on the Sabbath. Jesus' rebuttal was that it was the Father who healed the man; therefore, any work that He had done was really the Father at work. What a wonderful way to understand our role as men and women in the kingdom of God. Yes, we have lots to do and much to accomplish; however, if we are doing things God's way, we really aren't working because our efforts are nothing more than manifestations of the Lord working through us. It is God at work and we are simply partnering with Him as hands and feet through which He can operate.

When we learn that principle, all stress and pressure to perform evaporates. Our only task is to be sensitive to hearing His direction as to how to release His presence in our environment.

September 2
Why Mosquitoes?

Before I actually discuss why God created mosquitoes, I have to share with you a very interesting fact about these little pests. They are actually very selective about the people they choose to annoy. Certain people secrete a scent that attracts them while others seem to actually repel them. Although the story is about leeches rather than mosquitoes, I had an experience once that verified this principle very clearly. After hiking through some tall grass in Nepal, one of the guys in my group noticed that he had a leech attached to his ankle. When he pulled up his pant leg to remove the uninvited guest, he discovered that both his legs were covered with these bloodsuckers. No one else in our group had even one of the parasites. Apparently, he exuded an inviting scent that summoned the leeches to dinner.

Well, back to the mosquitoes. God created them to feed the fish. Their unwelcomed role as bloodsuckers and their annoying buzz around your ears when you're trying to sleep are apparently results of the Fall. Another result of the Fall is the very fact that fish eat them. It seems that prior to the Fall, all animals were herbivores, eating only plants. Mosquitoes didn't bite Adam and Eve, and fish didn't dine on mosquito larvae. But the fascinating point here is that God had a plan in advance even before the fish would need their non-vegetarian dietetic supplement. Even more astonishing is that God's plan couldn't have been set in motion without the devil's having a hand in it. Wow! Even mosquitoes prove the sovereignty and all-knowing wisdom of God.

In John chapter nine, we read the story of a man who was born blind. When the disciples asked whose sin had caused the man's disability, Jesus answered that it happened so that the works of God's glory could be displayed. God did not blind the man, but His ultimate purpose was fulfilled even through the devil's cruel attempt to hurt him and his family.

September 3

Christians and Money

Someone once divided the Christian world into three categories based on their relationship to money: "Bless Me Christians" are those who want God to give them everything; "Work Ethic Christians" are those who expect that they actually earn what they get from God, even if their work is simply exerting faith (they establish such regulations around manifesting faith that they turn it into a work); and "Wealth is Evil Christians" who actually contradict their own theology in that they will work hard to earn money even while preaching against what they call the "Prosperity Doctrine."

I think that we can see error in all three of these categories in that they are all off center in one aspect or another. The Bless Me Christians have certainly tapped into the truth of God's Word in terms of God's desire to bless His children and have an understanding of the promises that are available to them. Unfortunately, they are all too often motivated by greed rather than the true nature of God in their quest for these blessings. The Work Ethic Christians have come to understand a second principle about biblical prosperity – that although everything we obtain is a gracious gift from God, we are expected to practice good stewardship as we put forth our efforts to maintain and increase the resources God has given us. Unfortunately, these believers who have put their hands to the plow can let the pendulum swing too far the other way from the Bless Me Christians who live with their hands out open, waiting for them to be filled. The "Wealth is Evil Christians" are obviously in error in denying much of what the Bible teaches about God's desire to bless and prosper His children; however, we must give them credit for one thing – their desire to correct the error of the greediness of the Bless Me Christians. In fact, it is likely that there would never be any Wealth is Evil Christians if there were no abuses in the camp of the Bless Me Christians. So, where does this analysis of the categories of Christians lead us? To the necessity of taking the good from each category and rejecting the bad as we develop our own faith.

September 4

Filthy Rich

I'm sure that we've all heard the term "filthy rich" and have, therefore, had at least some inkling of the suggestion that that having money is evil. Of course, we've also heard the saying that money is the root of all evil. Even those of us who know our Bibles well enough to understand that it is the love of money, not money itself, that is the source of evil (I Timothy 6:10) still have some misgivings about how money might be a source of corruption.

Actually, there is nothing inherently evil about money. The evil is with the person who is holding it. How much wealth can be evil varies with several factors related to the person who is in control of the money. These factors include character, calling, and culture.

The character of the person is, of course, the major factor. It has been said that every man has his price, implying that every person will sell out his convictions at some point. The person with an evil character will commit a crime for unimaginably small compensation while others will hold out for higher stakes. I personally believe that there are those who cannot be "bought" for any price, but we can see the general principle at play that one's character dictates how much money it takes to corrupt.

The second factor is calling. This means that different people need different amounts of money to flow through their hands because they have different purposes in life for the money that they control. If an individual is called to run a large business or ministry, he can have millions of dollars passing through his hands each year without a second thought. He is focused on how that money is to be allocated to fulfill the mission he has set out to accomplish. Those with lesser callings and visions can be more readily tempted to misappropriate funds when extra money flows their way because that extra money is beyond the scope of their calling.

The third aspect is the culture in which he are working. Some cultures are so rife with corruption that it is impossible to put resources into the system without it becoming corrupted.

September 5
Questions to Ask Your Money

We've all heard the statement, "Money talks." Of course, the idea behind that statement is that those who have money will also have influence. But today, I'd like to think of that statement in another light – that of what your money actually says directly to you. Oh yes, it does talk, and it tells us a lot – more about ourselves than about itself or the economy. Therefore, I'd like to suggest that we develop a bank of questions (pardon the pun) to ask our money so that we can get its input on some significant areas of our lives:

1) Are you helping or hindering me in my efforts to win people and disciple them for Christ?
2) Can I make my decisions concerning what God wants me to do without letting you cloud my thinking?
3) Do I have you or do you have me?
4) Are you working as hard for me as I worked for you?
5) If I lose you, will you send your ghost back to haunt me with fears of how you got away or what I would do with you if you had not escaped from my hand?
6) Are there more of you where you came from?
7) Can you do more for someone else than you are doing for me?
8) What is your real value? Is it your intrinsic worth of what you are in and of yourself or is it what you can do for me, for others, and for the kingdom of God?
9) Are you loyal to me? If I send you out on an errand, will you come back? If I send you out with a purpose to accomplish, will you make it happen and send your benefits back into my life?
10) Do I have as much influence over you as you do over me?

September 6
Quick Thoughts about You and Your Money

God wants you to live in a way that makes you happy and complete as long as you put Him first in everything. We have a nice home, but we rarely have it to ourselves because we are always using it as a tool of expressing hospitality to others.

Romans 13:8 tells us to be up-to-date on paying our bills.

God is more interested in changing us into His image than in feeding us.

Gratitude for what He has already given us is a great part of our learning His ways and character.

Our pocketbooks can get our attention even when we ignore the clanging alarms of our conscience. God sometimes withholds provision until we repent and seek Him. Maybe we should add an addendum to all our prayers: "God, don't provide this request until I have learned the lesson You need to teach me."

Often, we notice God's daily provision for us only when it stops.

Learn to be thankful for all provision.

Don't blame others for your need.

God's provisions are both-and, not either-or. The fact that one man is rich does not cause another to be poor. There is enough to go around.

Creative ideas are a primary source of creating wealth. We are created in the image of God, the original idea man!

Natural resources are not wealth in and of themselves. Oil was worthless until someone invented the internal combustion engine.

There are seven relationships we can have with money:

Earn it
Spend it
Save it
Invest it
Share it
Waste it
Lose it through greed and covetousness

September 7
African Wisdom for Believers

The following short snippets of wisdom came from my good friend, Dr. Tunde Bakare of Nigeria:

It is one thing to hear the voice of the Lord and another to become that voice.

A voice out of timing is just a noise. (Jeremiah 46:17)

If you close your eyes while bad people pass by, they will still be closed when good people come along.

Every storm in life reveals the real storm inside of you.

If God makes a covenant with us, He becomes totally responsible for the outcome – even if we mess up.

When you enter a new territory, pave the way for others.

How would you live if you had no limitations? Remember: limitations are learned.

Those who see everything as spiritual warfare must remember that if everything is a struggle, they have no energy to enjoy the victory.

God will measure the man, not the ministry.

If you can't envision what God intends for you to have, you won't be willing to pay the price to get it.

Negative emotions are holes in your vessel that let the oil of God leak out.

If you are born again into the stature of Christ, all else is just a gift to help you mature in it.

You can't advance the kingdom of God by looking back at old institutions any more than you can drive a car by looking in the rear view mirror. John the Baptist was the *beginning of the gospel of Jesus Christ* (Mark 1:1) and he broke the pattern from his very naming ceremony. Instead of receiving a name that looked backward to his heritage, he was given a new name for a new generation.

Denominational doctrines tell you where they want you to stop growing spiritually.

A law without consequences is only advice.

Laziness is on the same plane with gluttony and drunkenness in the Bible. (Proverbs 23:21)

September 8
African Wisdom for the Church
The following are observations on the church from the great Nigerian church leader, Dr. Tunde Bakare:

The church must be an oasis in the wilderness of confusion, an intensive care unit of the spirit in a world of wounded soldiers, and a center for promoting revelatory truth.

If the fountain from which ministry flows is polluted, everyone who drinks is poisoned.

David was anointed three times before he realized that he had a wicked heart. (I Samuel 16:13, II Samuel 2:4, II Samuel 5:3)

Joshua did not have an inheritance for himself; it was given to him by the volition of the people. (Joshua 19:49)

America serves the spirit of amusement and entertainment. We can't take the city the unless we pull down the spirit of the city. Unfortunately, we have been possessed by the same spirit.

What our fathers cast out, we counsel.

Too many ministers believe in God's selective integrity: when others do it, God judges them; when I do it, God understands.

The giants in the land in Genesis corrupted the land; today's giants (corporations) are still corrupting the land.

The church today needs a discipleship process, not just a discipleship program.

What the world says about you is your reputation; what God says about you is your character.

God gives us the power to get wealth, not wealth itself. (Deuteronomy 8:18)

Don't be a plastic saint; people need to know that you have real problems. If Paul and Jesus needed prayer; so do you.

Why do we talk about discipling nations when we can't even disciple the members in our churches?

It's okay to walk while preaching and praying because the eye of the Lord goes to and fro. (II Chronicles 16:9)

Ministers must learn to make disciples, not devotees.

September 9
Quick Thoughts that Deserve Careful Contemplation

Is my life a justification of the price that was paid for it?

To what degree is my life a reflection of my potential?

Am I a challenge to or an advertisement for the kingdom?

The church must teach people to follow Him as part of its follow-up program.

We must not indiscriminately "blab" about our revelations from God. He has a select audience who will receive them as from Him. Nehemiah kept his revelation a secret except for certain people. (Nehemiah 2:12)

Keep your dream in prayer until you have the place of influence to make it come to pass. God gave a little slave girl an audience with Naaman's wife so she could share her idea about the captain's healing. (II Kings 5:1-4) He gave Joseph an audience with the butler who took him to the king of Egypt. (Genesis 41:9-16) When we have something to say, God will give us a platform from which to say it.

Good fathers not only provide for their children; they also answer their children's questions. Learning to have faith in God means learning to ask questions. Job was not afraid to ask questions. His whole book is full of questions, and it also contains the record of a powerful encounter with God when He showed up to answer the queries of His servant.

The human spirit is the primary source for creation of wealth. True creation of wealth is to meet human need, not selfish ambitions.

Israel bankrupted Egypt by taking away all its skilled laborers. Even though they suffered under slavery, they became the artisans necessary to make society work.

Don't use your health to gain wealth only to spend the wealth you have gained to reclaim the health you lost in the process.

Paul's credentials were not about his degrees but about his lifestyle. (I Thessalonians 1:5; Acts 20:26-27, 20:32)

There is water inside a coconut even before the rains come.

September 10

Stopping the Sun

I recently heard a preacher minister on the story of how Joshua stopped the sun over Gibeon and made the moon stand still over the Valley of Ajalon. (Joshua 10:12-14) He was stressing the fact that God often intervenes in our lives and does things that seem contradictory to the natural order of things just so that He can help us through our problems. To that, I said, "Amen!"

Once, I had gone to Sri Lanka to minister at a youth camp. Upon arriving, I was informed that the men in charge of the camp were on the verge of calling off the event. I, of course, objected and insisted that I wasn't about to come all the way to Sri Lanka for nothing. They explained that there had been a lengthy draught and that there was no water available at the camp. Without water, there was no way to cook and clean for the several hundred teens who were scheduled to come to the camp. I asked for one day's delay in making the decision and asked the Lord for a solution. That night, one of the strongest storms I have ever experienced struck the island nation. The next morning, the report came in that the cisterns at the camp were full and actually overflowing! The sun might not have stood still, but a draught turned into a world-class rainstorm overnight.

On another mission, we were taking musical instruments and sound equipment to a church in Kenya when the customs officer decided that we needed to pay a heavy import duty to get the equipment into the country. We argued with him that the instruments were going to a church and should, therefore, be exempt under a clause for religious organizations. He wasn't about to budge. That is until his superior officer came through the airport on his way to the restroom. Seeing that we were having a bit of a disagreement, he stopped by the customs station to see what was happening. When we explained, he waved us through without our having to pay a cent in taxes. The moon may not have stood in place that day, but God caused the right man to have to go to the bathroom at exactly the right minute!

September 11

The Power of Intercession

I woke up one morning while ministering in Nigeria with terrible back pain. Something had somehow gotten twisted out of joint, resulting in excruciating pain when I lay down, stood up, or sat in a chair. In other words, there was absolutely no comfortable position for me. To top it all off, I had a full day of teaching ahead of me at the conference where I was ministering. I fired off a quick email to one of our ministry partners who had promised to pray daily for me during the trip, and, gritting my teeth, headed into the conference for the day's sessions. The pain continued throughout the day until exactly 2 PM when it suddenly disappeared. When I got back to the hotel room that evening, I emailed my friend to ask if she had received the email and prayed for me at 7 AM, the time in Colorado that would have corresponded to the time of my healing in Africa. She promptly replied that it had been exactly 7 AM when she had read her email and prayed for me. Prayer and faith know no limitations in distance. The only limitation is our obedience. When she was obedient to pray, the healing came, even though I was thousands of miles away.

I've heard many other exciting testimonies of healings and deliverances that happened exactly when people on the other side of the world took time to pray. Missionaries Bud Sickler, Reinhart Bonke, and Lester Sumrall all had miraculous healings that occurred at the very hour when someone at home prayed for them. One missionary was surrounded by seventeen angels to protect him from armed bandits at the exact moment when seventeen men in the prayer group in his home church were interceding for his safety. The amazing point in all these stories is that they all happened without the knowledge that the missionaries were in need of prayer. God prompted the intercessors to pray and then miraculously intervened when they obeyed.

> *As thou hast believed, so be it done unto thee. And his servant was healed in the selfsame hour.* (Matthew 8:13)

September 12
Fellowship

I recently read something disturbing about two of the great Christian leaders in England during the late nineteenth century. Both William Booth and Charles Spurgeon lived in the city of London yet they never had fellowship together. Known as the "prince of preachers," Spurgeon pastored the Metropolitan Tabernacle, the largest church of the time with seating for five thousand and standing room for an additional one thousand. William Booth founded the Salvation Army that continues as a major evangelical force in the world until today. However, these two great men never fellowshipped together because Booth refused to accept Spurgeon because he smoked. Seeing how much they accomplished individually, I can't help but wonder what might have happened had the two men joined their faith together. Remember the principle that if one can chase a thousand, two can chase ten thousand.

Certainly, we must set standards to regulate our lives else we can become "guilty by association" in certain activities. However, we must be ever so careful not to reject the rest of the Body of Christ that we so vitally need.

But now are they many members, yet but one body. And the eye cannot say unto the hand, I have no need of thee: nor again the head to the feet, I have no need of you. Nay, much more those members of the body, which seem to be more feeble, are necessary: And those members of the body, which we think to be less honourable, upon these we bestow more abundant honour; and our uncomely parts have more abundant comeliness. For our comely parts have no need: but God hath tempered the body together, having given more abundant honour to that part which lacked: That there should be no schism in the body; but that the members should have the same care one for another. (I Corinthians 12:20-25)

September 13
The Dowry
I've had the privilege of being invited to engagement ceremonies in Nepal and in Africa, a practice that is foreign to our American culture. Similar to the betrothal ceremony of biblical times, this ceremony is the time when two families agree upon the marriage of the daughter of one family and the son of the other. In times past, such ceremonies might actually be the first time the couple are actually introduced to one another. In the engagement ceremonies I have had the privilege of witnessing, there were no surprises because the young men and women had already dated and decided on their own to be married. They were simply going through the ritual for their culture's sake. One significant part of these ceremonies was the offering of the dowry, a bride price to be paid by the groom-to-be or his family to the girl's parents. Part of the tradition is that the girl is to examine the offering and determine if it is appropriate. If she doesn't feel that the dowry is sufficient, she has the right to refuse the proposal. The dowry is placed on a table and covered with a cloth. When the bride-to-be enters the room, she is supposed to remove the cloth and examine the offering before pledging herself to the young man. The interesting thing about the ceremonies I had the privilege of witnessing was that the girl simply lifted the corner of cloth and took a cursory peek underneath. Within a second, she had made her judgment that the dowry was sufficient and had given her official acceptance to the marriage proposal. She was after the man, not his goods!

As the bride of Christ, why can't we be more like these Eastern young maidens? Why can't we be more interested in Christ Himself than in what He has to "bring to the table"? Certainly, we need to help the sinner understand that, in coming to Christ, he will receive forgiveness of his sins; we must let the addict know that, in surrendering to Christ, he can find deliverance from his habit; and we must make it plain to the sick man that, in Christ he will find his healing – but, at the same time, we must not try to sell the dowry and overlook the bridegroom's love.

September 14
The Oriental Restaurant
Our service had run very late and most of the restaurants in the area had closed, but my host was not concerned. He had called ahead to one of his favorite spots and asked them to stay open especially for us. I guess you could call it "clout" or possibly "favor," but there is a story behind it. My friend, who happened to be black, had brought a large group of his guests there for a meal and everyone was happily ordering without much concern for the price tags on the entrees. In fact, most of the meals were some of the priciest items on the menu. The little oriental shop owner became concerned and slipped around to the one white member of the party to ask if "these people" could really afford to pay the bill that they were racking up. As a matter of fact, he was actually about to ask that they pay in advance to ensure that he wasn't going to get stuck that night. When the lady assured him that the host that evening was a very successful businessman who could actually buy the whole restaurant as easily he could pay for the meals, the shop owner was finally at ease and happily placed the order. After the meal, my friend paid the bill in cash and left a generous gratuity. It didn't take a second visit for the owner to decide that my friend was one of his favorite and most valued customers.

There's a lesson to be learned from this little example. In fact, there are probably more than one lesson if we want to think of the stereotyping and racism elements of the story. But the thing I want to consider is the symbolism of how most of us look at God. Even though we might not envision it exactly that way, we are like the restaurant owner taking the orders that evening. We hear what God is reading off the menu but we are questioning if He can really "foot the bill." Well, the truth is that God can pay for anything He orders. If He directs you to go on a mission, He has the resources to supply the ticket. If He wants you to feed orphans, He will not come up short when the check is presented. If He asks you to build a church, He will take care of every invoice.

If it's His will, it's His bill!!

September 15
The Bride of Christ vs. The Body of Christ

I was once accosted by a young "theologian" who challenged a statement I had made concerning the symbolism of the church as the bride of Christ. He challenged each verse that I presented in my defense. To him, John 3:29 – where Jesus compared Himself to the bridegroom and John the Baptist to the best man – was only a figure of speech, not a definitive statement that the church is the bride of Christ. John's revelation of the New Jerusalem adorned as a bride was an expression of the church as the actual city and the bride was only a descriptive term to express the beauty of that city. (Revelation 21:2) I don't remember the arguments he presented against my interpretations of Revelation 21:9 and 22:17 where specific mention is made of the bride and the Lamb's wife in direct relationship to the church or to the references to the marriage supper of the Lamb in Revelation 19:7-9 where the church is presented as the bride. His main objection was based on Paul's statement in Ephesians 5:25-30 where Paul tells men to love their wives the way that Christ loved the church and that a husband's love for his wife should be as genuine as his love for his own body. My opponent went on to stress that the real measure of love is the love that we have for our own bodies. It is from this love that we are able to extrapolate the degree of love a husband should have for his wife. Thus, the real relationship that Paul was emphasizing was the love of a man for his own body, symbolizing that the true divine love is the love of Christ for His body – the church. From this, he drew the conclusion that our real relationship with Christ is not one of a groom and his bride but that of the individual and his own body.

Even though the passage specifically says that in marriage, the two become one flesh, he still couldn't seem to understand that both symbolisms were intended to help us understand the mysterious relationship we have with Christ. Eventually, I suggested to him to consider the fact that Adam married his own rib. At that, his mouth dropped open and his arguments ceased.

September 16
Did Moses Sabotage the Faith of His Spies?

Today, I want to examine an interesting thought that may bring us to an entirely new perspective on a very significant event in Old Testament history. I'd like to suggest that the whole experience of the people of Israel's forty years of wandering in the desert may have been a result of Moses' faltering in faith. In Numbers chapter thirteen, God specifically directed Moses to send spies into the land, but He did not tell Moses to ask them to determine if the land was worth fighting for or if they felt that it was within their power to take it. It was only in Moses' directions to the spies that these ideas were introduced.

> Get you up this way southward, and go up into the mountain: And see the land, what it is; and the people that dwelleth therein, whether they be strong or weak, few or many; And what the land is that they dwell in, whether it be good or bad; and what cities they be that they dwell in, whether in tents, or in strong holds; And what the land is, whether it be fat or lean, whether there be wood therein, or not. (verses 13:17-20)

God did not tell Moses to <u>check out</u> the land, but to <u>spy it out</u>. It was Moses who added the instructions about seeing if the inhabitants were strong or numerous. God simply said to spy out the land with the likely implication of developing the best strategy on <u>how</u> to take the land, not to determine <u>if</u> they could take it. God had repeatedly declared that He was going to give them the land flowing with milk and honey and that the opponents would be driven out. (Exodus 3:8, 3:17, 13:5, 33:3; Leviticus 20:24) Is it possible that Moses' words turned the mission of the twelve spies into a venture of doubt because they went in with questioning minds ready to place their confidence on what they saw rather than living in unwavering faith based on the Word of God? Notice that when Joshua sent his spies in forty years later, he didn't give them any directions to evaluate the land or the people in it. He simply told them to bring back a reconnaissance report. (Joshua 2:1)

September 17

The Birth of Revelation

When Jesus gave the Parable of the Sower, He specifically explained that the seed that was sown was the Word of God. (Mark 4:14) Interestingly enough, He used the term *logos* when speaking of the Word in this context, signifying that the Word of God as it is entering into the hearts and minds of the hearers is simply general ideas. However, when Paul spoke of the Word of God that produced faith in the hearts of the believers, he used the Greek term *rhema*, meaning the specific individually spoken Word of God. (Romans 10:17) It seems that there is an intentional message here. The preached word is general information that can fall on hard soil and produce nothing, on stony or thorn-infested soil and fail before it becomes productive, or on fertile soil where it can bring forth a harvest. It is when those general ideas get into the fertile soil that they change from *logos* words to *rhema* words. One minister used the terminology of a precept becoming a concept based on the idea of conception in pregnancy. When the general precept or idea actually enters into the heart of a believer, that believer can become spiritually pregnant with the idea or truth to the point of conception of a concept. That spiritual seed impregnates the believer with a reality that can eventually be born into the physical world. The bridge between a precept and a concept is the communication of the Word into the heart of the believer in such a way that he actually believes it as a literal infallible truth from God. In other words, just because we hear sermons on salvation or healing doesn't mean that we will be saved or healed. It is only when we believe the truths that they can produce change in our lives. Notice that in Luke's explanation of the parable, he specifically tells us that the reason for the unproductive seed was the lack of believing on the part of the hearers. *Those by the way side are they that hear; then cometh the devil, and taketh away the word out of their hearts, lest they should believe and be saved. They on the rock are they, which, when they hear, receive the word with joy; and these have no root, which for a while believe, and in time of temptation fall away.* (verses 8: 12-13)

September 18
Will of God

The will of God gets a lot of bad rap because the most quoted verse is from Jesus' prayer in the Garden of Gethsemane when He surrendered to going to the cross, *Not my will but Thine be done.* (Luke 22:42) Because we have emphasized this verse so much, many believers have the feeling that God's will is going to be hurtful to them. I have met many people who were afraid that, if they surrendered to the will of God, they would have to give up all their possessions and pleasures to become missionaries in Africa or perhaps they would suffer from some serious disease.

Actually, the opposite is true. First John 5:14-15 teaches us that we can have a confidence in the will of God that leads to favorable answers to our prayers. Ephesians 1:5-6 instructs us that there is good pleasure in God's will and that it will *bring praise of the glory of His grace.* Paul goes on to say in Ephesians 1:9 that God has made His will known to us and adds that it is according to His good pleasure. From these passages, we can clearly understand that God's will is not something to fear or dread but should be welcomed and invited into our lives, and even sought for.

God's will comes in three ways:

His ultimate will for us is to know and love God, to become more like Christ, to serve Him with our gifts and abilities, and to tell others about Christ.

His moral will has to do with how we should think, believe, and live. We often skip right past this in trying to figure out what God wants us to do in a given situation. God's moral will is more like a compass to direct our lives than a detailed road map for a specific destination.

God's specific will never will contradict God's moral will. If those two seem to be in conflict, we have misread God's specific will. The Lord says to His people, [You] *will be led by one who loves* [you]. (Isaiah 49:8) We can be released from the fear that God's will is a deep, dark mystery that we may never be able to understand. Instead, it is a blessed privilege.

September 19

Are Adultery and Murder Okay?

*Now the works of the flesh are manifest,
which are these; Adultery, fornication,
uncleanness, lasciviousness, Idolatry,
witchcraft, hatred, variance, emulations,
wrath, strife, seditions, heresies, Envyings,
murders, drunkenness, revellings, and such
like: of the which I tell you before, as I have
also told you in time past, that they which do
such things shall not inherit the kingdom of
God.* (Galatians 5:19-21)

I know that, when you read the title to today's Ditty,
you were thinking that I've lost all my marbles. Why would I
even entertain such a question – and especially when I
immediately quote a passage that lists both those actions as
works of the flesh. Well, the reason I bring up the topic is that
many translations of the Bible drop these two things out of the
list of the works of the flesh. The suggestion is that many of
the ancient Greek texts did not list them in Paul's original
listing and that scribes took the liberty to add them in as they
transcribed the passage. Well, let's avoid the argument of the
possibility of scribal additions or edition of the scripture and go
straight to the question, "What if these two sins were not in
Paul's original list?" The loss of the word for adultery is no
problem since the word used for "fornication" is *porneia*,
which includes every form of sexual indiscretion from
pornography to fornication to adultery to prostitution to incest.
If we drop "murder" out of the list, we still have a long list of
words describing interpersonal hostilities and ill will to deal
with: hatred, variance, emulations, wrath, strife, seditions, and
envyings. From the words of Jesus, we will realize that these
heart attitudes are actually tantamount to murder.

*Ye have heard that it was said by them of old
time, Thou shalt not kill; and whosoever
shall kill shall be in danger of the judgment:
But I say unto you, That whosoever is angry
with his brother without a cause shall be in
danger of the judgment.* (Matthew 5:21-22)

September 20

Chastening of the Lord

And ye have forgotten the exhortation which speaketh unto you as unto children, My son, despise not thou the chastening of the Lord, nor faint when thou art rebuked of him: For whom the Lord loveth he chasteneth, and scourgeth every son whom he receiveth. If ye endure chastening, God dealeth with you as with sons; for what son is he whom the father chasteneth not?...Now no chastening for the present seemeth to be joyous, but grievous: nevertheless afterward it yieldeth the peaceable fruit of righteousness unto them which are exercised thereby. (Hebrews 12:5-7, 11)

A lot of contemporary Christian teaching centers around the love of God and also includes the concept that because of His gracious undeserved love, He never does anything harsh to His people. In reaction to some of the judgmental teaching of the past that emphasized the idea that God would send sickness, poverty, and calamity upon people to punish them for disobedience, the teaching has swung to the far extreme with the idea that God would never do anything hurtful to His children. Unfortunately, such a teaching is actually in contradiction with itself in that if we believe in the love of God, we must also believe in His correction. Revelation 3:19 clearly states, *As many as I love, I rebuke and chasten.* When God corrects, punishes, and chastens us, it is not an expression of His anger, but of His love. He loves us so much that He cannot allow us to continue in our errors that will eventually lead us to harm and destruction. The word "chasten" means to educate, so we can understand that much of our correction will come through the educational process of the Word of God that is profitable for doctrine, for reproof, for correction, for instruction in righteousness. (II Timothy 3:16) Yet, the word also carries the meaning of scourging (even as in the crucifixion). The wonderful truth is that Jesus has already taken that scourging if we will only appropriate it.

September 21

Little Tidbits from the Word

After they were come to Mysia, they assayed to go into Bithynia: but the Spirit suffered them not. (Acts 16:7) The word "assayed" means that they tried very hard. It's interesting how often in life that some of the things we are striving the hardest at are hard because we are going against the direction of the Holy Spirit.

Not as though I had already attained, either were already perfect: but I follow after, if that I may apprehend that for which also I am apprehended of Christ Jesus. (Philippians 3:12) The term "follow after" literally means to persecute as in having a strategic plan and pursuit of God's plan for your life. In other words, God's purpose for your life isn't going to come with only casual concern.

If any of you lack wisdom, let him ask of God, that giveth to all men liberally, and upbraideth not; and it shall be given him. (James 1:5) The phrase "lack wisdom" refers to a scarcity like waiting for rationed supplies. Notice the dramatic contrast between living in our own wisdom and letting God give us His wisdom – going from standing in a ration line to living in liberal abundance.

Likewise, ye wives, be in subjection to your own husbands; that, if any obey not the word, they also may without the word be won by the conversation of the wives. (I Peter 3:1) When Peter spoke of husbands who do not obey the Word, he was actually referring to ones who are defiant against what they know is right. When he said that they could be won, he used a term that spoke of playing one's cards correctly, as in to act cleverly. What a wonderful promise that even the men who are defiantly resistant can be won over by careful and discrete maneuvers by their wives.

Likewise, ye husbands, dwell with them according to knowledge, giving honour unto the wife, as unto the weaker vessel, and as being heirs together of the grace of life; that your prayers be not hindered. (I Peter 3:7) Peter gives us a descriptive picture here when he says that prayers are hindered by using a word picture depicting being elbowed out of the race.

September 22

Insights into the Word

For he that will love life, and see good days, let him refrain his tongue from evil, and his lips that they speak no guile: Let him eschew evil, and do good; let him seek peace, and ensue it. (I Peter 3:10-11) One thing that is often overlooked about this verse is that it is actually in the context of instruction on marriage. How much more pleasant life will be if both partners decide to really live their lives, watch their tongues, do good things creatively, and seek peace zealously. The term used for "ensue" means to stalk after it like a hunter who looks through lots of places where game is <u>not</u>, trying to find the place where game <u>is</u>! In other words, when there isn't peace in the home, keep searching until you can find a common ground on which to build a happy relationship.

Wherefore we would have come unto you, even I Paul, once and again; but Satan hindered us. (I Thessalonians 2:18) When Paul spoke of Satan's having hindered him, he used terminology that referred to being delayed like through-road construction. Such a delay is not always a bad thing. Once we were delayed due to a landslide that blocked the mountain pass in Nepal. While waiting for the construction crew to clear the blockage, we had the opportunity to present a gospel drama for a bus full of school children who were also stranded.

Are they ministers of Christ? (I speak as a fool) I am more; in labours more abundant, in stripes above measure, in prisons more frequent, in deaths oft. (II Corinthians 11:23) In saying that he had experienced stripes above measure, Paul used the Greek word *huperballo* which literally means "out of ballpark." What a picturesque expression for his sufferings.

In journeyings often, in perils of waters, in perils of robbers, in perils by mine own countrymen, in perils by the heathen, in perils in the city, in perils in the wilderness, in perils in the sea, in perils among false brethren. (II Corinthians 11:26) "Journeyings" means that he traveled by foot. To understand what he was saying, we need to realize that Paul walked hundreds of miles after having been beaten with rods three times, a torture that fractured the bones of the feet. (verse 25)

September 23

Going Where No Man Has Gone Before

And Moses said unto Hobab, the son of Raguel the Midianite, Moses' father in law, We are journeying unto the place of which the LORD said, I will give it you: come thou with us, and we will do thee good: for the LORD hath spoken good concerning Israel. And he said unto him, I will not go; but I will depart to mine own land, and to my kindred. And he said, Leave us not, I pray thee; forasmuch as thou knowest how we are to encamp in the wilderness, and thou mayest be to us instead of eyes. (Numbers 10:29-31)

This simple little story introduces some really interesting truths. On the surface, it seems a simple request by Moses that his brother-in-law would serve as a scout for the people of Israel as they journeyed into unknown territories. However, if we connect the passage with a statement about the same event that is recorded by the prophet Jeremiah (verse 2:6), we understand something very intriguing – nobody (apparently including Hobab) had ever been there before. How could Hobab be a guide in a land where no man – including himself – had passed? Apparently, Moses had had a lapse in his faith and was seeking to rely upon human wisdom and knowledge – even as faulty as it was – rather than God's divine hand. The glory of the story is found a couple verses later when we see that God supernaturally led the people even while Moses talked to Hobab.

And they departed from the mount of the LORD three days' journey: and the ark of the covenant of the LORD went before them in the three days' journey, to search out a resting place for them.

The moral of the story is that God is faithful even when our faith fails. He can take us safely where no man has ever been.

September 24

Witnesses

It was the Christmas season, and the stores were crowded with shoppers who were pushing their way through the crowds to get to the best bargains and elbowing their way into the checkout lanes. When my wife finally got to the cash register, she made a comment about the madhouse in the mall. It turned out that the sales lady who was helping her was Jewish, and she responded with the surprising retort that the Christmas hassle and aggravation she had experienced in the store was enough to make her not want to be a Christian.

On the other end of the spectrum was a comment from one clerk in a store where I often shop. Since I always greet her with a smile and an upbeat greeting by telling her that I am absolutely, incredibly, stupendously marvelous, she one day expressed to me, "Boy, you always make me feel better!" That gave me an opportunity to tell her that Jesus is the reason for my happiness. Because of that opening, I was able to eventually share healing scriptures and pray with her for a relative who was dying with cancer. When I checked on the relative a couple weeks later, he had been totally healed!

It's amazing how our lives can be a testimony for the Lord or a testimony against Him. Even more than the words we say, the way we act and the look on our faces reveals to those around us if Jesus is really the center of our lives.

> *And it shall come to pass, that as ye were a curse among the heathen, O house of Judah, and house of Israel; so will I save you, and ye shall be a blessing: fear not, but let your hands be strong.* (Zechariah 8:13)

It's our choice to either be a curse or a blessing among the people around us. Let's make the right choice today. Someone once said, "If Jesus is in your heart, make sure that your face knows it."

Interesting Insights

You cannot spell "success" without "u."

Hebrews 11:24 tells us that Moses was a man of faith because he refused the riches and prestige of the wealthiest nation on earth. Today, we consider our faith as an avenue for receiving prosperity and honor.

In Acts 7:23, we read the story of Moses' inspiration to set his people free. He had the right idea, but the wrong time. God's timing is just as much a part of His will as His direction.

Acts 7:22 tells us that Moses was learned in all the wisdom of the Egyptians and that he was mighty in words. Interestingly enough, when God met him at the burning bush, Moses confessed to being slow of speech, and of a slow tongue. (Exodus 4:10) What happened to his mighty words and Egyptian wisdom? The scriptures don't give us an explanation, but isn't it possibly that those forty years of exile in the backside of the desert (Exodus 3:1) totally deflated his human confidence to prepare him to humbly allow the Lord to manifest His mighty words and wisdom through him?

Peter, James, and John were already business partners before they became disciples and, therefore, kingdom partners. God often wants to redeem and build upon what we already have in the natural rather than to start over from scratch.

Sometimes, there are more men of vision in politics and business than in the church. We need to birth vision and incubate leadership in the Body of Christ.

Had not God interrupted, Samuel would have anointed David's brother as king in Israel. (I Samuel 16:7) Even prophets can miss God's direction, and there has never been a seer who knew everything. That's why we need more prophets who can correct the other prophets. *Let the prophets speak two or three, and let the other judge.* (I Corinthians 14:29)

If your vision doesn't embarrass you when you tell others, it's probably not from God.

You are in bondage to anyone you don't forgive

September 26
Scriptural Insights

In II Timothy 2:26, Paul wrote, *And that they may recover themselves out of the snare of the devil, who are taken captive by him at his will.* The Greek terminology for "taken captive at his will" actually communicates the thought that they are taken captive to do his will. What an awful thought – once an individual becomes captive to Satan, he becomes a slave or pawn in the devil's hand to do whatever the enemy desires to do through him.

The watchings referred to in II Corinthians 6:5, *In stripes, in imprisonments, in tumults, in labours, in watchings, in fastings,* speak of Paul's taking his turn at guard duty, watching for bandits and wild animals, as he traveled from place to place. Even though he was an apostle, he had to pitch in with all the menial chores just like all the rest of his team. When he was often in fastings, he was not talking about foregoing food for religious purposes. He was simply too busy to stop and eat or possible too financially strapped to be able to buy food. His reference to being cold and naked probably referred to his prison conditions. Paul was willing to bear much suffering to uphold his mission in life – not only what was forced upon him, but also what he willingly accepted.

The Greek word for "bishop" or "overseer" is *episcopes,* which comes from the two words *epi* and *skopos.* One of the mountains in Jerusalem bears the name of Mount Scopus because it is a sentinel point from which the surrounding territory and be viewed or <u>scoped</u> out. The prefix epi means around and, when added to the root *skopos,* gives us the picture of one who is always carefully scoping out the terrain all around him to ensure the safety of those under his charge. Thus, the bishop is not a position of privilege with the church but one of extreme responsibility, always caring for the wellbeing of his flock.

Moses struck the rock and got water but lost the Promised Land. Just because you get results, it doesn't prove that your ministry has God's approval.

Quips and Quotes

Churches are full of empty people.

Man's rejects are God's selects

The future belongs to those who plan for it.

Elephants don't give birth to rats.

Plan for posterity, not prosperity.

Strength is in seeds, not seats. (It is the power of giving, not the number of members in a church that makes it strong.

Who you know is your status; WHO you know is your stature.

Israel wanted a king like other nations; the church wants a success pattern like the secular world.

What the church needs today is leader shift – not leadership.

Our enemy attempts to wear out saints because they do not know the times and seasons of God's moving among them. (Daniel 7:25)

The gentiles came to the temple in Jerusalem because of what God had done. (I Kings 8:43) But instead of the Jews recognizing this as an evangelistic opportunity, they turned it into financial opportunity with moneychangers' tables and stalls for selling sheep and doves. (Matthew 21:12) Today, we turn the church into a market with book tables and other merchandizing.

Success has eaten the soul out of the church. God did not promise success – only fruitfulness.

America has more churches than supermarkets and schools, but we still are without true righteousness.

God bless America, but America must also bless God.

We want to have ministries, so we do things that are not our calling.

Truth can become the enemy of revelation. So, be careful where you get your facts. The media may tell the truth and present facts, but they may only give a one-sided viewpoint. In fact, it may be true that CNN stands for "Constantly Negative News." A half-truth is a whole lie if it neglects to present God's viewpoint on the topic.

September 28
Our Better Covenant
Favor in the Old Testament was limited to God's friends. In the New Testament, Christ died for His enemies and prayed for the ones who were even at that moment crucifying Him. (Romans 5:10, Luke 23:34)

Increase in the Old Testament could still leave the recipients discontented. (Ecclesiastes 5:10) In the New Testament, we have great gain with contentment (I Timothy 1:6), and we prosper as our souls prosper (III John 2).

Respect in the Old Testament meant that we were set on high above the nations. (Deuteronomy 28:1) In the New Testament, we are seated with Christ far above the principalities that rule the nations. (Ephesians 2:6, 1:20-22)

Having one's enemies subdued in the Old Testament meant that one could chase a thousand. Samson killed a thousand with the jawbone of an ass; but, when he wanted to kill three thousand, he had to sacrifice his own life. (Judges 15:15, 16:27-30) In the New Testamament, Jesus cast out two thousand demons with a single word. This explains why Jesus asked the demon's name. (Mark 5:9-13) We now have at least fourteen thousand times the power as a natural person – one demon overcame seven sons of Sceva (Acts 19:14-16), but we can cast out two thousand demons!

Now hath he obtained a more excellent ministry, by how much also he is the mediator of a better covenant, which was established upon better promises. For if that first [covenant] had been faultless, then should no place have been sought for the second. For finding fault with them, he saith, Behold, the days come, saith the Lord, when I will make a new covenant with the house of Israel and with the house of Judah. (Hebrews 8:6-8)

Let us therefore fear, lest, a promise being left [us] of entering into his rest, any of you should seem to come short of it. (Hebrews 4:1)

September 29
Unreached People Groups
An unreached people group is a people group in which less than 2% of the population are evangelical Christians. Whereas unreached people groups are scattered among various world cultures, the majority of them are primarily in five major cultural blocks located geographically in what some scholars call "The 10/40 Window" from West Africa across Asia between 10 degrees latitude north of the equator to 40 degrees north. Over two billion people live in these unreached people groups, and every day some 50,000 of them perish without having heard the gospel. That is about 26 million a year.

1) 3,276 unreached Muslim groups. (Over 1.3 billion individuals or one sixth of the world's population)
2) 2,550 unreached tribal groups. (Only about 140 million individuals)
3) (3) 2,425 unreached Hindu groups. (900   million individuals)
4) 450 unreached Mandarin Chinese groups. (793 million individuals)
5) 552 unreached Buddhist groups. (375 million individuals)

There are approximately one thousand churches for each unreached people group. American Christians spend 95% of offerings on home-based ministry, 4.5% on cross-cultural efforts in already-reached people groups. Less than one percent goes toward blessing the unreached. American evangelicals could provide all of the funds needed to plant a church in each of the 6,400 people groups with only 0.2% of their income. If all the missionaries needed came from the U.S., less than 0.5% of evangelicals aged 18-35 could form the teams required. The church of Christ has over 100 times the resources needed to plant native churches in these people groups.

How then shall they call on him in whom they have not believed? and how shall they believe in him of whom they have not heard? and how shall they hear without a preacher? And how shall they preach, except they be sent? (Romans 10:14-15)

September 30
Putting Our Money Where Their Mouths Are

The pastor stood up one Sunday and announced to the church that he had both good news and bad news to share with them that day. The good news was that the church had all the money it needed to pay off the mortgage on the building and to fund all the projects it had slated for the year. The bad news was that all the money was still in their pockets.

It is true that the Body of Christ already has all the money and other resources we need to complete the Great Commission. According to David Barrett in <u>Our</u> <u>Globe</u> <u>and</u> <u>How</u> <u>to</u> <u>Reach</u> <u>It</u>, two thirds of the world's wealth is under ownership and control of Christians. The major problem with the church today is that we have failed to embrace the advice of the Psalmist, *When riches increase, don't set your heart on them.* (verse 62:10) As a result, we have focused on our resources more than on why God has delivered those resources into our hands.

A generation ago, there was tremendous emphasis in the Body of Christ on what became known as the "Prosperity Gospel." It was a genuine revelation from God that He wanted His church to be blessed and live in prosperity; however, the teaching got off-center and much of the focus was on acquiring possessions rather than advancing the kingdom. As a result, many evangelicals became very critical of the movement and began to push the pendulum to the other extreme so much that they became afraid or embarrassed to talk about money. We failed to understand that the prosperity must be part of the evangelical message. Without resources, we'll never be able to reach the lost or feed the hungry.

At the height of this dilemma in the church, God spoke to Dr. Lester Sumrall, telling him that His biggest concern was the people all around the world who prayed the Lord's Prayer every morning and then looked back at Him every evening asking why He hadn't answered their request for their daily bread. The Lord's response was that He had answered it, but a few greedy Christians were holding it rather than releasing it.

Let's become part of the solution instead of the problem.

October 1

Days of Provocation

Harden not your hearts, as in the provocation, in the day of temptation in the wilderness. (Hebrews 3:8)

When the Israelite spies came back with an evil report from their forty-day reconnaissance mission in Canaan, the nation was sentenced to forty years (one year for each day) of wandering through the desert as punishment for their unbelief. (Numbers 14:34) God goes on to say that during that period the people would experience His "breach of promise," an expression that is translated with many different shades of intensity – from displeasure to estrangement or alienation to rejection. These forty years were known as the days of provocation, a period of rebellion that literally made God angry. However, there is much more to the story than the simple fact that God was angry, Psalm 95:10 explains that He also grieved over Israel during those forty years. Even though the following verse again emphasizes the anger of God, we are able to see that there was an element of compassion in the midst of this anger. Acts 13:18 adds another dimension to the emotion of the Father during these forty years by saying that He suffered during this period. Though some translations render this term to mean that He put up with their ways or bore with them during this time, there are also very legitimate reasons for seeing this term as others translate it meaning that He fed and tenderly bore them like a nurse or caring father. After all, He provided forty-five hundred tons of manna each day, ninety million quail per month, and fifteen million gallons of water per day. He even made sure that their clothes and shoes didn't wear out during this four-decade desert odyssey. (Deuteronomy 29:5) One other aspect is God's concern over the people's failure to properly worship during this period. In Amos 5:25 and Acts 7:42, the Lord questioned their faithfulness in offering sacrifices during this period. Even if they did follow the prescribed ritual, they were apparently insincere and half-hearted in their practice. It seems that God was not just angered by the spies but also by the entire congregation's lack of devotion.

October 2

What's in Your Wallet?

One of the credit card companies promotes itself with a commercial touting, "What's in your wallet?" Today, I'd like to change the emphasis of the sentence and ask, "What's in your wallet?" The story behind this question dates back a number of years to a time when all of our sons were in their teen and preteen years. One of our boys was beginning to show some signs that he was dealing with something a bit more serious than just adolescence, but we couldn't get a straight answer from him so we could help him handle the issues. One evening, Peggy and I were sitting with him, making futile attempts to get to the root of the matter, when I suddenly had an impulsive thought to ask him to let me see his wallet. It was one of those things that seems to come from "out of the blue" or "out of left field," but I knew that I had to follow that "gut instinct." Peggy looked at me with sheer dismay, certainly thinking that I had "gone off my rocker." But my son looked at me with utter horror because he knew that there was telltale evidence in his wallet. As soon as I opened his wallet, I found "the smoking gun," exactly what we needed to get on the track of his issues. What had happened that afternoon was not just a gut instinct, nor was it a clairvoyant moment or a psychic revelation. It was the operation of the gift of the Holy Spirit called the word of knowledge, the supernatural revelation of a necessary fact that would not have been by natural means. (I Corinthians 12:8) This supernatural gift, along with the rest of the supernatural gifts listed in this chapter are available to all Christians if we simply have faith to receive them and courage to act when prompted to use them. Unfortunately, there are two misconceptions that have robbed us of the wonderful benefits of these blessings. The first is that such gifts were only for biblical times and that they passed away long before our present time. The second misconception is that, even if such supernatural manifestations are available today, they are only for special people like pastors and televangelists and only for use within a church setting. The truth is that these gifts are available anywhere the Holy Spirit is – regardless of the time, person, or place.

October 3

Divine Choreography

I often joke that my favorite Bible verse is James 1:2 because I do count it joy when I fall into a diver's temptation. Just give a hint that we could head to the Bahamas and see how excited I'll get. Actually, I'm a snorkeler rather than a scuba diver, but I always find it fascinating to get under the sea and mingle with the fish. One thing that I really love is to find a school of fish swimming together and just watch as they move through the water. They will do what is called shoaling, swimming as if directed by an unseen choreographer. They will all be moving the same direction and suddenly change course – all at the same instant. It is amazing to see hundreds of fish make this transition without a single one getting off track.

I've also watched flocks of birds during migration do exactly the same thing in the heavens. Like one being, rather than an aggregation of hundreds of individual birds, they would rise and fall, turn to the right or left, and literally paint the sky as their dark sides suddenly disappeared when their light-colored breasts came into view. Amazingly, not one bird seemed to get disoriented and miss even one move in the elaborate maneuvers through the air.

Although I've only seen it on videotape, the swimming pattern of a pod of dolphins is so graceful that I could watch it for hours as they glide through the water, maneuvering in perfect orchestration, occasionally hurling themselves into the air, flipping and splashing as they reenter their ocean homes.

There is only one explanation to such beauty and wonder – God has choreographed them for His pleasure – but He lets us enjoy them as a fringe benefit.

Thou art worthy, O Lord, to receive glory and honour and power: for thou hast created all things, and for thy pleasure they are and were created. (Revelation 4:11)

October 4

Life's Ups and Downs

In the story of Joseph, we can learn a lot about the ups and downs of life. Joseph started out as the favored son in a family of twelve brothers. His father gave him special privileges and gifts. (Genesis 37:3-4) The result of the jealousy that was birthed out of this special treatment was that his brothers plotted against him and eventually sold him as a slave. (Genesis 37:28) That was certainly a fall from the pinnacle of his father's favor to the chains of slavery; however, he eventually rebounded and found himself as the chief official over the house of the wealthy businessman in whose house he served. (Genesis 39:4) This position of authority was actually more significant than his position in the father's house. Although he was the heir apparent, he had not actually "come into his own" in the father's estate at the time he was spirited away. But, like a yoyo, almost as soon as he reached the apex of his position in Potiphar's household, he was suddenly plunged to the depths of a prison cell because of false accusations leveled against him by his master's wife. (Genesis 39:20) After a long and grueling ordeal in the prison, God again thrust His servant on another upward journey. This time, he became the second most powerful man in the most powerful nation on the planet. (Genesis 41:40-41) This positioned him as the second most powerful man in the world politically, but he was also in first place spiritually because he was the spiritual father to Pharaoh. (Genesis 45:8) Notice that each time he went down, God caused him to rebound and actually took him up higher than his previous level.

I believe that the power behind his amazing ability to bounce back was his faith in the vision he had of his brothers bowing before him (Genesis 37:6-10) – or more accurately, his faith in the God who gave him that vision (Genesis 39:2, 21, 41:39, 45:7, 50:20). No matter what happened in his life, Joseph knew that the vision had to be fulfilled; therefore, he expected God to turn all the negatives in his life into positives. You can have that same faith too; and, if you do, He'll turn your downs into ups!

October 5
Worthy to Fulfill God's Good Pleasure

When he shall come to be glorified in his saints, and to be admired in all them that believe (because our testimony among you was believed) in that day. Wherefore also we pray always for you, that our God would count you worthy of this calling, and fulfil all the good pleasure of his goodness, and the work of faith with power: That the name of our Lord Jesus Christ may be glorified in you, and ye in him, according to the grace of our God and the Lord Jesus Christ. (II Thessalonians 1:10-12)

God's full intent for the Body of Christ is that one day He will be glorified in us. His objective is that our lives be such a magnificent manifestation of His presence that the world will stand in awe and reverence of the holiness and power that exudes from our very lives. Paul declares that he is continually praying that our lives would really match up to this divine expectation so that we can indeed be conduits of God's goodness and power to the world around us. He then adds that all this will happen in accordance to the grace of God, meaning in direct proportion to His Grace. Since His grace is unlimited, then the potential of this kind of divine life being manifested in us is also unlimited. Someone commenting on this truth expressed his feeling this way, "Ones that others think aren't even worth the time of day are ones chosen by God."

Notice in his commentary that the key word in the hindering of our moving into the fulfillment of this high calling is that we think we are unworthy. That's why Paul also admonished us that we must renew our minds in order to begin to manifest the perfect will of God in our lives. (Romans 12:2)

The term "sound mind" in II Timothy 1:7, *For God hath not given us the spirit of fear; but of power, and of love, and of a sound mind,* refers to a saved mind that is no longer affected by illogical, unfounded, or absurd thoughts. What a blessing that most of us have failed to fully appropriate.

October 6
Is the Word of God Comfortable in Your Life?

Colossians 3:16 says, *Let the word of Christ dwell in you richly in all wisdom; teaching and admonishing one another in psalms and hymns and spiritual songs, singing with grace in your hearts to the Lord.* The Greek wording for "dwell" in this verse means to feel comfortably at home, not like an unwelcome and ignored guest or intruder. In my own life, there are times when the Word of God doesn't feel really comfortable in my life because I realize that the way I'm conducting my life at the moment is not in exact alignment with the standards of the Word. Ever happen to you?

In I Timothy 6:3-5, Paul wrote, *If any man teach otherwise, and consent not to wholesome words, even the words of our Lord Jesus Christ, and to the doctrine which is according to godliness; He is proud, knowing nothing, but doting about questions and strifes of words, whereof cometh envy, strife, railings, evil surmisings, Perverse disputings of men of corrupt minds, and destitute of the truth, supposing that gain is godliness: from such withdraw thyself.* A graphic translation of what he was saying would tell us that envy and strife lead to confusion, and a know-it-all attitude leads to a party spirit that produces a stinking mess! To really understand what Paul was saying, we need to look back at the first two verses in this passage to comprehend what it was that Paul said people should not teach against. He was telling us how we have to relate to other members of the Body of Christ who might just happen to be from different socio-economic circles. *Let as many servants as are under the yoke count their own masters worthy of all honour, that the name of God and his doctrine be not blasphemed. And they that have believing masters, let them not despise them, because they are brethren; but rather do them service, because they are faithful and beloved, partakers of the benefit. These things teach and exhort.* When we remember that, in Paul's day, any person who purchased a slave had the right to beat him to see how much he could endure, we see that Paul was injecting the church with a radical doctrine of interdependence and respect even in the harshest of scenarios.

October 7

Gossip

A monk told his monastic leader, "I am troubled in spirit, and I want to leave this place." The old man said, "Why?" The young monk replied, "I have heard unedifying stories about one of the brothers." The elder monk then asked, "Are the stories true?" The young monk answered back, "Yes, Father. The brother who told me is a man of trust." The old man settled the discussion with, "The brother who told you is not a man of trust. For if he was so, he would not have told you these stories."

> *The words of a talebearer are as wounds,*
> *and they go down into the innermost parts of*
> *the belly.* (Proverbs 18:8)

Although we can get some real-life applications from the contemporary English wording of this verse by saying that gossip hurts people like a serious blow to the gut, there is really much more to Solomon's words that we see on the surface. The word "wound" in 1611, when the King James Version of the Bible was translated, was the name of a kind of pastry. With this in mind, we see that the wise king was not really talking about injuries inflicted by gossip. Instead, he was trying to communicate the irresistibility of gossip. Did you know that the number one culprit in causing people on diets to break their willpower is donuts – not chips, ice cream, or fast-food burgers. Apparently, it was the same way three thousand years ago as the book of Proverbs was being penned. Solomon was trying to communicate how tempting it is to listen to gossip, no matter how strongly we have our will set against it, we just can't resist hearing "the goods" on our fellowman. Once that gossip enters our ears, it goes down into our inner man and becomes a part of us just like those tempting donuts instantly show up on our waistlines.

When it comes to gossip, we need to remember the three little monkeys: See No Evil, Hear No Evil, and Speak No Evil.

October 8

The Baseball

I once heard a story of a baseball enthusiast who had been going to professional baseball games and trying to get a souvenir baseball many years. For him, a foul ball, a home run ball, or even a batting practice ball – anything would do. He tells of a day when he was taking in batting practice for the St. Louis Cardinals. As he watched Mark McGwire and his teammates, he became acquainted with James, a five-year-old boy who was also trying to get a ball. He tried hard to pronounce the players' names as he politely asked for a ball: "Mr. Timwin (Timlin), can I have a ball, please?"

Before he knew it, the gentleman's mission became getting a ball for James. For about twenty minutes, he told James the names of the players who had a ball near the fence they were standing behind, and the players turned and smiled as James tried to say their names. Still, no ball. Finally the gentleman told James he could have his ball if he caught one. Of course you have to remember that he had been unsuccessful in catching a ball for almost twenty-eight years!

Obviously, I wouldn't be retelling this guy's story if you didn't know what happened within the next five minutes. Yes, he caught a baseball and gave it to James. The gentleman who told this story ended it with one observation, "I wonder how often God waits to give us something until we are willing to give it away."

> *For whosoever will save his life shall lose it: and whosoever will lose his life for my sake shall find it.* (Matthew 16:25)
> *But many that are first shall be last; and the last shall be first.* (Matthew 19:30)

October 9

Stormy Seas

We all know that the Bible was not originally written with chapter and verse breaks. However, the fact that they are there today sometimes influences us to segregate sections simply because the chapter breaks stop the flow in the reading. One significant example of such an interruption occurs in the story in Mark of Jesus' journey across the Sea of Galilee. Chapter four tells us that Jesus gathered His disciples onto a little ship with the direction that they were going to go to the other side. As Jesus took a much-deserved nap after His extensive teaching earlier in the day, an unexpected hurricane-force windstorm appeared without any previous indications of stormy weather. The disciples, fearing for their lives, woke Jesus and begged for His intervention. He, of course, calmed the storm raging in the sea and also the storm raging inside the hearts of the disciples (Why are ye so fearful? how is it that ye have no faith?). At this point, we generally think that we have come to the conclusion of the story simply because the chapter ends. If we ignore the chapter break and read on, we'd see that the story actually continues in the following chapter because the next verse says that they came to the other side. Since the same wording was used when they got into the boat, we must understand that there is a deliberate attempt here to link the journey with the arrival. In other words, the events that are to happen on the other side were the express purpose for the journey.

What happened on that other side was the deliverance of Legion, the demoniac of Gadara. With this in mind, we can't help but ask if the storm at sea wasn't the devil's deliberate attempt to stop Jesus from getting there because he (the devil) didn't want Jesus tampering with the great influence he held over that region through this possessed man. One paradox in the story is that Jesus did not drown in the sea, but the demons in the man sent a whole herd of swine to a watery grave in that same lake. Jesus overcame the storm, set the man free, and then left him there to spread the news among the local people. It was because of his influence that four thousand people would be saved on Jesus' next visit.

October 10
Did You Know that Christopher Columbus...

...did not sail to prove that the earth was round? Most educated Europeans and mariners already knew that.

...estimated the size of the Atlantic Ocean partially from reading his Bible? He had read in the Second Book of Esdras (in the Apocrypha) that God created the world in seven parts, six of them dry land and the seventh water. He thus calculated that the ocean separating Portugal from Cipangu (Japan) was one-seventh of the earth's circumference, or about twenty-four hundred miles. He figured that by sailing a hundred miles per day, he could reach the Indies within a month.

... never used profanity?

...insisted that the ships' crews observe religious rites? Every time they turned the half-hour glass (their primary means of keeping time), they cried: "Blessed be the hour of our Savior's birth, blessed be the Virgin Mary who bore him, and blessed be John who baptized him." They finished each day by singing vespers together (although reportedly they sang out of tune).

...believed he had encountered the Garden of Eden because he discovered four rivers flowing from the landmass when he finally landed on the American mainland on his third voyage?

....was nominated for sainthood? Irish and French Catholics have argued that Columbus, who "brought the Christian faith to half the world," should be named a saint. Though the move had the approval of Pope Pius IX (reign 1846–1878), Columbus was never canonized because he fathered an illegitimate child, and there was no proof he had performed a miracle.

...prompted a missionary movement to the New World? Between 1493 and 1820, Spain sent more than fifteen thousand missionaries to the Americas. Typically the government of Spain paid their full expenses. Because of Columbus' voyage and the resulting Spanish evangelistic efforts, Latin America has a higher percentage of professing Christians than that of any other region in the world.

October 11

Insights into the Word

James 4:5, *Do ye think that the scripture saith in vain, The spirit that dwelleth in us lusteth to envy?* The reference to the spirit inside us in this passage is not talking about the Holy Spirit, but our own human spirit. When James says that it lusts, his wording speaks of yearnings like those of a drug addict craving his next fix. In other words, it is not something that can be casually or nonchalantly controlled. It takes the true weaponry of God to subdue it.

II Timothy 1:7, *For God hath not given us the spirit of fear; but of power, and of love, and of a sound mind.* Historically, Timothy had a reason for having to deal with a spirit of fear. He was the pastor of the largest church in the Roman Empire (Ephesus) at the time Nero was in a lunatic rage against Christians. Thank God, he had a three-fold solution available.

II Peter 2:10, *But chiefly them that walk after the flesh in the lust of uncleanness, and despise government. Presumptuous are they, selfwilled, they are not afraid to speak evil of dignities.* When Peter spoke about walking in the flesh, he used a term that communicated the idea of being so accustomed to walking a certain way that we can do it with our eyes closed.

Hebrews 12:1, *Wherefore seeing we also are compassed about with so great a cloud of witnesses, let us lay aside every weight, and the sin which doth so easily beset us, and let us run with patience the race that is set before us.* The reference to a cloud of witnesses suggests that the bleachers are packed right up to the top row so high that they are literally sitting in the clouds. What a testimony we have to glean from.

I Corinthians 1:5, *That in every thing ye are enriched by him, in all utterance, and in all knowledge.* Being enriched in this verse refers to being a plutocrat, a member of the ruling class who is in that position because of his wealth. It does not refer to buying a political position but to the practice of gaining position because your resources prove that you have the wisdom and ingenuity to make the decisions necessary to run the government. Faith in Christ puts us in this category.

October 12

The Jubilee Singers

In the years immediately following the War Between the States, the American Missionary Association founded Fisk University, a college in Nashville, Tennessee, to educate freedmen and other young African Americans. Facing bankruptcy and closure, the treasurer and music director, George L. White, a white Northern missionary, gathered a nine-member student chorus to go on tour to raise funds. They faced extreme difficulties due to the prejudice of the days. Often, they were refused hotel accommodations, meals, and even seats on the train as they traveled from city to city. Ridiculing articles in the local newspapers discouraged people from coming out to their concerts as well as discouraging the team from continuing with its mission.

After a concert in Cincinnati in October 1871, an announcement was made that news had just been received that a devastating fire had destroyed most of the city of Chicago that day. The group responded by donating their total profit from the concert to the relief effort. Penniless, they had to decide if they should continue their efforts. It was at that point that they came up with the name Jubilee Singers in memory of the Jewish year of Jubilee, referencing the year of jubilee when all the slaves in Israel were set free. Since most of the students at Fisk University and their families were newly freed slaves, the name seemed fitting. As the tour continued, audiences came to appreciate the singers' voices, and the group began to be praised. The Jubilee Singers are credited with the early popularization of the Negro spiritual tradition among white and northern audiences in the late nineteenth century. They were invited to perform at the White House for President Ulysses S. Grant and made a tour of Great Britain and Europe where they sang for Queen Victoria. Their efforts financed the construction of Jubilee Hall, Fisk's first permanent building, which is now listed as a National Historic Landmark.

They came out of slavery, poverty, and discrimination to make an indelible mark on society and history. So can you!

October 13

Redeemed

Two different Greek words are used in the New Testament to speak of being redeemed. *Exagorazo* refers to buying a slave out of the slave market, and *lutroo* makes reference to ransoming an individual from the hands of kidnappers. Paul uses the slave market terminology four times – twice referring to our redemption from the bondage of the law (Galatians 3:13, 4:5) and two times speaking of redeeming the time (Ephesians 5:16 Colossians 4:5). The kidnapping term is used three times in the New Testament, once each by Jesus, Paul and Peter. Luke 24:21 speaks of the redemption of Israel. Titus 2:14 speaks of our redemption from iniquity. First Peter 1:18 tells us that our ransom was not paid with silver and gold but with the precious blood of Christ.

There seems to be a slight nuance of meaning displayed in these various usages. When a person is held in slavery, he is held in forced conscription. This is exactly what happens when we fall into the bondage of the law and what happens when we do not purposefully use our time. The law will make us feel that we must do certain rituals and live up to set standards in order to be worthy before God. If we do not divinely order our time, we will find ourselves in the continual "rat race" of always having something to do. The references to the kidnapper's ransom are different in the sense that a kidnapper does not force his victim into labor. He may be abused and deprived while held by the kidnapper, but he is not generally forced to work. The objective of holding a hostage is not to earn money by his work but to earn money by having someone pay for his release. The passages where ransom is referenced have to do with exactly that concept. Because Israel was the apple of God eye, Satan wanted to take them hostage to insult the great worth that God had placed on them. Sin and iniquity degrade and devalue believers, making them seem worthless in spite of the fact that God has loved us enough to give His Son for us. The fact that God was willing to pay the price of His Son's blood demonstrates how much He valued us and wanted to ransom us from the kidnapper's clutches.

October 14

He Knows You

On hearing of the death of Pulitzer Prize-winning cartoonist Jeff MacNelly, creator of the comic strip <u>Shoe</u>, fellow cartoonist Walt Handelsman of <u>The Times-Picayune</u> (New Orleans) wrote: "I once received a call from (editorial cartoonist) Mike Peters, complimenting me on a cartoon and saying that he and Jeff MacNelly had just been talking about how much they liked it, and when I got off the phone I told my editor that that was the highlight of my career – just knowing that Jeff MacNelly knew who I was."

It's hard to explain, but to have someone great know who you are brings a sense of significance to life. God, the greatest One in the Universe, knows us by name. In fact, he knows everything about us. And he loves us.

Several times in the scripture, God made a point to call individuals specifically by their names. (Exodus 31:2, 33:12, 33:17, 35:30) In John 10:3, Jesus specifically said that He calls all His sheep by their own names. God is individually interested in each one of us. (I Peter 5:7)

> *Henceforth I call you not servants; for the servant knoweth not what his lord doeth: but I have called you friends; for all things that I have heard of my Father I have made known unto you. Ye have not chosen me, but I have chosen you, and ordained you, that ye should go and bring forth fruit, and that your fruit should remain: that whatsoever ye shall ask of the Father in my name, he may give it you...If ye were of the world, the world would love his own: but because ye are not of the world, but I have chosen you out of the world, therefore the world hateth you.* (John 15:15, 16,19)

October 15

In Him and He in Us

The New Testament repeatedly speaks of believers being in Christ and the Holy Spirit being in believers. Colossians 3:3 even tells us that our life is hid with Christ in God. The imagery presented here is that of a fish and water in a tank. The fish is in the water and the water is in the fish at the same time. This is unlike a scuba diver who is in water but the water not in him. The relationship we have with God is not a one-way street. The life of God is inside of us and flowing through us at the same time we are living in His presence.

The imagery of the fish versus the scuba diver may also help us understand the difference between the two Greek words *baptzo* and *baptizo*. *Baptzo* refers to dipping into a liquid, whereas *baptizo* means to submerge, to dye, or even to drown. If water gets inside the scuba diver, he suddenly shifts from one verb to the other – not to mention that he also shifts from earth to heaven! When something experiences a true *baptizo* encounter, he has a permanent change. To dunk a cucumber in vinegar will have no effect, but to submerge it for a long duration will change it into a pickle. God's plan for us is that we be submerged, literally drowned, in the Spirit – but not to become pickled!

In Hebrews 4:12, *For the word of God is quick, and powerful, and sharper than any two-edged sword, piercing even to the dividing asunder of soul and spirit, and of the joints and marrow, and is a discerner of the thoughts and intents of the heart*, the word speaking of the two-edged sword can actually be translated "double-mouthed." The power of the Word of God is that it is in two mouths at the same time – God's mouth and your mouth. Romans 10:8 shows us the power of the Word of God when it is in our mouths, and Revelation 1:16 declares that the Word of God in His mouth is powerful enough to subdue all enemies.

October 16

You're in the Army Now

For the US Marines, it takes only a few good men to get the job done. For the US Army, it's the tough who get going when the going gets tough. For the US Navy, they do the difficult immediately even though it might take them a little while to do the impossible. Just imagine the possibilities for the Spirit-empowered Army of God!

> *Finally, my brethren, be strong in the Lord, and in the power of his might. Put on the whole armour of God, that ye may be able to stand against the wiles of the devil. For we wrestle not against flesh and blood, but against principalities, against powers, against the rulers of the darkness of this world, against spiritual wickedness in high places. Wherefore take unto you the whole armour of God, that ye may be able to withstand in the evil day, and having done all, to stand. Stand therefore, having your loins girt about with truth, and having on the breastplate of righteousness; And your feet shod with the preparation of the gospel of peace; Above all, taking the shield of faith, wherewith ye shall be able to quench all the fiery darts of the wicked. And take the helmet of salvation, and the sword of the Spirit, which is the word of God: Praying always with all prayer and supplication in the Spirit, and watching thereunto with all perseverance and supplication for all saints.* (Ephesians 6:10-18)
> *Thou therefore endure hardness, as a good soldier of Jesus Christ. No man that warreth entangleth himself with the affairs of this life; that he may please him who hath chosen him to be a soldier. And if a man also strive for masteries, yet is he not crowned, except he strive lawfully.* (II Timothy 2:3-5)

October 17
The Persecuted
In a recent article on the suffering church, FaithWorks listed the degrees of persecution one could face for practice of religious faith:

1) Disapproval
2) Ridicule
3) Pressure to conform
4) Loss of educational opportunities
5) Economic sanctions
6) Shunning
7) Alienation from community
8) Loss of employment
9) Loss of property
10) Physical abuse
11) Mob violence
12) Harassment by officials
13) Kidnapping
14) Forced labor
15) Imprisonment
16) Physical torture
17) Murder or execution

In my ministry around the world, I've had opportunity to meet many people who have suffered severely for their faith. One lady who is always on the front row in our services in Nepal has her entire face disfigured as the result of her Hindu husband's rage when he learned that she had become a Christian. He threw a bottle of acid on her. In Niger, I met a young man who had been kicked out of his home to fend for himself as a teenager because he told his Muslim parents that he was a believer. A young Jewish girl I led to the Lord while in college was disowned because she received Christian baptism. A lady in Nepal was allowed to continue to live with her family but not allowed to come to the table and join them for meals because she attended a Christian church. One young lady and an older woman died when a bomb went off just a few weeks after I had ministered in the same church.

Though we have a hard time imagining their suffering, we are commanded to intercede as if suffering with them.

October 18

The Power of a Name

With a name like "Delron," I've certainly had my share of questions and difficulties over the years. I'm constantly asked if it is a family name or a foreign name. The truth is my mother made up the name. She thought that those particular syllables sounded good together. Of course, there's always the issue of how to properly pronounce or spell it. In fact, I was at one meeting where the guy who was trying to introduce me pronounced it so many ways that I was almost confused myself by the time I took the microphone. One pastor in India finally decided to shorten my name to Del with the explanation that he had a Dell computer and that every time he needed to remember my name, he just needed to look at his laptop. Of course the fact that my last name sounds like a lady's name doesn't help matters either. I often get junk mail addressed to Miss Shirley Delron. To add to all this, Delron is actually my middle name. So on official documents like my passport and insurance papers, I'm known as Randall. It often causes problems overseas when the expected Delron shows up as Randall. Perhaps the biggest problem I ever encountered was on the first "real" job I ever had. My supervisor almost fired me the first day because he kept calling me Randy which he assumed would be the name I would answer to since my employment file had my name listed as Randall. Every time he called me I simply ignored him, thinking that he was speaking to another employee. Finally, he "got in my face" and demanded, "Young man, are you deaf?" I had no clue what the problem was until he again referred to me as Randy.

Some years later, I learned that there is a powerful connection between who we are and what name we answer to. If we answer to negative nomenclature such as "Stupid," we take that image into ourselves and actually become like that image! There is real power in our names – even to some amazing scenarios. Students whose names begin with C or D are more likely to get poor grades than students whose names begin with A or B. Baseball players whose names begin with K (the strike out symbol) are more likely to strike out when at bat.

October 19

The Important Role of Servants

I once heard a prominent Bible teacher make the comment that if you visit the home of an important person, your first impression will be determined by the attitude of the lowest servant. He went on to explain that the first person you meet will be a servant and that it is through him that you'll get your first sense about the overall organization and, therefore, the man behind the operation. I remember taking note of the comment but not being particularly impressed by it. However, over the years, I've come to recognize the validity in the observation. I've never met Queen Elizabeth or the Pope, but the impressions made by the Royal Guard at the gates of Buckingham Palace and the Swiss Guard at the entrance to the Vatican certainly left me with a feeling of the importance of these two world leaders.

We can see this principle exemplified in even such a simple matter as going to a restaurant. We will not meet the CEO of the restaurant chain or even the manager of the local establishment. We won't even meet the chef of the line cooks. The only person we will interact with will be the lowest paid employee in the place – our waiter. Yet, it is that person who will determine how we feel about the restaurant and will be the major factor in whether we will ever return.

Notice that twice in the story of the Queen of Sheba's visit to King Solomon we see reference to the fact that she was impressed by the state of Solomon's servants.

> *And the meat of his table, and the sitting of his servants, and the attendance of his ministers, and their apparel, and his cupbearers, and his ascent by which he went up unto the house of the LORD; there was no more spirit in her...Happy are thy men, happy are these thy servants, which stand continually before thee, and that hear thy wisdom.* (I Kings 10:5, 8)

As servants of the Lord, we need to be aware of exactly how important it is for us to properly represent the King we serve.

October 20
All Creatures Great and Small
Please don't misunderstand what I'm about to say. I am not in any way opposed to trying to save the rain forest or protect whales. And (God forbid) I am certainly not advocating any less diligence in trying to capture and prosecute the evil men who poach elephants, rhinos, and tigers. I just want to take a minute to point out one interesting little-known fact. As we are bringing high-profiled attention to the fact that extinction of various species of animals and plants is occurring in our world today at the rate that hasn't been known since the end of the age of the dinosaurs, new species are being discovered at the rate that far exceeds any period in history with the exception of the day that Adam named all the animals. New species have been cataloged at a rate of about one every three days for the past ten years. The World Wildlife Federation counted twelve hundred new species – including six hundred thirty-seven plants, two hundred fifty-seven fish, two hundred sixteen amphibians, fifty-five reptiles, sixteen birds, and thirty-six mammals that were discovered in the Amazon Basin alone during the first decade of the new millennium.

Certainly, the discovery of one species does not counterbalance the loss of another. The only point I'm trying to make is that God has filled the earth with more than we have ever been able to understand or even dream about. As we worry about the loss of one thing, God is graciously lifting His hand to reveal that He has even more in store for us to discover.

> *O LORD, how manifold are thy works! in wisdom hast thou made them all: the earth is full of thy riches. So is this great and wide sea, wherein are things creeping innumerable, both small and great beasts.*
> (Psalm 104:24-25)

But this principle works in all of life, not just in the world of fauna and flora. Never worry about what you might lose in life. Just keep your eyes open for what He is going to give you in its place!

October 21

One-liners That Pack a Punch

Talk to God about men, then talk to men about God.

Alexander the Great would say of his brave soldiers that he was proud to call them brothers. Jesus does too. (Hebrews 2:11)

The church needs a backbone, not a wishbone.

The evils in America are the ones that couldn't make it on the overseas mission field.

Be an organ donor; give your heart to Jesus.

Paganism asks for people to sacrifice children to their gods. God gave His son for us.

Abortion is the sacrifice of children to the god of convenience.

God is not Pharaoh. He does not ask us to make bricks without giving us straw.

The chief end of man is to glorify God and enjoy Him forever. This present life is the classroom and dressing room for eternity.

Travel is fatal to prejudice, bigotry, and narrow-mindedness. – Mark Twain

When Jesus showed up, there was a revival or a riot – but never indifference.

Wisdom is the principle thing, but it is not everything.

Bad boys need to be watched; good boys don't mind being watched. Keep an eye on all of them!

Thanks to the interstate highway system, you can travel from coast to coast without seeing a thing.

Vision leads to provision.

Enjoy the tempo of a God-directed life as Jesus sets the pace.

God is present in the present.

Friends are very expensive, but they are priceless.

People who get healed if you pray for them while you are living in error are proof of the love of God.

I've lived on the north side, south side, east side, west side; now I'm living on the Lord's side

October 22
The Sabbath Was Made for Man
Forty-five percent of Americans rate Sundays much more enjoyable than other days. The percentage of the fondest childhood memories associated with Sunday include:

Church/Sunday school: 36
Special dinners: 24
Special family outings: 17
Watching Disney or 60 Minutes as a family: 9
Watching sports: 6
Wearing Sunday-best clothes: 3

The Jewish leaders of Jesus' day developed a set of regulations to ensure that the sabbath would be preserved. These rules, no matter how good their original intentions were, became a burden. The gospels recite incident after incident where that protection of the sanctity of the sabbath became more important than human life as the religious leaders attacked Jesus for healing individuals on the holy day. Eventually, Jesus answered these challenges with the conclusion that the sabbath was made for man, and not man for the Sabbath. (Mark 2:27) It is intended to be a day of rest so that the physical body can be renewed, a day of worship so the spirit can be restored, and a day of fellowship so the soulical man can be refreshed.

Six days thou shalt labour, and do all thy work: But the seventh day is the sabbath of the LORD thy God: in it thou shalt not do any work, thou, nor thy son, nor thy daughter, nor thy m
anservant, nor thy maidservant, nor thine ox, nor thine ass, nor any of thy cattle, nor thy stranger that is within thy gates; that thy manservant and thy maidservant may rest as well as thou. (Deuteronomy 5:13-14)
Six days thou shalt do thy work, and on the seventh day thou shalt rest: that thine ox and thine ass may rest, and the son of thy handmaid, and the stranger, may be refreshed. (Exodus 23:12)

October 23

Stories That Make a Point

In the book <u>The Ascent of a Leader</u>, Bruce McNicol and Bill Thrall tell of a woman who had a dream in which she wandered into a shop at the mall and found Jesus behind a counter. Jesus offered, "You can have anything your heart desires." Astounded but pleased, the lady asked for peace, joy, happiness, wisdom, and freedom from fear. Then she added, "Not just for me, but for the whole earth." Jesus smiled and replied, "I think you misunderstand me. We don't sell fruits, only seeds."

In a commencement speech given at Emerson College in Boston, multi-billionaire Ted Turner talked about success: "It's all relative...I sit down and say, 'I've only got ten billion dollars, but Bill Gates has a hundred billion.' I feel like I'm a complete failure in life. So billions won't make you happy if you're worried about someone who's got more than you...So don't let yourself get caught in a trap of measuring your success by how much material success you have."

Jamey Ray of New York was born with only one arm; yet, has pursued his desire to play classical music on the piano. He is so accomplished that his audiences never notice that he is only playing with one hand until he stands to take his bow after the performance.

A five-year-old girl had disobeyed her mom and had been sent to her room. After a few minutes, the mother went in to talk with her about what she had done. Teary-eyed, the little girl asked, "Why do we do wrong things, Mommy?" The mother replied, "Sometimes the devil tells us to do something wrong, and we listen to him. We need to listen to God instead." To this the lass sobbed, "But God doesn't talk loud enough!"

When Drew Carey was asked by <u>Ladies' Home Journal</u> if he considered himself ambitious, Carey answered, "Now, yes. But before, I always thought I was going to win the lottery or get lucky. I had no idea what I was going to do. Now I would never buy a lottery ticket – that would be like slapping God in the face."

October 24

Some Things in Life Just Can't Be Taken Seriously

In Houston, Texas, a man robbed Family Dollar Store dressed in Spongbob Squarepants pajamas.

In Cleveland, Ohio, a man dressed in a gorilla costume to promote cell phones was attacked by an assailant dressed in a banana suit.

In Peterborough, Ontario, Canada, a bank robber fled via cab but stopped at a coffee shop a few blocks away for his morning coffee.

In Sacramento, California, David Senk took two big bites out of another man's three-foot pet python.

The sign warning drivers of commercial vehicles that they use snow chains under snowy conditions read, "Chain station two miles if flashing." I couldn't help wondering how far the station would be if the sign were not blinking.

I always wonder about the evangelists who tell everybody bow head and close eyes. Then they go around the church, section by section, asking people who want prayer to raise their hand. How do they expect people to know what section they are pointing to if they have their eyes closed?

A driver in Portland, Oregon, was stopped three times in a one-hour period for speeding: 105 MPH, 98 MPH, and 92 MPH. He was in a hurry to appear in court on charges of possession of meth.

When the pastor's children were called in for dinner, their mother reminded them, "Be sure to wash your hands." The little boy scowled and said, "Germs and Jesus. Germs and Jesus. That's all I hear, and I've never seen either one of them."

In Glasgow, Scotland, a pizza delivery man was robbed of his pizza, cash, and phone. He ran to the first house with lights on and asked to come in to call the police. A few minutes later, the robber showed up. It was his mother's house.

Chen Wei-yi of Taipei married herself as a protest to the fact that the country is putting pressure on young women to marry as a way of addressing the country's dwindling birth rate. Chen says, "You must love yourself before you can love others."

October 25
Blessings Shall Chase After You (Deuteronomy 28:2)

Peggy and I had a couple days free before heading home after ministering in England and Ireland, so we decided to do a little exploring. In one of the shops we visited, Peggy found a darling little ceramic memento of the Emerald Isles and thought that it was fairly priced, so she decided to purchase it. We had walked about a block and a half down the street after leaving the store when we suddenly heard the clerk from the shop calling out for us to stop. Curious as to what was the problem, we came back and asked what was the matter. The clerk responded that she hadn't realized that the item was on sale and that she had charged us full price. She was running after us to give us our money back. I've often thought that she didn't need to give us the sale price since we were happy with what we had paid and that even if she did want to adjust the price she could have simply personally pocketed the money.

But that isn't the only time we have been chased down like that. A good friend of ours had a daughter who was living in Hawaii and was going to be married in the islands. The father stopped me one day to say that we would be receiving an invitation to the wedding. I politely thanked him and said that we would be sending a nice card or gift to the couple. He then repeated to me that we were going to be invited to the wedding. Again, I politely thanked him, and again he insisted that we were going to receive an invitation. After the strange repetition of the conversation, he finally interrupted to explain that what he meant by "receive an invitation" was that airline tickets and hotel accommodations would be included with the invitation. After I picked my jaw up from the floor, I called Peggy over to hear the news. Of course, we were elated to accept the invitation and had a great time at the wedding. But there was more to the story. After the reception, we were walking back to our car when I heard my friend's voice calling my name from across the parking lot. When we looked back, I saw him running after us just like the little lady in Ireland. When he caught up with us, he shoved a handful of cash into my hand with the explanation that he had failed to include spending money with the tickets!

October 26

Inadequate

My first mission trip was to Japan with a Japanese friend from seminary. He would go back home to minster during each summer break, and always asked me to join him. The first summer, I politely nodded when he extended the invitation and promptly dismissed the idea. The second summer, I also politely thanked him for the invitation and ignored the request. When he made the offer the third summer, there was something different about his invitation, he concluded the request with, "and I've already booked your tickets." No, he didn't pay for them; he simply put them on hold under my name. Well, that was enough to make me decide to be serious about the request. As I prayed about it I gave God all the excuses I could think of as to why I shouldn't go. When I got to, "I'm not adequate," He responded with such a distinctly clear reply that to this day I still wonder if it might have been an actual audible voice. When God speaks, He can say just a few words but convey volumes of meaning. That is exactly what He did that day. His words were, "I know that you're not adequate. That's why I'm sending you." The commentary on the actual words communicated that if I were adequate I'd go in my own ability rather than relying upon His ability working through me.

Well, I did go to Japan that summer and had one of the most unusual experiences imaginable. I was scheduled to speak for a week at a youth camp in a rather remote area where no one spoke English. Of course, that many years ago, very few Japanese outside the major cities were bilingual. My friend was to serve as my translator; however, his wife fell seriously ill and he had to take her back to the hospital in Tokyo. The result was that I was stranded for the full week and couldn't minister in any of the sessions. When my friend came back at the end of the week to pick me up, the director of the camp asked him to translate a message of thanks to me for being with them for the week. In the salutation, he said, "We've learned so much from you." I interrupted to ask how since I had not ministered. The response was that they had learned from the Spirit in me. Thank God, I was inadequate!

Words of Wisdom

Live so the preacher won't have to lie at your funeral.

Success comes from good decisions; the ability to make good decisions from experience; experience from having made bad decisions.

Money comes, and money goes. Some folks blow it like a runny nose.

Without the bread of life, you're toast.

You were given your free will for one choice – to choose God.

There is enough for every man's need, but not enough for a few men's greed.

Those afraid to make mistakes will never make anything.

There is no progress without process. Adam was created full grown but fell within one chapter.

What you drive isn't as important as what's driving you.

If you want to enjoy the ministry of angels, you first have to endure the harassments of demons. (Matthew 4:11)

If this world is not your home, pass through quickly and get out of the way of those of us who are here to change the world.

Business is not competition. It is alternative. Give your customers options.

GOD – Great Organized Designer

When the church becomes absolutely different from the world, she invariably attracts it. It is then that the world is made to listen to her message though it may hate it at first.

Build the kingdom, not your own empire.

The Swswswsw principle works well in sales and in witnessing: Some will; some won't. So what, someone's waiting.

October 28
Anecdotes That Teach Life Lessons

A young man had gotten into some trouble with the law and hired a prominent lawyer to plea his case. When the "not guilty" verdict was handed down, the young man felt that he could continue to break the law and continue to get by. Eventually, he was apprehended again, and again brought to court. When he walked into the courtroom and saw that the judge was the same man who had defended him so brilliantly during his first trial, he felt even more confident that he would again get by. But to the young man's surprise, the judge explained, "Before, I was your lawyer. Today, I am your judge. You are sentenced to be hanged by the neck until dead." Today, Jesus is our advocate, but there will be a day when He will judge this world's sinners. Come to Him for grace today so that you can stand before Him in confidence in that day.

Norman Schwarzkopf took over command of a battalion near front lines during the Vietnam War. After training and encouraging the men, they intercepted a message from the enemy that stated that the previous inept force must have been replaced by a much tougher and more highly skilled unit. The Holy Spirit is standing willing today to encourage and instruct us in the spiritual battles we face. Allow Him to empower you.

English cuckoo birds lay their eggs in the nests of other birds. The unsuspecting mothers will sit on the eggs even though they are larger and different from their own eggs. These surrogate moms will feed the hatchlings, but since the cuckoo chicks are much larger than the rest, they will get all the worms. These invader chicks will eventually push the others out of the nests. So it is with the devil. Once he plants his thoughts and opinions in our hearts, we unwittingly nurture them to the point that they rob us of our own thoughts and the truths that God wants to develop in us, pushing them totally out of our hearts and minds. We must constantly be on guard that these eggs not get laid in our "nests."

October 29

Some of These Stories Are Made Up, But Some Are True

I met the Surgeon General, and he offered me a cigarette.

I knew I was in trouble with my girlfriend when she told me that she had to get off the phone because there was a telemarketer on the other line.

In a movie theater, I couldn't hear the dialogue over the chatter between two ladies in the row in front of me. Finally I tapped them on the shoulders and said that I couldn't hear. One retorted, "Well, I hope not! This is a private conversation!"

A blond and her boyfriend were walking down the street when the guy said, "Oh, look. A dead bird." The girl looked up into the sky and asked, "Where?"

An Afro-American friend of mine told me that he never believed in Santa Claus because he knew that no white dude would come into his neighborhood after dark.

I was puzzled when the clerk asked if my payment would be paper, plastic or rubber. Then he pointed to the sign explaining the store's returned check policy.

As the cashier was ringing up my pint of Haagen-Dazs ice cream, I asked, "How do you pronounce that?" She slowly and deliberately enunciated, "Four dollars and ninety-five cents."

In Haverstraw, New York, a man walked into the Taco Bell, robbed the cashier, and went into the manger's office to apply for a job.

In Chandler, Arizona, an ecofriendly program has started recycling gray water to flush their toilets. Hence, signs in the bathrooms warn that the toilet water is not safe to drink.

When the 911 dispatcher asked if the lady on the call had an address, she replied, "No, just slacks and a blouse."

When the 911 operator asked what the caller was doing before he started experiencing the severe chest pains and shortness of breath, he answered, "Running from the police."

It was no surprise to find her dead body stretched across the bed with her clothes piled on the floor beside her. After all, she was not about to get caught dead in last year's fashions.

October 30

You Decide if These Stories Are Fact or Fiction

They actually built a small cemetery in the mall parking lot for the women who shopped until they dropped.

When little boy, who was the in the hospital after being hit by a car when chasing a ball, was asked by the rehab counselor what he would do next time his ball went into the street, he answered, "Send my sister after it."

The doctor was trying to explain the dangers of an unhealthful lifestyle to a non-English speaker. When the interpreter told the gentleman that his drinking and smoking was slowly killing him, he replied, "Good, I'm in no hurry to die."

My friend asked my grandmother if she ever had kids.

It has been scientifically proven that men fall asleep faster and sleep more soundly in a rocking hammock than in a solid bed.

A company is producing underwear with the Fourth Amendment (the one about being protected from unreasonable search) printed at strategic spots on the underwear. It shows up on the screen when the wearer is subjected to full-body scans at airport security lanes.

Two men – one a believer and one not – were having an argument. Eventually, the unbeliever suggested, "Let's stop this conversation because I don't believe you, and I'm convinced that you don't believe yourself. If you really did believe what you're saying, you would put every penny into fulfilling the message."

A preacher asked a farmer, "If you had two hundred dollars, would you give one hundred dollars to the Lord?" "Sure would," said the farmer. Next, the preacher asked, "If you had two cows, would you give one cow to the Lord?" "Yeah, I would," came the farmer's reply. Next, the preacher questioned, "If you had two pigs, would you give one of them to the Lord?" The farmer replied, "That's not fair. You know I have two pigs."

When John the Baptist went beyond his ministry of announcing the coming of the messiah to become a marriage counselor, King Herod was his first client.

October 31

A True Horror Story

It happened during one of those Rockwellian moments: a grandmother making cookies with her seven-year-old granddaughter. It was the kind of moment a grandmother wraps around her like a handmade shawl, to keep her warm months later, when the smell of Snickerdoodles no longer fills the kitchen, and the child has returned to another time zone. The little girl, the grandmother noticed, was engrossed in the flour. She had a knife and, with the intensity of a sculptor – a sculptor whose little tongue suggested she was deep in concentration – carefully shaped the fine powder into a pattern of neat, narrow lines. "How cute," the woman remembered thinking. Then the little girl looked up at her. "Look, Grandma," she said, "this is how Mom and Gary cut their cocaine."

But this is just one of a plethora of scenes that paint a startling picture of the drug culture's legacy on American home life: A teenage girl shares her hopes and dreams with her mother – as they binge on methamphetamines. A boy bonds with his father over a marijuana-filled bong. For the vast majority of families, scenes such as these are hard to fathom. But counselors who deal with teen addicts across the country say that parents' complicity has become a significant factor in putting kids on a path to drug dependency. A new survey of nearly six hundred teens in drug treatment in New York, Texas, Florida, and California indicated that twenty percent have shared drugs other than alcohol with their parents, and that about five percent of the teens actually were introduced to drugs – usually marijuana – by their moms or dads.

November 1
Fullness of Time

I'm sure that we have all heard the expression of something or someone being "ahead of its/his time." We also use the expression, "Your time has come." And of course, there is the wine company that touts the idea that they will sell no wine before its time. Actually all these thoughts are based on the biblical truth that there is an appointed and set time for everything in God's economy.

> *To every thing there is a season, and a time*
> *to every purpose under the heaven.*
> (Ecclesiastes 3:1)

Galatians 4:4 and Ephesians 1:10 speak of the fullness, of time, suggesting that we might sometimes want to make things happen before they have had their full-term gestation period. Just like a premature baby will face critical – or even fatal – complications or fruit picked before it is ripe will not have its full flavor, anything that we try to rush ahead of God's schedule will not have His full blessing.

Jesus told us a parable in Mark 4:26-29 in which He said that the kingdom of God is like seed that needs to go through the full developmental steps of sprouting, growth and maturity until it produces the full corn in the ear. Let's take one biblical story as an example of what this means. In Acts chapter three, we read about a crippled man who had spent his entire life begging at the Beautiful Gate in the temple in Jerusalem. No doubt, Jesus and His disciples had walked past him many, many times. They had probably even tossed an occasional coin or two into his begging cup as they passed by. Even though His ministry was characterized by miraculous healings in every place He visited, Jesus apparently walked right past this poor man and never even asked if he wanted to walk. It was only after the death, resurrection, and ascension of Jesus and the outpouring of the Holy Spirit on the Day of Pentecost that this man was healed. Why? Five thousand souls were won to the Lord as a result. The man's time and the time for the kingdom of God had finally come.

Election Day
We Need Some New Men in Office
The following story will help illustrate why it is so important that we prayerfully decide which men and women to vote into office. We need some new (new as in new creatures in Christ) in office in this country.

Homeowners Chuck and Stephanie Fromm were fined $300 for holding a home Bible study in the city of San Juan Capistrano, which was ironically founded as a mission in the late 1700s. In fact, San Juan Capistrano is home to California's oldest building still in use, a chapel where Father Junipero Serra celebrated mass.

A hearing officer told Fromm that regular gatherings of more than three people require a conditional use permit. Officials also stated that further religious gatherings in the home would be subject to a $500 fine per meeting. Although the group is not affiliated with any particular church, nor is it seeking to establish a church in the home, the city is insisting the home Bible study is not allowed because it is a "church," and churches require a Conditional Use Permit in residential areas. "Imposing a heavy-handed permit requirement on a home Bible study is outrageous," says Brad Dacus, president of Pacific Justice Institute. "In a city so rich with religious history and tradition, this is particularly egregious...An informal gathering in a home cannot be treated with suspicion by the government, or worse than any other gathering of friends, just because it is religious...We cannot allow this to happen in America, and we will fight as long and as hard as it takes to restore this group's religious freedom."

Fromm says there was no noise beyond normal conversation and quiet music on the home stereo system. The Christians met inside the Fromm's family room and patio area. Many neighbors have written letters of support, denying that they were disturbed by the presence of the Bible study. Fromm appealed, but the city rejected the appeal.

November 3
Athens vs. Corinth
In Acts 17:15-34, we read the story of Paul's ministry in the city of Athens. I find this particular episode in Paul's ministry very intriguing in that it is the only visit to a city that didn't result in a permanent planting of the gospel. The summation of his visit was that a few people found his message curious while others ridiculed it outright. A few people believed, with only three individuals specially mentioned. We really don't have to look very hard to see why he was so unsuccessful in his ministry there. The account of his evangelism methodology in Athens is a classic model for what we know today as the "seeker sensitive approach." He tried to relate to the people on their level by talking about their culture and even quoting their own secular philosophers.

When Paul left Athens, his next stop was in Corinth, just a little over fifty miles away. Although there was only a short distance between the two cities, Paul's ministry in Corinth and the results he achieved there were light years ahead of what had happened in Athens. Even though the church was rife with problems of almost every description, it was a strong and vital church that made an impact on the city and church history. We find his key in the first letter he sent back to the congregation he established in the city.

> And my speech and my preaching was not with enticing words of man's wisdom, but in demonstration of the Spirit and of power: That your faith should not stand in the wisdom of men, but in the power of God. (verses 2:4-5)

The real question I have about the whole scenario is why Paul ever tried to use human tactics in Athens when he had already established a powerful and effective method in Thessalonica, one of the last cities he visited before Athens.

> For our gospel came not unto you in word only, but also in power, and in the Holy Ghost, and in much assurance; as ye know what manner of men we were among you for your sake. (I Thessalonians 1:5)

November 4

Need a Good Laugh?

If so, try these on for size:

Procrastinate now – don't put it off.

The television series I Love Lucy was born out of Desi and Lucy's decision to profit from their own mistakes rather than letting the divorce lawyers make the money.

A thief broke into a slot machine and rushed into the street. In his attempt to commandeer a slow-moving vehicle outside the place as a get away car, he jumped into a police car that was patrolling the block.

When a pickpocket was accosted, he shoved the wallet back and ran away. The only problem was that he gave the victim his own wallet instead – complete with his ID.

A man who stole six laptops from a company that sells second-hand electronics was apprehended when he posted the "hot" merchandise on the website of the very company he "lifted" them from.

A man tripped on an ascending escalator and fell down the steps for almost an hour. Okay, so this one is a little exaggerated.

Actual excuses submitted for not coming to work:

My twelve-year-old daughter stole my car.

A bat got stuck in my hair.

I injured my back while chasing a beaver.

I was bitten by a deer.

My brother-in-law was kidnapped by the drug cartel.

I had a headache after attending too many garage sales

President Franklin Delano Roosevelt thought that people really never heard what he was saying because they were too nervously worrying about what they were supposed to say that he often muttered, "I murdered my grandmother this morning." He had only one person who actually noticed what he said. The gentleman replied, "I'm sure that she deserved it."

November 5
Acceptance in the Body of Christ
In I Corinthians 12:17, Paul is discussing the necessity of accepting all the members of the Body of Christ without prejudice. *If the whole body were an eye, where were the hearing? If the whole were hearing, where were the smelling?* Someone once looked at that verse and then, after looking at the condition within the church, offered an answer, "We all smell." Yes, it is true. We all have a tendency to reek with prejudice against others within our own family of God.

When I was a freshman in college, the Christian group I fellowshipped with set a spy in my dorm to watch me because they knew that I spoke in tongues and they wanted to find proof that I was actually a cult member trying to infiltrate their ranks. Some good friends of mine from seminary were kicked off the mission field by their denomination because they became Spirit-filled – just when they were probably ready to be the most effective workers that the denomination could have sponsored. On the other hand, the shoe fits just as snuggly on the other foot. I've also known some Pentecostals who were "too good" to work with other Christian churches to help minister at a local Billy Graham crusade.

Sometimes, the divisions are over a lot less significant things than doctrinal issues. I remember taking a college group to tour a tract-publishing ministry in the heart of the Amish-Mennonite country in Indiana. A number of the volunteers working in the ministry were dressed in the traditional black clothing of these ultra-conservative groups, and the women were wearing the lacy head coverings characteristic of their Anabaptist background. Several of the students were so intimidated by believers from a heritage that was so different from their own that they were literally afraid to talk with the workers. Of course, I have to admit that I even find myself falling into a judgmental attitude toward some of the younger ministers who show up in the pulpit with hair that looks like they just crawled out of bed – even though I now understand that they might have spent half an hour getting it to look that way.

Let's try to remember to use our spiritual deodorant.

November 6
Though the Vision Tarry, Wait for It. (Habakkuk 2:3)

I had known for a number of years that my ministry was to encompass the entire world, but there was no way that it could ever happen because the position I served in at the Bible school demanded that I be there essentially 24/7. Even my summers were not free because I had to maintain all the administrative work even when classes were not in session. At one point, I tried to convince myself that I did not have to personally go around the world as long as I was able to teach students who would eventually take my message to the far corners of the globe; however, no matter how much my brain would rationalize the argument, my spirit would not accept the excuse. Finally, I decided that I would have to resign from that position in order to follow my calling. I reasoned that the logical time to make that move would be when Dr. Lester Sumrall, the head of the ministry, would pass away. When he did go on to his reward, I asked the Lord if it was now time for me to make my move, but the Lord answered back, "You need to stay to help Steve through the transition." Of course, that seemed totally logical. As Dr. Sumrall's son stepped into leadership, he would need the support of the staff who had been with his father for the last many years. Strangely enough, there was never any request for my input or assistance in the transition period. I questioned what was happening, but I never questioned the voice. I knew that it was the Lord's explicit direction that I help Steve through the transition although I never saw anything happen that needed my help. Weeks turned into months, and months into years – nine years to be exact. But I couldn't make a move because I knew that I had to fulfill that last command concerning the present phase of ministry before I could take on a new phase of ministry.

When Steve decided to leave his father's ministry and start his own ministry, he asked me to be one of the handful of men who went with him to establish the new work. Instantly, I knew that the word the Lord had given me so many years before was finally coming to pass. I was helping him through the transition – just not the one I thought the Lord was talking about!

November 7
The Kingdom of Heaven is at Hand

There are presently approximately two hundred thousand new births each day globally. That means that the new birth rate is three times the natural birth rate. Here are a few quick stories about how the kingdoms of this world are becoming the kingdom of our God.

It was probably about a century and a half ago that a missionary asked an African man if he knew Jesus. When the man immediately responded in the affirmative, the missionary delved a bit deeper to find out that what the man really meant was that he knew David Livingstone. What a wonderful testimony that would be – to be at the place spiritually where people would actually confuse you with Jesus Himself!

In one of the countries where I've had the opportunity to share the gospel, Christianity is still under persecution to the point that sharing one's faith can be very dangerous. One friend there described his evangelism technique of taking two gospel tracts with him when he rides the bus. He has one in his backpack and keeps on in his shirt pocket. As he sits on the bus, he will take the tract out of his pocket and read it with extreme concentration, hoping that his seatmate will notice the intensity with which he is engrossed in the tract and ask about the contents. If the conversation does materialize, he will begin to explain the message and answer any questions. If the listener seems interested, my friend will say that he thinks that he might happen to have another one in his pack. He will then scramble through his bag looking for the other tract. Since he never initiates a conversation and since he doesn't carry a large supply of literature, he can safely dodge accusations of proselytizing.

The gospel first came to one African country after a local man had a dream of albinos with a book. Months later, Christians came to the very place and offered the people copies of the Bible. When the man met these foreigners, he immediately knew that they were the fulfillment of his dream and readily accepted the gospel.

A gospel tract may be the passport to someone's future.

November 8

Double for Your Trouble

All of us who have ever worked an hourly-paid job are familiar with the time-and-a-half policy for overtime work and the double-time policy for holiday pay, but did you know that there is actually a biblical precedent for double payment? Exodus 22:4, 22:7, 22:9, Deuteronomy 15:18, and I Timothy 5:17 all make reference to double payment for losses or for special labor, but the really interesting example is found in the story of Job who lost all that he had because of his relationship with God. When Satan appeared before God, he seems to have come to taunt Him about how he had the world under his control. God countered Satan's boast by holding up His "poster child" – Job. Satan retaliated that Job was only loyal to God because of all the riches that God had given him. At that point, God – confident that Job's relationship was not based on his toys but on true love for God – gave the devil permission to take everything that Job owned. At the end of the story, God restored exactly everything that Job lost. He had twice as many sheep, camels, oxen, and asses. He also had another set of seven sons and three daughters to go with the first family who, though dead, were alive in heaven. The only thing he didn't get doubled was his wife – and I'm certain that he didn't want another one like her! In fact, I wonder if he might have regretted that he wasn't able to trade her in and get a new one like he did with all his children.

The point of this story is that anything we lose because of our stand for the gospel never leaves our lives even though it may leave our hands. God keeps meticulous accounting records and never fails to repay with benefits.

> *There is no man that hath left house, or brethren, or sisters, or father, or mother, or wife, or children, or lands, for my sake, and the gospel's, But he shall receive an hundredfold now in this time, houses, and brethren, and sisters, and mothers, and children, and lands, with persecutions; and in the world to come eternal life.* (Mark 10:28-30)

November 9

These are True Stories About Real People

When filling in the blank on the application, one lady answered the "Person to contact in case of emergency" question with "A doctor."

In India, candy is called sweets. Therefore a man put a placard in front of his house, "Home, candy home"

In Zagreb, Croatia, there is a museum dedicated to broken relationships. Among its exhibits are a set of fake rubber breasts, an arm cast (You can imagine how broken <u>that</u> relationship must have been!), an axe that the man used to hack up the furniture in his home when his wife left him, a garden gnome that the woman threw at her husband, and a prosthetic leg from a man who fell in love with his therapist.

The US death rates dropped during the 1974 and 1982 recessions and rose during the recovery of the 1980s. The theory is that time is more valuable when the economy is good, so people work more and spend less time exercising and being with family, leading to stress, which can be bad for health. During downturns, people spend more time taking care of themselves and their children, which is good for health. The love of money <u>is</u> the root of all evil after all!

Louise Estes gave birth to her third leap-year baby in 2012. The first one in 2004 was coincidence, but the second one in 2008 and the third one in 2012 did have a little family planning. Third baby was five days late, and labor was induced. Louise tied a record that was set by a lady in Finland who had babies on successive leap years in 1960, 1964, and 1968.

One lady I know has two Bibles – her study Bible and one she calls her "fun Bible." The fun Bible has paper clips marking probably a hundred different pages that have her favorite verses highlighted. When all she wants is to be uplifted, she reads the special verses from the fun Bible, saving the rest of the book for her more serious time in her study Bible.

UFO Phil from Colorado Springs wants to build a four-hundred-eighty-foot-tall pyramid on Pikes Peak as a power plant and landing strip for aliens.

November 10

Truisms

The King of Hearts enables you to play with a full deck.

If the grass is greener on the other side of the fence, you need to fertilize yours.

Hats off to the past; coats off to the future.

When people pray, God releases more money to supply the Word of God to more people who then pray and start the cycle all over again on a larger scale.

In Acts 18:10, God told Paul that He had many people in that place, but this was before the city had been evangelized. God is the only one who can count His chickens before they hatch.

My friend who was not accustomed to a Pentecostal service remarked that he had gotten saved "the Billy Graham way."

Do not argue with an idiot. He will drag you down to his level and beat you with experience.

We never really grow up; we just learn how to act in public.

A lot of us think we want a career. It turns out that what we really want is paychecks.

You don't need a parachute to skydive. You just need one if you want to skydive twice.

I used to be indecisive; now I'm just not sure.

You're never too old to learn something stupid.

When tempted to fight fire with fire, remember that the fire department uses water.

What God is saying is superior to what He has said. Abraham would have killed Isaac if he had not heard second the command to stop.

If an insane man steals the clothes of a sane man while he is bathing, and the naked man chases him through the public street – how will you tell who is mad?

If God needed our help, He would have created Adam sooner than the last thing on the sixth day.

The Sabbath is the only day that isn't described in Genesis as having evening and morning because God went into perpetual rest.

November 11

Points to Ponder

Live your life knowing that you are on a collision course with a miracle.

Your miracle will just "show up" – like a wire transfer to your bank account.

Jesus told the lame man to rise up and walk, not to take up his bed and limp.

Don't let the devil set up an upset in your life.

Democracy commits suicide. – John Adams

If you ask God for a bike, but don't get it; the solution isn't to steal a bike and ask God for forgiveness.

Jesus told us to make peace with our enemies – not to agree with them. Then we would both be wrong.

War doesn't determine who is right, just who is left.

Prosperity knits man to world. It makes him feel that he is finding his place in the world, but it is really finding its place in him. – CS Lewis

If there's no transformation, there is no move of God.

Don't live a dial-up life in a broadband world.

God will not alter truth on the altar of consistency.

Good does not need to take permission for evil to express itself.

Prosperity won't send you to hell. If so, the devil would double your salary tomorrow.

Tithing breaks the power of greed.

The whole universe is one entity. Everything is interrelated.

In the Body of Christ, we must learn to complete – not to compete.

Be ruthless in kicking out the devil. – Dick Eastman

A new broom will sweep clean, but the old one knows corners.

You may be out of God's will, but you are never out of His reach.

The best way to get rid of your enemies is to make friends of them.

We call God holy because He is; He calls us holy because we shall be.

November 12
A Kinder, Gentler World

One researcher has made a case that a smarter, more educated world is becoming more peaceful in several statistically significant ways. Stephen Pinker of Harvard University noted that the number of people killed in battle – calculated per one hundred thousand population – has dropped by one-thousandfold over the centuries as civilizations evolved. Before there were organized countries, battles killed on average more than five hundred out of every hundred thousand people. In nineteenth century France, it was seventy. In the twentieth century with two world wars and a few genocides, it was sixty. Now battlefield deaths are down to three-tenths of a person per hundred thousand. The rate of genocide deaths per world population was fourteen hundred times higher in 1942 than in 2008. He also noted that fewer than twenty democracies existed in 1946. Now there are close to one hundred. Meanwhile, the number of authoritarian countries has dropped from a high of almost ninety in 1976 to about twenty now.

He surmised that one of the main reasons for the drop in violence is that we are smarter. IQ tests show that the average teenager is smarter with each generation. The tests are constantly adjusted to keep the average at 100, and a teenager who now would score a 100 would have scored a 118 in 1950 and a 130 in 1910. So this year's average kid would have been a near-genius a century ago. "As we get smarter, we try to think up better ways of getting everyone to turn their swords into plowshares at the same time," Pinker said. "Human life has become more precious than it used to be."

He argues that our everyday lives are also less violent. The professor estimated that there are almost one and a quarter million deaths detailed in the Old Testament. He noted that murder in European countries has steadily fallen from near one hundred per hundred thousand people in the fourteenth century to about one per hundred thousand people today.

November 13
The Bible – Only A Museum Piece

I first heard the story from Dr. Lester Sumrall who claimed to have actually personally seen Bibles stacked from floor to ceiling in the former home of the great Enlightenment philosopher Voltaire. Though modern historical scholarship argues the point that the accounts about the presses used to publish his books and the house in which he lived and wrote may be exaggerations or even outright mythological or apocryphal, there is quite a message in the story.

Voltaire (1694-1778), an outspoken atheist who ridiculed the Bible and faith in God, once said, "While it took twelve men to write Christianity up, I will show that it takes but one man to write it down!" Taking his pen, he dipped it into the ink of unbelief and wrote against God. But, the very room in which he made that statement was soon used after his death as a Bible storehouse! The printing press that published Voltaire's works was later used in Geneva to print Bibles, and Voltaire's house was used by the Geneva Bible Society as a distribution center for Bibles.

Voltaire stated that within one hundred years of his death a person would be able to find a copy of the Bible only in museums because the Bible would become a dead book; however, only twenty-five years after his death, the British and Foreign Bible Society was organized and the very presses which had been used to print Voltaire's writings were used to print copies of the Word of God. Since Voltaire's death, millions of copies of the Bible have been printed. The demand for Bibles increases, and the eternal Book lives on while Voltaire's works have yet to reach a complete English edition!

Even if his home and presses were not converted to tools for spreading the gospel, the fact remains that his proclamation of the death of the Bible has failed. In fact the Bible is being distributed more widely and in more languages today than at any previous point in history.

November 14
Lessons from the Tropical Rain Forest
While traveling through the tropical rainforest of Belize, I learned of two very interesting botanical oddities in the region.

The first is a native species of tree that contains both a powerful toxin and its antidote. Very appropriately named, the "give and take" tree is covered with razor-sharp thorns that inject a poison into the person unfortunate enough to touch the tree. Paradoxically, the only known antidote to this poison is found in the tree's own sap, which can relieve the pain of the sting as well as stop the bleeding and disinfect the wound!

The Black Poisonwood tree exudes a highly irritating sap that produces a severe rash similar to poison ivy, poison sumac, and poison oak that will often turn into extremely painful itchy and burning blisters that will spread the infection to other parts of the body. Even after the tree is chopped down and dried, the poison still can be potent. The sawdust in sawmills where the wood is being cut can produce the same burning affect, and smoke from burning old poisonwood logs can spread the poison through the air. As hostile as the poisonwood tree may seem, there is one fascinating lesson to be learned from it. There is a companion tree that is always found growing within ten feet of the poisonwood – the Gumbo Limbo tree. Amazing as it may sound, the Gumbo Limbo is the natural antidote to the poisonwood's toxin. The sap of the Gumbo Limbo relieves the rashes, stings, and burns caused by the poisonwood, and tea made from its leaves reduces fever and helps regulate blood pressure. Victims who have touched the poisonwood can cut a piece of the Gumbo Limbo bark and wipe the inside on the affected area. They can also boil the bark to make a paste that can be applied to the burn.

It is fascinating how God planned an immediate cure to accompany each of these dangerous plants. Of course, He has always done so. Remember that He planted not only the Tree of the Knowledge of Good and Evil in the midst of the Garden of Eden – He also planted the Tree of Life right next to it.

November 15

With Eyes of Faith

It is often easy to read biblical passages with certain images in our heads and not take the time to consider if those mental pictures are accurate. I realized one day as I was reading the Psalms that I often imagined King David standing, kneeling, or even whirling about in exuberant worship inside the courts of the temple. After all, he mentions the sanctuary fourteen times (verses 20:2, 63:2, 68:24, 73:17, 74:3, 74:7, 77:13, 78:54, 78:69, 96:6, 102:19, 114:2, 134:2, 150:1) and the temple ten times (verses 5:7, 11:4, 18:6, 27:4, 29:9, 48:9, 65:4, 68:29, 79:1, 138:2). However, it took a genuine reality check for me to place the Psalms in their proper chronological context – the period before the temple was even built! How is it that David could write so explicitly and so eloquently describe his emotions as he worshiped in a temple that didn't even exist? The answer is simple – he was there in the spirit. He had entered into the faith realm to the point that he was experiencing the yet-to-be-built temple as genuinely as if he was in the actual building and experiencing the sanctuary prophetically in preparation for the fulfillment of the vision.

Andrew Wommack describes his experience of walking through the unfinished building of his headquarters when it was nothing more than a shell. As he walked through the open cavern, he imagined every wall and door that was yet to be built as he cautiously avoided walking through the "solid" walls and was careful to turn the handle on each door as he went through them. He said that he was actually less excited when he walked into the finished building than when he "experienced" it by faith.

Lester Sumrall built a hangar at the South Bend airport to house a C-130 aircraft that he saw by faith even when the US government was still insisting that they would never grant him the permit to own such an aircraft.

It is said that one speaker at the dedication of Disney World lamented that he wished Walt Disney had lived to see the place. Another of the guests corrected him by saying he did see it and that is the reason they were there to experience it.

November 16

Tabatha, Arise!

It was one of those moments when you genuinely expect that the next thing to happen will be for Alfred Hitchcock's silhouette to appear or for Rod Sterling to step forward to announce that you have just entered the Twilight Zone.

I had come to the funeral home to show respects to one of my students who had lost her daughter. When I walked into the mortuary, I could find only one viewing room open – and the deceased displayed there was a young man, about the right age, but obviously the wrong gender. I walked back out the front door and totally circled the building, wondering if there might be a side entrance that led to another part of the building. Finding no other way in, I reentered the front entrance and began opening the doors to all the closed off areas. As a man on a mission, I wasn't about to be stopped simply because the doors were closed! Finally, I found my student and her family huddled in prayer in one of the closed rooms. They were so excited to see me, saying that God had sent me there at just the right moment. They then explained that a lady had just showed up, saying that she was from our ministry and that God had sent her there to raise the daughter from the dead. I then asked where this lady was and was taken to another closed off area. There, dancing around the casket, doing some bizarre incantation was a woman I'd only seen once in my life. She had been at the church service the previous night when the announcement had been made about the visitation hours and funeral arrangements. I remembered having seen her in the service and having been a bit unsettled by some of her actions during the worship time. Now, here she was, invading these hurting people's tragedy with the lie that she was from our ministry and that God had sent her to raise the dead daughter. I calmly – but authoritatively – stopped her and confronted her over the lie of misrepresenting herself as being part of our ministry. Once I got her to confess her deception and apologize to the family, she left. I was then able to have a time of healing prayer and counseling with my friends. The girl didn't come back to life; but at least their faith did.

November 17

Beaver It or Not

During World War II, the US Marines spent two million dollars trying to train bats to drop tiny bombs across Japan.

A group of owls is called a parliament, and a group of frogs is called an army.

George Washington's teeth were not wooden. They were made of elephant ivory and walrus tusks.

Humans share over ninety-eight percent of their DNA with chimpanzees, but we also share seventy percent with slugs.

Cats have thirty-two muscles in each ear.

Ostriches can outrun horses, and male ostriches can roar like lions.

Bats cannot walk on their legs. They crawl using the claws on their wings.

Jellyfish are ninety-eight percent water and will evaporate in the sunlight.

Giraffes and humans have the same number of bones in their necks.

The Indian giant squirrel is usually about three feet long.

While it is illegal to keep foxes and raccoons as pets in Colorado, you can have as many kangaroos as you like.

A chicken with white earlobes will lay white eggs, and one with red earlobes will lay brown eggs.

A polar bear's body gives off no detectable heat and is invisible in infrared vision.

Cows from different regions have different accents when they moo.

Ants do not have lungs. Their exoskeletons have tiny valves called spiracles that draw oxygen into an internal system of tracheae. Queen ants sleep an average of nine hours every day in relatively long stretches. Worker ants sleep half that much by taking about two hundred fifty power naps a day with each one being about a minute in length. A queen ant can live for years; workers a few months.

November 18
More Global Warming Debate
Have you noticed the recent shift in terminology in the news? We're hearing a lot about "climate change" now as opposed to being constantly bombarded about "global warming." I suspect that there is a hidden agenda. Is it possible that the "Al Gore"s of the world are finally catching on to the fact that they haven't been able to fool us after all?

Now, I don't deny the fact that the polar icecaps are melting away, but I am also aware that this planet has been through several bouts of Ice Ages followed by thawing of ice at not just the poles but over the majority of the globe. In fact, I question if what we are seeing now is not just a continuation of the undoing of the last Ice Age. After all, who ever said that the climate as we knew it a few years back was supposed to be the permanent state of affairs? We have to realize that someone is trying to "pull the wool over our eyes" when they explain that global warming brings cold winters like the really severe weather we have experienced in some recent years. They have tried to explain that the loss of Arctic ice creates circulation changes that block weather patterns, dumping snow on northern parts of the continents and spurring cold surges. Or is it just a plain and simple truth that the weather really isn't that much different? And then they counter your question with the really brilliant statement that climate and weather are not the same thing! If not, then I think we really need some explanation! The bottom line is that people seem to be waking up to the inconsistencies in the argument. A recent survey indicates that the percentage of people who believe in human-generated global warming has dropped from forty-seven to only thirty-six.

Now, a new twist to the whole issue – recent research had shown that relying too heavily on wind and wave power as an alternative to fossil fuels can be as detrimental to the environment as using traditional non-renewable energy sources. Harvesting large amounts of energy from the winds will change precipitation, turbulence, and the amount of sun reaching the surface. The overall effect could be as serious as the current greenhouse gas emissions.

November 19
Mooning the Street Preacher

I had not heard his testimony before, so, when he began to share by asking the audience in Nepal if they understood the term "mooning," I was really taken aback. As my friend went on with his story, he explained that as a rebellious young man, he and his friends were out "cruising" one Saturday night when they drove past a street preacher who was proclaiming the Word of God to the people on the "strip." My friend said that he told the driver of their convertible to go to the end of the block and turn around so they could circle past the street preacher another time. As they passed the young evangelist, my friend stood up in the passenger seat, turned his backside toward the preacher and pulled down his pants as an intended insult to the messenger and his message. However, that wasn't the end (pun totally intended) of the story. Something about the whole episode just wouldn't let him forget the event. It kept gnawing at his conscience and tormenting his thoughts. Within just a few weeks, my friend found his way to someone who could complete the work that had begun that night when he passed the evangelist on the strip. Not only did he become a Christian, he eventually became a preacher of the gospel himself.

I've heard similar stories from a good friend who has spent many years as an open-air evangelist. He has shared so many stories with me about how the most violent and antagonistic members of his audiences – the ones who hit him in the face with pies, broke chunks of ice over his head, spat in his face, or punched and slapped him – are the very ones who responded to his challenge to come to Christ as Savior.

Perhaps this is one reason why Jesus told us that we should rejoice and be glad (Matthew 5:12) when people persecute us for our gospel message – the ones who are agitated enough to harass us over our message are the ones who are most convicted by it, and are therefore the closest to coming into the kingdom. We can see a great example in the life of Saul of Tarsus who violently went after believers as the Holy Spirit was violently going after him.

If you get mooned, rejoice that the sun is about to rise!

November 20
Of Course, There is Logic
When asked where the Declaration of Independence was signed, the student answered, "At the bottom."

Aborigines are the Native Americans of Australia.

The soothsayer warned Julius Caesar to beware of the March of Dimes.

My hometown was so small that our square was a triangle.

There will be short deacons meeting today. The tall deacons will meet later.

Don't give up. After all, both Moses and the Apostle Paul were once basket cases.

Keep using my name in vain; I'll make rush hour longer. – God

People who are only married once live in monotony.

We should blame God for overeating because He gave us mouths.

Once a man died in church; when paramedics came, they couldn't figure which one to take.

Why did Moses go up the mountain to get to the two tablets? The people had given him a bad headache

Smorgas-wear is elastic-waisted pants.

Cleopatra was the queen of denial.

The Low Self-Esteem Support Group will meet Thursday at 7 PM. Please enter through the back door.

Every man should have some female friends – married and past eighty years old.

Hypochondria is very hard to cure.

There is a curse of competence – everyone always expects you to help them.

Donuts help keep you pleasant to be around.

Sermons on legal pads are easier to haul around than engraved on stone tablets.

Why doesn't the word umlaut not have an umlaut in it?

I'm not bossy; I just have a better idea.

What happens if you get scared half to death twice?

I'm actually in shape. Round is a shape.

November 21
Let God Fight Your Battles

A couple years ago, my youngest son and a friend were driving to Denver for a ball game. Since my son had been up late the night before studying for a test, he asked his friend to drive. They were traveling north on the interstate at the seventy-five-mile-an-hour speed limit when they came upon an accident in the southbound lane. As my son's friend glanced over to see what had happened, all the other drivers apparently did the same. By the time he looked back up, the traffic was beginning to pile up and it was too late for him to stop before crashing into the car in front of him. My son's car was a total loss as well as several other vehicles involved in the pileup. The insurance company settled the vehicular claims and medical coverage, so we thought that everything was over. However, several months later we received a summons informing us that we were being sued by the driver of the car that was struck from behind. Knowing that the law determines that you are automatically at fault if you collide from the rear, we assumed that there was little we could do.

People "in the know" began giving us advice as to how to protect ourselves and our assets. One doctor who had been involved with a number of such cases with his patients spent a very lengthy conversation trying to convince us that we shouldn't simply rely on the lawyer that our insurance company had appointed to defend us. He was insistent that simply because it was our car that was involved in the accident – even though neither one of us was personally involved by being in the vehicle (in fact, I was actually in India at the time of the accident) – we could be sued for our life's savings. No matter how much everyone tried to get us to worry and be anxious over the situation, I couldn't help relying upon the motto that was on my inspirational calendar the day we received the summons: Let God Fight Your Battles. We didn't hire extra attorneys or do anything out of the ordinary, but we were dismissed from the case and even the claims against the driver were dropped.

Stand ye still, and see the salvation of the LORD. (II Chronicles 20:17)

Thanksgiving

Thankfulness

Giving thanks is a very powerful tool. Jesus healed ten lepers, but the Bible says that only one was made whole because he came back to give thanks. (Luke 17:11-19) The Bible says that the other nine were healed, but it gives us no indication that the parts of their bodies that had been eaten away by the leprosy were ever restored. If they had already lost earlobes to the leprosy, when they were healed there was no more leprosy, but the earlobes would still be missing. However, the one who came back and gave thanks was made whole. This means that he received a creative miracle in his body and his missing earlobes grew back.

A dear friend of mine who served as director of Nepal Leprosy Fellowship for more than fifty years explained that the mission had two objectives – to heal the patients and to reconstruct their disfigured bodies. I obviously understood the significance of the first objective, but had never really considered the importance of the second thrust. For these leprosy patients to be able to be accepted back into their homes and re-integrated into society, it is just as important that their deformities be dealt with as it is for their contagious conditions to be treated. Without reconstructive plastic surgery, these victims are doomed to the same miserable lives as outcasts that they had previously known. So it was with nine of the men who came to Jesus that day; they may have received certification from the priests that they were cured, but they were not to be welcomed back by their wives, families, or employers. Only one – the thankful one who was made every whit whole – was able to find welcoming arms waiting for him when he made his way back to his village.

God will do so much for every Christian, but it seems that He does more for those who are thankful. When we get to the point of thanking God for what we do have rather than grumbling over what we do not have, we will find out how much more He is willing to bless us.

November 23
Living in Two Time Zones
When you travel as much as I do and work with people in other parts of the world, you have to get accustomed to functioning in different time zones. More times than I would wish to remember, I've been awakened in the middle of the night by a phone call from someone in Asia or Africa who didn't realize that it wasn't the middle of the day here just because it was there. Some people I know even travel with two watches so they can keep one set to the time at home while they have the other set on the local time. I'll never forget the time I missed a connecting flight because I failed to reset my watch when I landed in an intermediate city en route or the time I arrived at security with what I thought was a comfortable hour prior to the flight but wound up barely slipping onto a flight just as the plane was leaving because I had not realized that the airport was in a different time zone from our home.

Of course, we don't have to leave home to have problems with time zones. All we need to do is wait for each spring and fall when we switch onto and off of daylight saving time. How many times have you held your clock in your hand, wondering which way you are supposed to turn the dial, or how many times have you failed to make the change and wound up either early or late for church the next morning? Granddaddy always kept two clocks in his home, one set to standard time and one set to daylight time. That way, he didn't have to make any readjustments; he simply switched clocks twice a year.

But the real problem we have with timing is that we must remember that we are also living in two different spiritual time zones. There is our timing of things and God's timetable. Many things that we think need to happen now must wait for God's time and things that we think shouldn't happen until much later in our lives are in His perfect timing today. Just as we must constantly be aware of the proper time zones here on earth, we must also be sensitive to living in God's set time.

One day is with the Lord as a thousand years, and a thousand years as one day. (II Peter 3:8)

November 24

Integrity

Today, let's look at a story from the Old Testament. It is part of a very familiar section of scripture, but not a part of the narrative that is usually emphasized when recounting the tale. In the course of events when David committed adultery with his neighbor's wife (I almost said that he "slept with her," but the real problem wasn't sleeping – it was what happened when they were awake.), the king tried to cover up the whole affair by having the husband called home from the frontlines. His plan was to get Uriah to go home to his wife so that it would look like the child was his. As the story unfolds, Uriah decided to stay with the sentries at the gate of the royal palace rather than spending the night in his own bed. When David got the news the next morning, he called Uriah before him again and asked him about the night. The soldier answered, *The ark, and Israel, and Judah, abide in tents; and my lord Joab, and the servants of my lord, are encamped in the open fields; shall I then go into mine house, to eat and to drink, and to lie with my wife? as thou livest, and as thy soul liveth, I will not do this thing.* (II Samuel 11:11) David's scheme had failed but he wasn't about to give up so easily, so he had him stay another day and got the poor man drunk in hopes that in his drunkenness he would forget his honor and stagger into his home that evening. His plan failed as Uriah stood his ground on his commitment to solidarity with his comrades in battle.

The point of the story is that Uriah was a better man drunk than David was sober. This whole scenario had been instigated by David's decision to stay back when all the other kings were at war. (II Samuel 11:1) It was normally David's practice to lead, rather than send, his men into battle – but on this occasion, he preferred the comforts of home instead. Although he had a harem of wives and concubines, the sober king chose to totally abandon integrity and commitment to the team by taking another man's wife during this time of leisure at home while his men suffered on the battlefield. In contrast – Uriah, even while his physical senses were impaired, held to his spiritual veracity.

November 25

Count Your Blessings

1) Clean water: One in eight people in the world (that's 884 million people) lack access to clean water supplies. Your five-minute shower uses more water than a typical person in a developing country uses in a whole day.

2) A bathroom: About 40 percent of the world's population (2.6 billion people) do not have toilets. More than 2 million people die annually of diarrhea.

3) Electricity: A quarter of humanity (1.6 billion people) live without any electricity. At least 2 billion people on earth don't have any light at night.

4) A roof over your head: One billion people (one-sixth of the world's population) live in slums. They live in cardboard boxes, tin-roofed shacks, one-room mud huts or filthy, crowded tenements. Here in the US, 2.5 million people are homeless.

5) Food on your table: Approximately 790 million people in the developing world are chronically undernourished, and almost 28 percent of all children in developing countries are estimated to be underweight or stunted while 22,000 children die each day due to poverty.

6) A stove: In developing countries, some 2.5 billion people use fuel wood, charcoal, or animal dung for cooking. Indoor air pollution resulting from the use of these fuels claims the lives of 1.5 million people each year, more than half of them below the age of 5.

7) A regular income: At least 80 percent of humanity lives on less than $10 a day.

8) Education: Nearly a billion people entered the 21st century unable to read a book or sign their names.

9) Healthcare: In the developing world, more than 2.2 million children die each year because they are not immunized. Forty million people in developing countries are living with HIV/AIDS. Every year there are 350–500 million cases of malaria, with at least 1 million fatalities.

10) Freedom to worship God: More than 400 Christians die for their faith every day around the world.

November 26

Thoughts to Live By

God wants full custody, not weekend visits.

Make sure your testimony is not just moany about your test.

We are to dwell in Him. He is our permanent address, not our weekend vacation cottage or our eventual retirement home.

God loves you enough to accept you as you are, but too much to leave you that way.

If you work hard on your job, you will become rich; if you work hard on yourself, you will become wealthy.

God won't bless you more than you are willing to be a blessing.

Small prayers dishonor God.

Your seed will produce more than your money could ever buy.

There is no life in the scriptures themselves, but if we follow where they lead, they will bring us to Him, and so we will find life, not in the scriptures, but in Him through them. – G. Campbell Morgan.

The promise of the Father is the Holy Spirit – not just His gifts.

For some people, failure is more acceptable than change.

Rome wasn't built in a day, but it burned down overnight.

Time is the only non-renewable resource.

A great motto for facing life's problems: "So what?"

If you are not a liberal by the time you are 25, you have no heart. If you are not a conservative by the time you are 45, you have no brains. – Winston Churchill

If God were guilty of all the things we blame Him for, there isn't a civilized nation on the face of this earth that wouldn't convict Him of crimes against humanity. – Andrew Wommack

Hard work spotlights the character of people: some turn up their sleeves, some turn up their noses, and some don't turn up at all.

In real life, I assure you, that there is no such thing as algebra.

Obedience is a response, not a requirement for salvation. It is our reasonable response. (Romans 12:2)

If you don't want to miss the boat, join the crew.

If you sow it, God will grow it.

November 27

Take Heed

In Colossians 4:17, Paul instructed us to take heed to the ministry and to see that we fulfill it. He followed up that directive in I Timothy 4:16 with instructions to take heed of ourselves. Obviously, our Christian lives and ministries are not just casual, nonchalant activities, but commitments to be taken most seriously. Most of us are aware of what it means to take heed to ourselves in watching out for things that can harm our physical bodies, our relationships, our finances, and our spiritual development. However, we may not be as alert to all the areas we need to be aware of in terms of cautiously watching after our ministries.

In thinking about taking heed of our ministries, I'd like to make a couple suggestions of areas that we need to guard. Sometimes, we feel that we can and must solve every issue that we encounter. However, we must remember that even Jesus could not do miracles at Nazareth. (Mark 6:5) If even Jesus couldn't solve every problem that He encountered, why should we feel that we must resolve every issue that presents itself to us? Instead, we need to have an accurate vision of our specific calling and ministry in life. It is only then that we will be able to fulfill the mission we have been given. If we err in our vision, we will stumble in ministry. If we have a clear vision of our calling and stick to it, we will be able to fulfill it. There will always be more needs in ministry than we can fulfill; therefore, we have to have discernment as to which ones are for us to tackle and which ones we need to leave for others. Jesus didn't heal the lame man at the Gate Beautiful because He wanted to leave that task for His disciples. The result was much more impactful than if He had healed the man. So, there is a second benefit in not taking on every challenge we meet – not only does it save us from being diverted from our own mission, but it also allows others to develop into their callings.

Mark 1:32 tells us that Jesus began His day with prayer, apparently seeking His assignment for the day and the resources to fulfill it. With clear vision and fresh anointing, He was able to finish the job without letting the job finish Him. (John 4:34)

November 28

The Blessing of Enemies

Jesus gave us some pretty radical commands about our relationships with those people that we would consider to be our enemies. In Matthew 5:44, He told us to love our enemies, bless those who curse us, do good to those who hate us, and pray for those who despitefully use us and persecute us. He reaffirmed this command in Luke 6:27, and in verse thirty-five added the directive to even lend them money with no anticipation of being repaid. Paul, in Romans 12:20, reiterated Solomon's advice in Proverbs 25:21 that we must feed our enemies when they are hungry. But other than the general, "Well, it's the Christian thing to do" and the "Remember, they are human beings, too" answers, is there any reason that we should show kindness to our enemies?

Although the Bible is full of statements about conquering, destroying, and even obliterating our enemies, there are a few select passages that might give us a little glimpse into a beneficial purpose that having enemies can serve in our lives.

Two passages in Psalms suggest that having enemies may help us to be better Christians. It seems from these passages that the very fact that we have opposition can draw us to a place of more clearly understanding God's ways and more closely following them.

> *Lead me, O LORD, in thy righteousness because of mine enemies; make thy way straight before my face.* (verse 5:8)
> *Teach me thy way, O LORD, and lead me in a plain path, because of mine enemies.* (verse 27:11)

Psalm 8:2 suggests the fact that enemies have risen up is grounds enough for God to cause the weak, and even children, to rise up in a new strength and power to oppose them. And Psalm 23:5 suggests that it is because of – not in spite of – the opposition of our enemies that God lavishes His blessings upon us.

Take a good look at your life and see if there isn't a blessing waiting for you through loving your enemy.

November 29
Notes from What's Happening Around the World

One pastor I know asks all his congregation to bring their iPads and smartphones to church each Sunday and post a Bible message on their Facebook pages during service. He gives a short message, called Face the Book, that goes out to an average of one hundred thirty-three friends for each person actually in the service.

NASA Jet Propulsion Laboratory employee David Coppedge, who was the team lead on the Cassini mission to Saturn and its moons, was dismissed after fifteen years of employment with suspicion that the cause was his belief in intelligent design.

Black churches in Harlem are becoming the object of international tourism by groups wanting to hear their music. The tourists often leave before or during the message.

One minister friend of mine was healed by watching himself pray for the sick on television.

One minister friend told me that he had a dream about a man who was about to be swept away in a storm at sea. In the dream, the pastor grabbed him just in time to save his life. He was so impacted by the dream that he interceded for the man for several months. In an even more unusual twist to the story, he even knew the young man's name. One day, when the pastor was having his car worked on, the mechanic looked up and noticed a friend of his drive past. When he called out to his friend, the name was the same as the individual in the dream. Even though the man did not stop, the pastor knew that there really was a real person to go with the man in the dream. A few days later, a friend request from this individual showed up on the pastor's Facebook page. When the pastor contacted him, the man said that he didn't know how the request got posted, but he was willing to meet with the pastor. But the most amazing part of the story was still ahead. The total period of time that the pastor was praying for the man coincided with a period of backsliding in his life when he even entertained thoughts of suicide.

November 30
More Notes from What's Happening Around the World

A friend of mine who has lived her whole life in South Africa said that the first time she ever felt like she was in Africa was when she went on a safari in Zimbabwe.

One of my friends in the ministry was looking for a new location for his church when he happened upon a vacant storefront. The front window of the building had been blocked off with newspapers, so he thought that he would try to take a peek inside by looking through cracks between the sheets that were taped to the glass. The first thing that he saw when he approached the window was his own picture and an article he had published in the newspaper more than a year before! He obviously rented the building.

A Christian couple in the United Kingdom was deemed unfit to have foster children because of their religious beliefs against homosexuality.

Workers with children from Muslim backgrounds discovered that they did not know how to sing except in the one flat note used in the Islamic call to prayer.

Judy Zmerold wrote in the Minneapolis Star-Tribune: Three-year-old Katie was taken to her pediatrician during a recent bout with the flu. As the doctor examined her ears, he asked, "Will I find Big Bird in here?" Apprehensively, Katie replied, "No." Then, before examining her throat, he asked, "Will I find the Cookie Monster in here?" Again she replied, "No." Finally, listening to her heart, he asked, "Will I find Barney in here?" With innocent conviction, she looked him directly in the eye and said, "No, Jesus is in my heart. Barney is on my underwear."

When the minister who conducted the funeral for a man who had helped develop the Boeing 747 asked his widow about his career she replied, "The truth is that he spent fifteen years developing one little switchbox smaller than a bread box." That huge plane couldn't have lifted off without this man's breadbox-size contribution. We may see only our small efforts and feel we aren't very important. But when the great Kingdom of God "lifts off," we'll be thrilled to find out that all our efforts were essential.

December 1
Religion and Well Being
The most religious Americans also have the highest rates of well being, according to a new Gallup survey. The finding is based on a survey of more than half a million people about their physical and emotional health and their work environment. Overall, the very religious received a score on Gallup's well-being index of 68.7 percent, while both the moderately religious and the nonreligious received a score of 64.2 percent. The very religious were defined as those who said religion is an important part of their daily lives and they attend worship services at least every week or almost every week. The researchers did not determine why the very religious had higher levels of health and happiness. However, the Bible itself explains how that honoring God will produce well being in every area of life.

> *But his delight is in the law of the LORD; and in his law doth he meditate day and night. And he shall be like a tree planted by the rivers of water, that bringeth forth his fruit in his season; his leaf also shall not wither; and whatsoever he doeth shall prosper.* (Psalm 1:2-3)
> *It shall be health to thy navel, and marrow to thy bones.* (Proverbs 3:8)
> *When a man's ways please the LORD, he maketh even his enemies to be at peace with him.* (Proverbs 16:7)
> *This book of the law shall not depart out of thy mouth; but thou shalt meditate therein day and night, that thou mayest observe to do according to all that is written therein: for then thou shalt make thy way prosperous, and then thou shalt have good success.* (Joshua 1:8)

One issue really bothers me. Since faith is so vital to success in everyday life, why are so many people avoiding it? Less than two percent of the world's population could fit into all the church buildings and synagogues at any one time?

December 2

Power of the Word

While my roommate and I were waiting as our clothes were in the washers, we decided to post a gospel tract on the bulletin board at the laundromat. After thumbtacking it to the corkboard, we really didn't think any more about it. That is until several months later when we were holding a Bible study in our dorm room. After knocking on all the doors in our building to invite students to come for the study, we welcomed the few who responded by sharing some free literature with them. One of the pieces was the same tract that we had posted on the board. One of the young men excitedly responded that he had seen the tract before and told the story of having read it while waiting for his clothes to wash. He added that he had put it back on the board after having read it, thinking that others could benefit from it as well.

One of the things I miss about the modern online banking is the opportunity I had of slipping a tract into the envelope with my check when I paid my bills. Like casting bread on the waters and wondering what wave it will return on (Ecclesiastes 11:1), I always wondered who would read them and what impact they would have on the readers. The answer came one day when a call came in from a gentleman from one of the companies asking for extra copies of the tract. He had been touched by it and wanted to be able to share the message with others.

We never know exactly how much good so little effort can do and how much impact such a tiny investment can make. One of my friends shares the testimony that his mother accepted Christ because of a four-word testimony. I've often wondered what four words had so much impact as to change this woman's life and eternal destiny. Although I have no idea exactly what those words were, I do know the power of the God of the Word and have all confidence that He can use even the smallest of seeds to produce a tree that feeds and shelters many. (Mark 4:31-32) Those words changed not only the woman, but also her son who has impacted his whole nation!

December 3

Where is Our Nation Headed?

In spite of the fact that we can see signs of revival around us, there are some startling wake-up-call statistics that we need to bring into the equation. Today, there are three thousand fewer churches in America than there were a year ago. In proportion to the population, there are fewer than half as many congregations as there were a century ago. Over eighty percent of present congregations in our country are considered to be either stagnant or dying. Only one out of fourteen adults said that anything related to spirituality or faith in Christ would help achieve what they might term success. In fact, the US is considered to be one of the largest unchurched nations in the world, along with China, India, Indonesia, and Japan.

Bishop William Willimon summarized what he sees as the condition of the church in America in these words, "Here we are in the North American church cranking along just fine, thank you…managing the machinery, utilizing biblical principles, celebrating recovery, user-friendly, techno savvy…growing in self-esteem, reinventing ourselves as effective ecclesiastical entrepreneurs, and in general, feeling ever so much better about our achievements. Notice anything missing in this picture? JESUS CHRIST!"

Is it possible that we are just like Mary and Joseph on their way home from their visit to Jerusalem? (Luke 2:40-49) They traveled for three days without Jesus before they finally found Him in the temple dialoging with the doctors. As shocking as the story may be that Jesus' parents left Him behind and headed out on their journey without realizing that He was missing, the story has a great redemptive message in that they began to seek Him diligently as soon as they realized that He was not with them. They stopped at nothing until they found Him. Perhaps the church in America has been moving very well, headed down our self-determined course – all the while oblivious that we turned a corner somewhere along the line and left Jesus behind. Let's learn from the Holy Family and go back to where we last knew that Jesus was with us and start all over again.

December 4
Repent, Believe, and Be Baptized

A Hindu convert in India who had not yet been baptized asked me, "Who am I? I am not Hindu because I've accepted Jesus. But I'm not a Christian because I haven't been baptized yet." Of course, we reassured him that he was a true Christian from the moment he prayed the prayer to be saved, but his question did bring up a very valuable issue. Perhaps the modern church has failed to understand the significance of the sacrament of baptism. In New Testament times, baptism was considered an automatic part of the conversion experience. (Matthew 28:19; Acts 2:38, 8:36; Romans 6:3; Galatians 3:27)

To be baptized means an end of the old life. In Ephesians 4:22-24, Paul makes reference to putting off the old man and putting on the new man, an allusion to the first century practice of taking off the old tattered and stained street garments and being clothed in a clean new robe at the time of baptism. Thus, baptism was an outward sign of the inward transformation that had occurred at conversion. Notice also how Paul used baptism as the cornerstone of his argument in I Corinthians 1:10-18 concerning solidarity within the Body of Christ. It was baptism that determined membership, not just in the physical church but also in the universal spiritual church.

It is also worth noting that, in his encounter with the disciples at Ephesus recorded in Acts 19:1-4, Paul made a real distinction between the baptism of John and baptism in the name of Jesus. Even though John's baptism signified repentance and remission of sins (Mark 1:4), it did not constitute membership in the Body of Christ (Romans 6:3, Galatians 3:27); therefore he required them to be baptized again.

In Acts chapter eight, we see two powerful truths about baptism. In Samaria, the people experienced many wonderful spiritual blessings but still needed to confirm their belief in the gospel through baptism. (verse 12) Immediately upon the heels of that revival, Phillip ministered to an Ethiopian, leading him to believe with all his heart. (verses 35-37). It was only at that point that he consented to baptize the eunuch. He was a genuine member of the family and could now receive initiation.

December 5

Accountability

A recent survey indicated that only about five percent of Americans feel that their church exercises any accountability in their lives. The Barna Group study showed that most American Christians have no one holding them accountable for their Christian walk. The vast majority of church members answered that they don't see the church taking an active role in requiring them to be responsible for integrating biblical beliefs and principles into their lives – nor did they really want or expect it to do so. "Americans these days cherish privacy and freedom to the extent that the very idea of being held accountable by others – even those with their best interests in mind, or who have a legal or spiritual authority to do so – is considered inappropriate, antiquated and rigid," said George Barna, director of the survey. "Overlooking a principle as foundational as accountability breeds even more public confusion about scriptural authority and faith-based community, as well as personal behavioral responsibility."

The biblical pattern, on the other hand, is that church leadership has an obligation to take responsibility for the lives of the congregants. Obviously, this oversight is not for the benefit of the leaders' egos. It is rather for the security of the believers' souls.

> *The elders which are among you I exhort, who am also an elder, and a witness of the sufferings of Christ, and also a partaker of the glory that shall be revealed: Feed the flock of God which is among you, taking the oversight thereof, not by constraint, but willingly; not for filthy lucre, but of a ready mind; Neither as being lords over God's heritage, but being ensamples to the flock.* (I Peter 5:1-3)

One individual I was mentoring had a challenge with turning to internet pornography. The issue was instantly cured by linking up my computer so that every site on his computer immediately registered on mine. Accountability does work!

December 6
Fat

I live in Colorado, the thinnest state in the union even though we still have a rate of fifty percent of the population as being overweight. One recent study has linked the state's fitness level with our altitude, noting that Colorado has the highest mean elevation and the lowest adult obesity rate. I suppose that that extrapolates to an explanation of the weightlessness on the moon.

Another explanation links obesity with religion. It has been observed that the areas of the nation that are the most religious are also the most obese areas: Mississippi, Alabama, South Carolina, Tennessee, Louisiana, Arkansas, Georgia, North Carolina, Oklahoma, (Kentucky/Texas tie). Colorado is number thirty-seven. To validate the study, it is interesting to note the claims of the residents of various regions. Twenty-three percent of the people in Jacksonville, MS, claim to be born again, and sixty-seven percent of the population of Alabama lists itself as born again. There are ten large metropolitan areas in America (all in the South) where sixty percent or more of the citizens are born again. I think that these Christian folk just take some Bible verses a little too literally.

> *Ye shall eat the fat of the land.* (Genesis 45:18)
> *Go your way, eat the fat, and drink the sweet, and send portions unto them for whom nothing is prepared.* (Nehemiah 8:10)
> *They did eat, and were filled, and became fat, and delighted themselves in thy great goodness.* (Nehemiah 9:25)
> *All they that be fat upon earth shall eat and worship.* (Psalm 22:29)
> *The liberal soul shall be made fat.* (Proverbs 11:25)

Go ahead and claim these verses for yourself during this holiday season. After all, what you eat between Thanksgiving and New Year's is exempt!

December 7
Burn, Devil, Burn
At six o'clock this evening, the devil will be eradicated! Well, at least Antigua Guatemala, and that at least in symbolism. Each year on December 7, a three-story tall figurine of the devil is set ablaze to mark the beginning of the Christmas season. The tradition traces its roots to colonial times when those residents of Guatemala City who could afford it adorned the fronts of their houses with lanterns in anticipation of the feast of the Immaculate Conception, their patron saint. Eventually, the poor who could not afford such lanterns began gathering their garbage and would burn all of the year's rubbish in front of their houses. Over time it was formalized and in addition to individual piles of garbage, communities started to burn the devil to clear the way for Mary's feast. The idea is to burn all of the bad from the previous year and to start anew from the ashes.

Other Latin American countries share similar traditions. Colombia has *Años Nuevos*. For the festival, life-size dummies are made to represent one's sinful self of the previous year. Often they are portrayed with bulging sex organs, a white nose (for those who struggled with cocaine during the year), and with bottles of liquor in their hands. When the year rolls over, these figurines are doused in gasoline and the old self brilliantly burns away to make way for the reformed.

When the devil goes up in flames in Guatemala, every injustice of the previous year is considered to have been corrected so that the feast day of the Immaculate Conception can begin the following morning without the devil's interference. Of course, the festivities last far into the night and the early hours of the morning with revelry that without fail proves that the devil's work is far from over.

December 8

Humor Makes the World Go 'Round

Why did Kamikaze pilots wear crash helmets?

Why is it that nobody is listening until you make a mistake?

When a mime is arrested is he given the right to remain silent? What about a monk?

How many animals went onto the Ark? One mail and one email.

In England, if you get off the train before the stop printed on your ticket, you can be fined more than the price of the ticket.

Carrots are now being packaged to look like junk food with the tagline: eat them like junk food.

Success is just a matter of luck. Ask any failure.

Doctor said, "Gee, I haven't seen you in a while." Patient's reply, "I've been ill."

I just discovered that I've been riding in a UFO. My car requires <u>u</u>nleaded <u>f</u>uel <u>o</u>nly.

Headlines:
>   Woman kidnapped, forced to shop
>   Pickle jar, mushroom soup used for evil
>   Fatal shooting victim got out of jail Sunday

Warning signs:
>   In the Federal Reserve Bank – In case of fire, do not use stairs, do not use elevator.
>   In the Department of Energy building – In case of nuclear attack, the only thing you need to do is go to the bottom of your swimming pool and hold your breath.
>   In the <u>El Paso Times</u> – Don't make luggage look like a bomb.

Twenty years ago, we could predict weather for three days. Now we can predict it to within seventy-two hours.

I had an autopsy last year. Luckily, it wasn't serious.

Text to Dad from Son: Can I borrow fifty dollars?
>   Dad's reply: The only time I hear from you is when you need money.
>   Son: If that's the way you feel, can I borrow forty dollars?

Without Jesus, you'll have one hell of an eternity.

December 9
More One Liners to Live By
The heaviest thing to carry is a grudge.

Don't listen to those who say you're taking too big a chance. If he had, Michelangelo would have painted the Sistine floor.

Look on every exit as being an entrance to somewhere else.

Don't complain about the weather. If it didn't change every now and then, most people wouldn't have any way to start a conversation.

You can't go anywhere in your body that you haven't already been in your mind.

God's will will never take you where His grace will not keep you.

When it comes to giving, some people will stop at nothing.

Even when you're in over your head, your situation is under your feet.

Confession is much cheaper than therapy.

Failure is just another way to learn how to do something right.

A lot of people want to have children the same way they own stock – with no personal responsibility, but they love to go to parties and brag about how well they are doing.

Kneel so as to be able to stand.

Telling a woman to be silent is like telling water not to be wet.

The power of God is too big to be kept in a bottle of oil.

UV light kills ninety-nine percent of germs, but the light of God kills one hundred percent.

Don't focus on your circumstances, but on your responses.

Faith gathers strength in waiting patiently.

How many times does it have to happen before you realize that it is not coincidence?

A parrot can speak English but he is not an Englishman. Just because you quote scripture does not mean that you are full of the Word.

Success has eaten the soul out of the church. God did not promise success, only fruitfulness.

God led His people to a land that flows with milk and honey. It was a good thing that He first healed all the lactose intolerant and diabetic ones. (Psalm 105:37)

December 10
Our Roots – Part I

Did you know that fifty-two of the fifty-five signers of The Declaration of Independence were orthodox, deeply committed Christians? The other three all believed in the Bible as the divine truth. This same congress formed the American Bible Society. Immediately after creating the Declaration of Independence, the Continental Congress voted to purchase and import twenty thousand copies of scripture.

Patrick Henry is still remembered for his words, "Give me liberty or give me death." But in current textbooks the context of these words is deleted. Here is what he said, "An appeal to arms and the God of hosts is all that is left us. But we shall not fight our battle alone. There is a just God that presides over the destinies of nations. The battle, sir, is not of the strong alone. Is life so dear or peace so sweet as to be purchased at the price of chains and slavery? Forbid it, Almighty God. I know not what course others may take, but as for me, give me liberty, or give me death." The following year, 1776, he wrote, "It cannot be emphasized too strongly or too often that this great nation was founded not by religionists, but by Christians; not on religion, but on the Gospel of Jesus Christ. For that reason alone, people of other faiths have been afforded freedom of worship here."

Consider these words that Thomas Jefferson wrote on the front of his well-worn Bible, "I am a Christian, that is to say a disciple of the doctrines of Jesus. I have little doubt that our whole country will soon be rallied to the unity of our Creator and, I hope, to the pure doctrine of Jesus also."

Consider these words from George Washington, the Father of our Nation, in his farewell speech on September 19, 1796, "It is impossible to govern the world without God and the Bible. Of all the dispositions and habits that lead to political prosperity, our religion and morality are the indispensable supporters. Let us with caution indulge the supposition that morality can be maintained without religion. Reason and experience both forbid us to expect that our national morality can prevail in exclusion of religious principle."

December 11

Our Roots – Part II

Was George Washington a Christian? Consider these words from his personal prayer book, "Oh, eternal and everlasting God, direct my thoughts, words and work. Wash away my sins in the immaculate blood of the lamb and purge my heart by the Holy Spirit. Daily, frame me more and more in the likeness of Thy son, Jesus Christ, that living in Thy fear, and dying in Thy favor, I may in Thy appointed time obtain the resurrection of the justified unto eternal life. Bless, O Lord, the whole race of mankind and let the world be filled with the knowledge of Thy son, Jesus Christ."

Consider these words by John Adams, our second president, who also served as chairman of the American Bible Society. In an address to military leaders he said, "We have no government armed with the power capable of contending with human passions, unbridled by morality and true religion. Our constitution was made only for a moral and religious people. It is wholly inadequate to the government of any other."

How about our first Court Justice, John Jay? He stated that when we select our national leaders, if we are to preserve our Nation, we must select Christians. "Providence has given to our people the choice of their rulers and it is the duty as well as the privilege and interest of our Christian Nation to select and prefer Christians for their rulers."

John Quincy Adams, son of John Adams, was the sixth U.S. President. He was also the chairman of the American Bible Society, which he considered his highest and most important role. On July 4, 1821, President Adams said, "The highest glory of the American Revolution was this: it connected in one indissoluble bond the principles of civil government with the principles of Christianity."

Calvin Coolidge, our 30th President of the United States, reaffirmed this truth when he wrote, "The foundations of our society and our government rest so much on the teachings of the Bible that it would be difficult to support them if faith in these teachings would cease to be practically universal in our country."

December 12

Our Roots – Part III

In 1782, the United States Congress passed this resolution, "The congress of the United States recommends and approves the Holy Bible for use in all schools." William Holmes McGuffey is the author of the McGuffey Reader, which was used for over one hundred years in our public schools with over one hundred twenty-five million copies sold until it was stopped in 1963. President Lincoln called him the "Schoolmaster of the Nation." Listen to these words of Mr. McGuffey, "The Christian religion is the religion of our country. From it are derived our notions on the character of God, on the great moral Governor of the universe. On its doctrines are founded the peculiarities of our free institutions. From no source has the author drawn more conspicuously than from the Sacred Scriptures. From all these extracts from the Bible I make no apology."

Of the first one hundred eight universities founded in America, all but two were distinctly Christian, including the first – Harvard University, chartered in 1636. In the original Harvard Student Handbook, rule number one was that students seeking entrance must know Latin and Greek so that they could study the Scriptures, "Let every student be plainly instructed and earnestly pressed to consider well, the main end of his life and studies is, to know God and Jesus Christ, which is eternal life, John 17:3; and therefore to lay Jesus Christ as the only foundation of all sound knowledge and learning. And seeing the Lord only giveth wisdom, let everyone seriously set himself by prayer in secret to seek it of Him (Proverbs 2:3)." For over one hundred years, more than half of all Harvard graduates were pastors!

December 13
Our Roots – Part IV
It is clear from history that the Bible and the Christian faith were foundational in our educational and judicial systems. However, in 1947, there was a radical change of direction in the Supreme Court. Here is the prayer that was banished: Almighty God, we acknowledge our dependence on Thee. We beg Thy blessings upon us and our parents and our teachers and our country. Amen." In 1963, the Supreme Court ruled that Bible reading was outlawed as unconstitutional in the public school system. The court offered this justification, "If portions of the New Testament were read without explanation, they could and have been psychologically harmful to children." Bible reading was now unconstitutional, though the Bible was quoted ninety-four percent of the time by those who wrote our constitution and shaped our nation and its systems of education and justice and government. In 1965, the Courts denied as unconstitutional the rights of a student in the public school cafeteria to bow his head and pray audibly for his food. In 1980, the Stone vs. Graham ruling outlawed the Ten Commandments in our public schools. The Supreme Court said, "If the posted copies of the Ten Commandments were to have any effect at all, it would be to induce school children to read them. And if they read them, meditated upon them, and perhaps venerated and observed them, this is not a permissible objective." James Madison, the primary author of the Constitution of the United States, said, "We have staked the whole future of our new nation, not upon the power of government; far from it. We have staked the future of all our political constitutions upon the capacity of each of ourselves to govern ourselves according to the moral principles of the Ten Commandments."

Today we are asking God to bless America. But how can He bless a nation that has departed so far from Him? Most of what you read in this article has been erased from our textbooks. Revisionists have rewritten history to remove the truth about our country's Christian roots.

December 14

The Slide Show

It was a wonderful spring weekend, and about a hundred college students had gathered at a seaside lodge for a spiritual renewal retreat. The schedule was filled with Bible studies, prayer sessions, testimony times, and teaching sessions. Very little free time for the beach had been scheduled. No one really minded because we were all there because of a genuine desire to grow in our faith and deepen our experience with the Lord. On the other hand, we were still kids in our early twenties and we had been corralled on campus all winter. So, needless to say, the precious little time we had for the sun, surf, and sand was exactly that – precious and little!

So when one of the group announced that he had something special that he wanted to present and asked the leadership if he could have part of the free time for his presentation, you can imagine the less than joyous response that reverberated through the crowd. It turned out that his special presentation was a slide show from his recent trip to Israel. At that point, I was reminded of the existentialist's presentation of the afterlife in which a man found himself in a locked room with an elderly couple and their stacks of slides of their grandkids and their travels around the world. When he exclaimed to the warden that he realized that he was in hell, the warden's response was that there was another room exactly like this one upstairs in heaven. Well, our friend giving the show may have been in heaven, but no one else in the room shared his elation. His photographs were not exactly on par with National Geographic. In fact, he had a series of shots from Caiaphas' house where a set of stairs with thirteen steps upon which Jesus had walked had been excavated. He had a shot from each one of the steps. In addition, he had taken many of the pictures at a forty-five degree angle in order to get a wider shot. The result was that he had to turn his projector on its side to show the diamond-shaped photos.

We all tried to politely encourage our brother, but you can't imagine how happy we were when his bulb blew up and we could head for the beach.

December 15
Some Days, You Just Have to Scratch Your Head

Our world today is facing all sorts of issues and problems that we could never have imagined just a few years ago. When I read that Jenna Talackova, a transgender woman had been permitted to compete for the Miss Universe Canada title, I thought, "Well, that takes the cake!" But when I read about the next issue, I had to say, "Well, that takes the whole bakery!"

An English man has had a baby! The "man" was able to carry the child after taking female hormones to reverse the effects of his female-to-male sex change treatment. The news reported that he is in a long-term relationship, but it is not clear whether his partner is male or female. Although he has legally changed his gender to male, he was able to have the baby because his womb was not removed during the original sex change procedure.

As unnerving as this news item was, it turns out that this is not just a singular incident. There has also been a man in the US and one in Spain who have also had babies. In fact, the American man had actually had three children to date. Some medical agencies have begun investigations into the possibility that there are other such cases that have been kept secret, with the patients having possibly gone for treatment in places like India where medical and ethical scruples are less stringent.

> *O Lord, to us belongeth confusion of face, to our kings, to our princes, and to our fathers, because we have sinned against thee.* (Daniel 9:8)

December 16

A Way of Escape

I ran across these two stories in different publications on the same day. Both are powerful testimonies to the wonderful grace of God. No matter how much the enemy may plot against us, our God always has a way of escape and even a way to vindicate us in the eyes of those who would try to stop us. The Bible tells us that Haman was hanged on the very gallows that he constructed to execute Mordecai (Esther 7:10) and that those who dig a ditch to trap us will fall into their own pit (Proverbs 26:27). There is no reason for us to be intimidated in our efforts to share the gospel. God always has a way out planned because He will never let His word go forth void (Isaiah 55:11) nor let it fall to the ground fruitless (I Samuel 3:19).

In Nepal, several evangelists were kicked out of a village and then followed as they left town to ensure that they didn't come back. As they traveled down the road near the village, they met a man who was very ill. In fact, he was on his way home from having visited several doctors and even a witch doctor in hopes of being healed. When the evangelists shared the gospel with him, he accepted the Lord and received prayer for healing. When the people who were following the evangelists saw the miracle, they rushed back to the village to report what they had witnessed. The evangelists were invited back to the village to share with the entire populous, with the result that a baby church with twenty members was birthed.

A minister who was distributing a shipment of gospel tracts that had just arrived for the Christian workers in Mexico was kidnapped by the drug cartel. They ripped open all his cases of literature, thinking that they would find something of value in the boxes. Disappointed, they yelled at the gentleman, "Don't you have anything more valuable than this?" He replied that the gospel was actually the most valuable thing in the world. When they realized that he was a minister of the gospel, the kidnappers decided not to hurt or kill him. They even took him back to town and gave him money for dinner and taxi fare to get home! Instead of robbing him, they gave him money!

December 17

Friday Afternoon Car

When I was growing up, there was an expression for cars that seemed to always have one mechanical problem after the other. They were called "Friday afternoon cars," based on the idea that the workers in the factory were tired from their long workweek and in a hurry to get home for the weekend and were, therefore, a bit haphazard about their work. Well, have you ever thought that man was the last thing that God made on a Friday afternoon after a long workweek? Here are a few stories that suggest that there might be some flaws in this Friday afternoon creation:

A man set out to sail around the British Isles but wound up circling one single island multiple times because he always kept land in sight on the starboard side of his little boat.

A Native American friend of mine explained her people's tradition of always holding the annual rain dance during the third week of August. She said that it always rains in the fourth week of August. That's why they scheduled their dance during the previous week.

The church bulletin announcement read, "The pastor would appreciate it if the ladies of the congregation would lend him their electric girdles for the pancake breakfast next Sunday morning."

The military policy manual read, "Intelligence forces have to take physical tests twice a year; others have to do them every six months."

My friend's neighbor worked unsuccessfully for hours trying to get his snow blower working. Finally, in frustration, he suggested to my friend that he could have the thing if he could just get it working. When my friend pushed the machine into his garage and put gas into the tank, it started up on the first try.

I paid for a service call for an electrician to come check out the circuitry in my house when none of the lights in one room would come on even though the breaker switch wasn't "blown." I never stopped to think that there was any possibility that all the bulbs in that particular room might have burned out at the same time.

December 18
I Can't Die. It Will Ruin My Image

Although I'm not exactly in the camp of people whose idea of a good exercise regimen is a good round of lifting their forks to their mouths, I'm certainly not a body builder or an exercise nut by any means. However, I've always had a liking for Jack Lalanne. I remember seeing him on television when I was just a youngster and being fascinated by the callisthenic program he advocated – a novelty back in that period of history. Of course, during my school PE classes, I did more than I care to remember of his invention – the jumping jack.

The story of how Jack became the man we all know is very interesting. As a fourteen-year-old, he traded his lunchtime sandwiches for doughnuts and chocolate bars, wore a back brace to support his weak shoulders and arch supports, was scrawny, and had severe acne. He said that even the girls could beat him up. By the age of fifteen, he was running backyard training for local firefighters and police officers who could not pass annual fitness tests. Imagine the change in just one year!

But the discovery that changed his life was not as obvious as we might think today. In fact, he was really a "fish swimming upstream" at the time. When he began to develop his workout program, doctors and athletic trainers warned their clients to stay away because it would cause men to lose their sex drive, become muscle-bound, and develop hemorrhoids.

In an interview given shortly before his death, he told the story of how he introduced himself to the young lady who eventually became his wife by warning her that the only thing good about the doughnut she was eating was the hole. Still strong and fit at 96, he remarked, "I can't die. It will ruin my image…Dying is easy; living is hard."

But physical fitness was not his only key to a good life. When he bumped into Dr. Lester Sumrall in an airport, he immediately recognized him from having watched his television broadcasts and remarked, "You work on their souls; I'll work on their bodies." Jack knew that we must have a healthy inner man as well as a strong outer one.

December 19

Discerning the Vision

The young man came to me with excitement written all over his face. God had spoken to him in a dream, and it was the clear direction he needed! In the dream, he saw himself and another pastor standing on the stage of an old theater that the young man wanted to purchase for a youth center. The pastor he was with had a growing congregation but no permanent church facility. In the dream, they were together before a large congregation with their hands clasped and lifted in what seemed to be an exclamation of victory. The only possible interpretation for him was that the two men had joined together and God had answered both their prayers by giving then the building. It all seemed so logical. The young evangelist had a lead on buying the theater, but no money. The pastor had a congregation and money to buy a building, but no lead on a property in the area of town he wanted to be in. It was a win-win situation. So the young man moved quickly to present his dream to the pastor and convince him that the idea had been birthed in heaven. The pastor responded by hiring the young man as his youth pastor and taking immediate steps toward acquiring the building.

As soon as the arrangements were made, the young man came to visit me to share the story. As I heard the dream, I interrupted his story with an alternate interpretation. Because their hands were clasped together in victory meant that they were to work together, not that he was supposed to join the pastor's staff. He was to work with him, not for him. I warned him that he had given up the dream the minute he had become the other man's employee. Now, he would have a comfortable salary and access to the building, but he had given up the freedom to have the youth ministry that was behind the whole vision. No sooner than the ink on their employment agreement was dry, the troubles began. Soon he had to resign from the position. He did continue with the attempt to secure the theater, but everything eventually fell through.

Many times, things aren't actually as they seem at first. That's why we need the counsel of others to help discern our visions before we act on them.

December 20

Victoria Falls

I had the privilege of being in Livingstone, Zambia, twice within a few months of one another. My first visit was in November when Victoria Falls was at its minimal flow. The next visit was in February when the water flow was almost at its peak. On the November trip, we walked the full length of the trail around the falls without being splashed by even a drop of water. On the February trip, we were issued raincoats before we approached the falls, but I soon wondered why. I was totally soaked even with the raingear. For more than half the time, my trip along the trail was like walking in a downpour. One friend who was exploring the falls with me remarked that he was amazed at the flood of water since he had seen the Zambezi River in his native Angola, and it certainly didn't seem to be the raging force that it proved to be here at the falls.

Later that day, some of the ministers were reflecting on our experience at the falls when one man mentioned that he understood that the promises of God are like the rain that fell in the plains of Angola to feed the Zambezi. They are refreshing and encouraging, but they are not very powerful in and of themselves. It is only when they are concentrated at the falls that they release their awesome potential and power. The minister went on to say that he could liken the falls to prayer because it is the falls that bring focus and intensity to the water just as prayer brings focus and intensity to the promises.

My experience of having seen the falls at "low tide" allowed me to understand an added level of symbolism to the story of the falls. When I saw the falls in November, it was awe-inspiring and majestic; however, it was nothing to be compared to its February glory. Prayer is also always a majestic experience, but if the words of our prayers are our own wishes and desires rather than the verbalization of the explicit promises of God, they will lack the power, splendor, and glory of Victoria Fall at her peak!

December 21
The World Ends Today – Again!
Here we are again – the last day of the world. The apocalypse is beginning to become almost a habit with Harold Camping's prediction for May 21 of last year and then his correction for October 21 (saying that the earlier date was the spiritual end of the world) and now the Mayan calendar that comes to an abrupt end today after clocking time for over five thousand years.

When I was in Belize earlier this year, I asked a man of Mayan descent what he thought about his ancestors' predictions. His answer was that if we consider the end of a calendar to be the prediction of the end of the world, Americans predict the world to end every December 31. But, instead of calling it quits, we simply go out and buy a new calendar. He explained the whole scenario as simply being the limitation of the tracking device, not the end of the universe.

I quite honestly expect to wake up tomorrow morning to pretty much the same world I awoke to this morning. I don't think that the Mayans had it figured out any better than Brother Harold, who – by the way – made a public announcement that he was retiring from the prognosticating business after his two recent failed attempts in addition to his earlier miscalculation of September 6, 1994. The truth of the matter is that not even the angels in heaven or Jesus Himself knows when the end will come. (Matthew 24:36) Although the exact details are not disclosed, we are able to know when the coming of the end is nearing by looking at certain signs in the world around us. Unfortunately, most people tend to misunderstand even the things that are plainly written in the scripture. Libraries have been written about how wars and natural disasters are preparing the way for the end. However, Jesus specifically said that such things did not indicate the end. (Matthew 24:6) He does go on to give us four distinct things to watch for:

Worldwide persecution of believers (verses 9-10)
False prophets (verse 11)
Widespread iniquity (verses 12-13)
Universal proclamation of the gospel (verse 14)

December 22

He's Not A Doctor

"He's not a doctor. He's not a doctor," those words kept ringing inside my heart every time I would hear Dr. Garner paged on the intercom system in our offices. He had first started working for the ministry as a volunteer and, therefore, did not need a resume or background check. Proving himself with the responsibilities he had been given, he was eventually asked to take a position with the organization. Since he had been around the operation for a while, the office manager assumed that we knew him well enough to simply accept his word about his background; so, no investigation was done.

It was a bit unusual that he requested that he be addressed as "doctor" when the position he held did not require that level of education, especially considering that I never asked to be addressed with my title even though the position of dean at the Bible college would have mandated a doctorate education. But every time he had to be paged to pick up a phone call or meet a visitor at the reception desk, the phone operator would page him as Dr. Garner, and my spirit would respond immediately that this was not a true title.

Eventually, he asked the principle of our Christian school if he could serve as the counselor for the young men in the school and boasted that this area was the specific focus of his training in graduate school. As a member of the school board, I was made aware of the consideration. My immediate response was that the principle needed to check into his credentials before making any consideration of the request. The research came back that, not only was he not a doctor, he hadn't even completed his bachelor's degree program. Much like Frank Abagnale, Jr., whose fake career as a doctor and airline pilot was popularized in the movie Catch Me If You Can, he had been able to slip through the cracks in the system time and time again. It was only by a word from the Holy Spirit that we were able to stop him. The real miracle is that we also learned that he had a record as a pedophile and wanted the position as a counselor in the school for all the wrong reasons!

December 23
Christmas Adam
Today is Christmas Adam. The logic is simple: since tomorrow is Christmas Eve, and since Adam came before Eve; then today must be Christmas Adam! I know: that one is even cornier than my usual joke. But at least it does introduce an important concept to consider during the Christmas season: why Jesus had to be born of a woman.

In a rather enigmatic statement, Paul links the fact that humans can be saved because Adam came before Eve.

For Adam was first formed, then Eve. And Adam was not deceived, but the woman being deceived was in the transgression. Notwithstanding she shall be saved in childbearing, if they continue in faith and charity and holiness with sobriety. (I Timothy 2:13-15)

The key to understanding this passage is the introduction of the idea of Eve's having been deceived while Adam was not. If you read the Genesis account carefully, you will notice that Eve had not even been created when God gave Adam the instruction not to eat of the Tree of the Knowledge of Good and Evil. There is no record of His ever repeating that directive after Eve came along. (Genesis 2:17-22) This leaves us with the assumption that she only knew about the injunction against the tree through second-hand knowledge through Adam. The result is that she could have legitimately been confused during the conversation with the serpent, whereas Adam had no excuse since he had direct first-hand information from God Himself. Even though we always accuse Eve in the story about the "apple," the truth is that the Bible distinctly puts the blame for the Fall and entrance of sin into the world squarely on the shoulders of Adam. (Romans 5:12, I Corinthians 15:22)

Since sin came to the human race through the man, God determined to use the woman as the avenue through which salvation would come, *And I will put enmity between thee and the woman, and between thy seed and her seed; it shall bruise thy head, and thou shalt bruise his heel.* (Genesis 3:15)

December 24
Random Christmas Thoughts
God placed His greatest gift on a tree, not under one.

Increasing numbers of churches and synagogues are protecting their nativity and holiday scenes with more than prayer. Upset with thefts of Baby Jesus and menorahs, many have put GPS systems inside their valuable figurines to relocate them if stolen. Most of the thefts are childish pranks. Those with an agenda to remove Christ from Christmas occupy themselves with the courts rather than Jesus figurines.

The children in the presentation were to each hold up a card with one letter to spell out the words "Christmas Love." Accidentally, the little girl with the "M" turned her card upside down. Now the message read, "Christ was love."

Did you know that God originally intended that Jesus be born in America? The problem was that He couldn't find three wise men or a virgin. Of course, He did have to import the original wise men from the Far East and the virgin from Nazareth to stage the nativity in Bethlehem.

The latest calculation on the gifts offered during the twelve days of Christmas is more than a hundred thousand dollars. However, you can trim your budget down to just twenty-four thousand dollars by giving just one of each item rather than duplicating them each day.

When a mom dropped a cookie on the floor, she brushed it off and replaced it on the saucer she had set out for Santa, telling her young child not to worry since Santa would never know. The little girl replied, "You mean he knows if I'm naughty, but not if his cookie has been on the floor!"

One child wrote the following letter to Santa, "Do you know that Jesus is the real reason for the season. Not to be mean, but he is!"

When Neil Armstrong stepped onto the moon, he made what will forever be remembered as "one small step for man; one giant leap for mankind." When Jesus stepped onto earth that first Christmas, He made one small step for God; one giant leap for mankind.

Christmas

Which Father?

In a movie Mary congratulated Jesus on one of His miracles by saying, "Your father would have been so proud of you." With a smile, Jesus responds with, "Which one?"

Earthly Dad	Heavenly Father
The seed of the Woman	Conceived of the Spirit
Son of Mary	Son of God
A star led the wise men to Him	Bright morning Star
A poor Jewish boy	The heir of all things
Came from Nazareth	Came from Glory
No beauty in Him that we should desire Him	Rose of Sharon and Lily of the Valley
Bar Mitzvah at 12 years old	Forevermore, eternal
Got hungry	The Bread of Life
Got thirsty	He's the Living Water
He walked in the dark of night	The Light of the world
Got tired and would fell asleep in the midst of storm	Commanded the waves to be still
Had no place to lay His head	Owns the earth and its fullness
He was meek and lowly	Almighty
The crowd tried to stone Him	The Living Stone
Wept at Lazarus' tomb	Raised Lazarus
Considered mad	The Way, Truth, Life
He was baptized by John	Baptizer with the Spirit
Man of sorrows	Joy unspeakable, full of glory
Stone the builder's rejected	The Chief Cornerstone
Crucified in agony	The Resurrection and Life
They gambled for His clothing at the foot of the cross	Ascended into heaven clothed with majesty and glory
Son of Man	The King of kings and Lord of lords.

December 26
The Optimists Are Coming – Part I
"The world has never been a better place to live in," says science writer Matt Ridley, "and it will keep on getting better." Ridley, author most recently of The Rational Optimist, has been a foreign correspondent, a zoologist, an economist, and a financier and brings a broad perspective to his sunny outlook.

1) We're better off now

   Compared with fifty years ago, the average human now earns nearly three times as much money (corrected for inflation), eats one third more calories, buries two thirds fewer children, and can expect to live one third longer. In fact, it's hard to find any region of the world that's worse off now than it was then, even though the global population has more than doubled over that period.

2) Urban living is a good thing

   City dwellers take up less space, use less energy, and have less impact on natural ecosystems than country dwellers. The world's cities now contain over half its people, but they occupy less than three percent of its land area. Urban growth may disgust environmentalists, but living in the country is not the best way to care for the earth. The best thing we can do for the planet is build more skyscrapers.

3) Poverty is nose-diving

   The rich get richer, but the poor do even better. Between 1980 and 2000, the poor doubled their consumption. The Chinese are ten times richer and live about twenty-five years longer than they did fifty years ago. Nigerians are twice as rich and live nine more years. The percentage of the world's people living in absolute poverty has dropped by over half. The United Nations estimates that poverty was reduced more in the past half a century than in the previous five centuries.

December 27
The Optimists Are Coming – Part II

4) The important stuff costs less

One reason we are richer, healthier, taller, cleverer, longer-lived, and freer than ever before is that the four most basic human needs – food, clothing, fuel, and shelter – have grown markedly cheaper. Take one example: In 1800, a candle providing one hour's light cost six hours' work. In the 1880s, the same light from a kerosene lamp took fifteen minutes' work to pay for. In 1950, it was eight seconds. Today, it's half a second. In these terms, we are forty-three thosand times better off than in 1800.

5) The environment is better than you think

In the United States, rivers, lakes, seas, and air are getting cleaner all the time. A car today emits less pollution traveling at full speed than a parked car did from leaks in 1970.

6) Shopping fuels innovation

Even allowing for the many people who still live in abject poverty, our own generation has access to more calories, watts, horsepower, gigabytes, megahertz, square feet, air miles, food per acre, miles per gallon, and, of course, money than any who lived before us. This will continue as long as we use these things to make other things. The more we specialize and exchange, the better off we'll be.

7) Global trade enriches our lives

By 9 a.m., you have shaved with an American razor, eaten bread made with French wheat and spread with New Zealand butter and Spanish marmalade, brewed tea from Sri Lanka, dressed in clothes made from Indian cotton and Australian wool, put on shoes of Chinese leather and Malaysian rubber, and read a newspaper printed on Finnish paper with Chinese ink. I have consumed minuscule fractions of the productive labor of hundreds of people. This is the magic of trade and specialization. Self-sufficiency is poverty.

December 28
The Optimists Are Coming – Part III

8) More farm production equals more wilderness
    While world population has increased more than fourfold
    since 1900, other things have increased, too – the area of
    crops by thirty percent, harvests by six hundred percent. At
    the same time, more than two billion acres of "secondary"
    tropical forest are now re-growing since farmers left them
    to head for cities.

9) The good old days weren't
    Some people argue that in the past there was a simplicity,
    tranquility, sociability, and spirituality that's now been lost.
    This rose-tinted nostalgia is generally confined to the
    wealthy. It's easier to wax elegiac for the life of a pioneer
    when you don't have to use an outhouse.

10) Population growth is not a threat
    Although the world population is growing, the rate of
    increase has been falling for fifty years. Across the globe,
    national birth rates are lower now than in 1960, and in the
    less developed world, the birth rate has approximately
    halved. This is happening in spite of the fact that people
    are living longer and infant-mortality rates are dropping.
    According to an estimate from the United Nations,
    population will start falling once it peaks at nine and a
    quarter billion in 2075 – so there is every prospect of
    feeding the world forever. After all, there are already seven
    billion people on earth, and they are eating better and better
    every decade.

11) Oil is not running out
    In 1970, there were five hundred fifty billion barrels of oil
    reserves in the world, and in the twenty years that followed,
    the world used six hundred billion. So by 1990, reserves
    should have been overdrawn by fifty billion barrels.
    Instead, they amounted to nine hundred billion – not
    counting tar sands and oil shale that between them contain
    about twenty times the proven reserves of Saudi Arabia.

December 29
The Optimists Are Coming – Part IV
12) We are the luckiest generation

This generation has experienced more peace, freedom, leisure time, education, medicine, and travel than any in history.

13) Storms are not getting worse

While the climate warmed slightly last century, the incidence of hurricanes and cyclones fell. Since the 1920s, the global annual death rate from weather-related natural disasters (that is, the proportion of the world's population killed rather than simply the overall number) has declined by a staggering ninety-nine percent. The killing power of hurricanes depends more on wealth than on wind speed. A big hurricane struck the well-prepared Yucatán in Mexico in 2007 and killed nobody. A similar storm struck impoverished Burma the next year and killed 200,000. The best defenses against disaster are prosperity and freedom.

14) Great ideas keep coming

The more we prosper, the more we can prosper. The more we invent, the more inventions become possible. The world of things is often subject to diminishing returns. The world of ideas is not. The ever-increasing exchange of ideas causes the ever-increasing rate of innovation in the modern world. There isn't even a theoretical possibility of exhausting our supply of ideas, discoveries, and inventions.

15) We can solve all our problems

If you say the world will go on getting better, you are considered mad. If you say catastrophe is imminent, you may expect the Nobel Peace Prize. Bookshops groan with pessimism; airwaves are crammed with doom. I cannot recall a time when I was not being told by somebody that the world could survive only if it abandoned economic growth. But the world will not continue as it is. The human race has become a problem-solving machine.

December 30
The Optimists Are Coming – Part V

16) This depression is not depressing

The Great Depression of the 1930s was just a dip in the upward slope of human living standards. By 1939, even the worst affected countries, America and Germany, were richer than they'd been in 1930. All sorts of new products and industries were born during the Depression. So growth will resume unless prevented by wrong policies. Someone, somewhere, is tweaking a piece of software, testing a new material, or transferring the gene that will make life easier or more fun.

17) Optimists are right

For two hundred years, pessimists have had all the headlines – even though optimists have far more often been right. There is immense vested interest in pessimism. No charity ever raised money by saying things are getting better. No journalist ever got the front page writing a story about how disaster was now less likely. Pressure groups and their customers in the media search even the most cheerful statistics for glimmers of doom. Don't be browbeaten – dare to be an optimist!

18) Optimism is good for you

Optimists are nine percent less likely to develop heart disease and seventy-seven percent less likely to be re-hospitalized after major surgery. Their blood pressure registers about five points lower than average, and they live about nine and a half years longer.

The optimists are coming. Make it your New Year's resolution to become one of them.

For I know the thoughts that I think toward you, saith the LORD, thoughts of peace, and not of evil, to give you an expected end.
(Jeremiah 29:11)

December 31

Deadliest Holidays

I'm sure that most of us grew up with the impression that New Year's Eve and New Year's Day were the most dangerous times to be out driving a car. That concern was strongly implanted in my teenage brain by my dad who gave the "lecture" every December 31 as I was headed out to welcome the new year. However, the truth is that these days actually fall pretty far down the list of the most lethal holidays.

Thanksgiving
Independence Day
Labor Day
Columbus Day
Memorial Day
Christmas
Presidents' Day
MLK Day
New Year's Day
New Year's Eve

My guess is that it is exactly because of all the lectures that our fathers have given us over the years and the resulting emphasis on having designated drivers on this particular day as opposed to other holidays that the holiday isn't at the top of the list.

Okay, so we've earned a bit of reprieve for the New Year's reveler, but we still can't escape the fact that alcohol consumption is the root cause for almost incalculable pain and sorrow in our society. The toll of excessive drinking works out to about two dollars per drink in medical bills, work loss, property damage from car crashes, incarceration of drunken drivers and criminals using alcohol. Eighty cents comes from the government and the rest from drinkers, families, health insurers, employers, crime victims, etc. The total annual loss calculates to approximately $224 billion.

Teach All Nations Mission

Teach All Nations Mission (TAN) is a global evangelical educational ministry birthed from the teaching ministries of Delron and Peggy Shirley. The name for Teach All Nations Mission was chosen to carefully indicate the exact heart of the Shirleys' mission. TAN's commitment is to establish a solid biblical foundation in national pastors and leaders so they can help enrich their own people. This vision is being accomplished by holding national leadership conferences and publishing and distributing Christian teaching materials in English and their local languages.

Someone accurately observed concerning the revival that is occurring in many parts of our world today that it is a mile wide but only an inch deep – the result of energetic evangelism by both missionaries and local Christians. Sadly, there is a marked shortage of teachers who are taking the next step in fulfilling our Lord's directive to teach them how to observe all that He has commanded. Therefore, Teach All Nations Mission has literally taken the words of Christ from Matthew 28:19, "Teach all nations," as its motto and mission statement.

TAN's commitment is to deepen that revival by training the pastors and leaders who then go back and strengthen their congregations. TAN pays for the travel and lodging of handpicked leaders because Delron and Peggy want to invest into their lives but know that these third-world saints could never afford to come at their own expense. TAN always provides the meals for all the guests during these conferences. The ministry also furnishes solid Christian literature in their local language or in English for those who understand the language.

Delron and Peggy realize that the challenge is much bigger than what they can accomplish in person; therefore, they have determined to expand the scope of their vision. One area of expansion includes a scholarship fund that will allow selected individuals to obtain a formal education in solid Christian colleges and Bible schools or through correspondence courses. The ministry has also assisted in building a Christian school in Zimbabwe and a Bible college in Nepal. Additionally, Teach All Nations assists the pastors and leaders they work with in times of need such as the tsunami in Sri Lanka, the earthquake in Nepal, and hurricanes in Belize and in the Turks and Caicos Islands. More recently, the ministry supported suffering Christians in twelve different nations who lost their source of income during the shutdowns during the COVID-19 pandemic.

Your gifts to and prayers for Teach All Nations will help the Shirleys continue their outreach to Christian leadership around the world.

Teach All Nations Mission
3210 Cathedral Spires
Colorado Springs, CO 80904
719-685-9999
www.teachallnationsmission.com
teachallnations@msn.com

Books by Delron & Peggy Shirley

Bingo, a Fresh Look at Grace
Christmas Thoughts
Cornerstones of Faith
Daily Bible Study Series (Five-Volume Set)
Daily Ditties from Delron's Desk
(Eight Volumes Available)
Doctor Livingstone, I Presume
Don't Leave Home Without It
Finally, My Brethren
Getting More UMPH out of Your Bible
Going Deeper in Jesus
The Great Commission – Doable
The IN Factors
In This Sign Conquer
Interface
Israel, Key to Human Destiny
The Last Enemy
Lessons Along the Way
Lessons from the Life of David
Living for the End Times
Maturing into the Full Stature of Jesus Christ
Maximum Impact
No Longer Bound
The Non-Conformer's Trilogy
Of Kings and Prophets
Passion for the Harvest
People Who Make A Difference
Positioned for Blessing and Power
Problem People of the Bible
Seeds and Harvest
The Seventh Man at the Well
So Send I You
So, You Wanna be a Preacher
Thirty-, Sixty-, One-Hundred-Fold
Tread Marks
Turning the World Upside Down and Back Again

Verse for the Day (Four Volumes Available)
Women for the Harvest
You'll be Darned to Heck
if You Don't Believe in Gosh
Your Home Can Survive in the 21st Century
Your Part in the Grand Scheme of Things

Available at:
teachallnationsmission.com